BASIC MECHANICAL ENGINEERING

FOR
FIRST YEAR DEGREE COURSE IN ENGINEERING
(COMMON TO ALL BRANCHES)

**According to Revised Syllabus of Shivaji University, Kolhapur
With effect from Academic Year 2013-2014**

Dr. V.M. DOMKUNDWAR
B.E. (Osm), M.E. (Cal.) Ph.D. (I.I.T. Madras)
"**Gold Madalist**", National and International Awards Winner"
MIE MISTE, MCI (India),
"**Ideal Teacher Award Winner**"
"Maharashtra Gaurav" and '"Bhushan Purashkar"
Member of IIIE (India); MIE (India) MCI (India)
Ex. – Principal COE, Aurangabad & Ex – Principal K.J. Somaiya COE (Mumbai)
Ex. Professor and Advisor, Jawaharlal Nehru Engineering College, Aurangabad.
Presently Professor, (Em) Government College of Engineering, Pune

Dr. A. T. PISE
ME Ph.D. (IIT kanpur)
FIE, LMISTE, LISHMT, ISHRAE
Professor and Head
Department of Mechanical Engineering
Government College of Engineering, Karad Dist. Satara.
Chairman, Board of Studies Mechanical Engineering &
Member, Management Council Shivaji University Kolhapur

NIRALI PRAKASHAN

N 2401

BASIC MECHANICAL ENGINEERING (FE SEM. II, SU)　　　　ISBN 978-93-83971-30-5

First Edition : January 2014

© : Authors

The text of this publication, or any part thereof, should not be reproduced or transmitted in any form or stored in any computer storage system or device for distribution including photocopy, recording, taping or information retrieval system or reproduced on any disc, tape, perforated media or other information storage device etc., without the written permission of Authors with whom the rights are reserved. Breach of this condition is liable for legal action.

Every effort has been made to avoid errors or omissions in this publication. In spite of this, errors may have crept in. Any mistake, error or discrepancy so noted and shall be brought to our notice shall be taken care of in the next edition. It is notified that neither the publisher nor the authors or seller shall be responsible for any damage or loss of action to any one, of any kind, in any manner, therefrom.

Published By :
NIRALI PRAKASHAN
Abhyudaya Pragati, 1312, Shivaji Nagar,
Off J.M. Road, PUNE – 411005
Tel - (020) 25512336/37/39, Fax - (020) 25511379
Email : niralipune@pragationline.com

Printed at
Repro Knowledgecast Limited
India

DISTRIBUTION CENTRES

PUNE

Nirali Prakashan
119, Budhwar Peth, Jogeshwari Mandir Lane
Pune 411002, Maharashtra
Tel : (020) 2445 2044, 66022708, Fax : (020) 2445 1538
Email : bookorder@pragationline.com

Nirali Prakashan
S. No. 28/25, Dhyari,
Near Pari Company, Pune 411041
Tel : (022) 24690204 Fax : (020) 24690316
Email : dhyari@pragationline.com
bookorder@pragationline.com

MUMBAI
Nirali Prakashan
385, S.V.P. Road, Rasdhara Co-op. Hsg. Society Ltd.,
Girgaum, Mumbai 400004, Maharashtra
Tel : (022) 2385 6339 / 2386 9976, Fax : (022) 2386 9976
Email : niralimumbai@pragationline.com

DISTRIBUTION BRANCHES

NAGPUR
Pratibha Book Distributors
Above Maratha Mandir, Shop No. 3, First Floor,
Rani Jhanshi Square, Sitabuldi, Nagpur 440012,
Maharashtra, Tel : (0712) 254 7129

BENGALURU
Pragati Book House
House No. 1, Sanjeevappa Lane, Avenue Road Cross,
Opp. Rice Church, Bengaluru – 560002.
Tel : (080) 64513344, 64513355,
Mob : 9880582331, 9845021552
Email:bharatsavla@yahoo.com

JALGAON
Nirali Prakashan
34, V. V. Golani Market, Navi Peth, Jalgaon 425001,
Maharashtra, Tel : (0257) 222 0395
Mob : 94234 91860

KOLHAPUR
Nirali Prakashan
New Mahadvar Road,
Kedar Plaza, 1st Floor Opp. IDBI Bank
Kolhapur 416 012, Maharashtra. Mob : 9855046155

CHENNAI
Pragati Books
9/1, Montieth Road, Behind Taas Mahal, Egmore,
Chennai 600008 Tamil Nadu, Tel : (044) 6518 3535,
Mob : 94440 01782 / 98450 21552 / 98805 82331, Email : bharatsavla@yahoo.com

RETAIL OUTLETS
PUNE

Pragati Book Centre
157, Budhwar Peth, Opp. Ratan Talkies,
Pune 411002, Maharashtra
Tel : (020) 2445 8887 / 6602 2707, Fax : (020) 2445 8887

Pragati Book Centre
Amber Chamber, 28/A, Budhwar Peth,
Appa Balwant Chowk, Pune : 411002, Maharashtra,
Tel : (020) 20240335 / 66281669
Email : pbcpune@pragationline.com

Pragati Book Centre
676/B, Budhwar Peth, Opp. Jogeshwari Mandir,
Pune 411002, Maharashtra
Tel : (020) 6601 7784 / 6602 0855

PBC Book Sellers & Stationers
152, Budhwar Peth, Pune 411002, Maharashtra
Tel : (020) 2445 2254 / 6609 2463

MUMBAI
Pragati Book Corner
Indira Niwas, 111 - A, Bhavani Shankar Road, Dadar (W), Mumbai 400028, Maharashtra
Tel : (022) 2422 3526 / 6662 5254, Email : pbcmumbai@pragationline.com

PREFACE

Basic Mechanical Engineering of First year Engineering introduces fundamentals of **Mechanical Engineering** course. This book is a straightforward guide to the subject. Eight chapters in this book cover all the contents as per **the revised syllabus of Shivaji University, Kolhapur with effect from Academic year 2013-14.** The specialty of the book is, it contains all the 6-chapter included in the Recent syllabus all the solved problems which are asked in previous University.

Easy language and figures in this book are easy to understand. Whereever possible, the 3D diagrams and photographs of practical applications are introduced. The students can easily correlate the theory with the applications.

Success in the exam depends on proper planning of studies and appropriate selection of material for the study. The authors have taken enough pains to arrange the material of the subject which will be helpful for exam and evaluate their practical knowledge. The authors, consider the usefulness of this text to the students is the success of the Text.

This book is also helpful to those who wish to appear for GATE.

Thanks to Nirali Prakashan, Pune whose untiring follow up has completed this text in shortest possible time.

Although, all attempts are made to avoid the errors and printing mistakes, but like in every human task, there are likely to be some mistakes in this book also, therefore any suggestions, modifications brought to notice will be highly appreciated and incorporated in next edition.

14 January 2014
Pune

Authors

SYLLABUS

SECTION - I

Unit 1 Thermodynamics (7 Hrs)

Thermodynamic State, Process, Cycle, Thermodynamics System, Heat, work, Internal Energy, First law of Thermodynamics, Application of First Law to steady flow and Non-flow processes, Limitations of First Law (Numerical Treatment) Statement of Second Law of Thermodynamics.

Unit 2 Introduction to I C Engine (7 Hrs)

Carnot Engine, Construction and Working of C. I. and S. I., Two stroke, Four Stroke Cycles, Air standard cycles, Carnot Cycle, Joule Cycle, Otto Cycle, Air standard efficiency (Descriptive Treatment only).

Unit 3 Introduction to Refrigeration and Air Conditioning (7 Hrs)

Cannot refrigerator, Refrigerant types and properties, Vapour compression and vapour absorption system, solar refrigeration, Window Air Conditioning, Psychometric properties of moistair, Applications of refrigeration and air conditioning (Descriptive Treatment only).

SECTION - II

Unit 4 Energy Sources and Power Plants (7 Hrs)

Renewable and nonrenewable, Solar-flat plate collector, concentric collector Parabolic and cylindrical, Photovoltaic cell, Wind, Geothermal, Tidal, Hydrapower plant, Steam Power Plant, Bio-gas, Bio-Diesel (Descriptive Treatment only).

Unit 5 Mechanical Power Transmission and Energy Conversion Devices

Type of Belt and belt drives, chain drive, Types of gears and gear trains, Types of Coupling, Types of Bearings (Numerical Treatment on belt drive), Types, Construction, working and applications of pumps, Compressor and Hydraulic Turbines.

Unit 6 Manufacturing Processes (7 Hrs)

Introduction to manufacturing processes – Casting Process, Steps involved in casting processes and their applications, Metal removing processes and their applications, Metal Joining Processes – welding, soldering and brazing and their applications.

CONTENTS

Section - I

Chapter 1 : Thermodynamics   1.1-1.58

Chapter 2 : Introduction to I C Emgine   2.1-2.48

Chapter 3 : Introduction to Refrigeration and Air conditioning   3.1-3.16

Section - II

Chapter 4 : Energy Sources and Power Plants   4.1–4.28

Chapter 5 : Mechanical Power Transmission and Energy Conversion Devices

    5.1–5.54

Chapter 6 : Manufacturing Processes   6.1–6.38

Section I

1
THERMODYNAMICS

1.1 Introduction
1.2 Working Substance
1.3 Thermodynamic System and Surrounding
1.4 Thermodynamic Equilibrium
1.5 Property, State and Process
1.6 Work, Power and Energy
1.7 Total Internal Energy and Forms of Energy
1.8 Zeroth Law of Thermodynamics
1.9 Law of Conservation of Energy and Joules Law
1.10 First Law of Thermodynamics
1.11 Applications of First Law of Thermodynamics
1.12 Limitations of First Law of Thermodynamics
1.13 Heat Engine and Heat Pump
1.14 Statements of Second Law of Thermodynamics
     Solved Problems
     Exercises

1.1 INTRODUCTION

Thermodynamics is a science which deals with the heat and work. Heat is a basic source of energy available naturally, whereas work is generally derived from heat. Heat is released by the combustion of fuels and it is converted into mechanical work with the help of an engine. A part of the heat energy is converted into work while the remaining is rejected at lower temperature to the surroundings. Thermodynamics decides the possibility and sets the conditions for the transformation of a maximum part of the heat into work.

A machine which is commonly used for converting heat into mechanical work is known as heat engine. The working substances which are commonly used in the heat engines are gases and vapours. A mixture of air and fuel is used as working substance in internal combustion engines and gas turbines, while steam is used in steam engines and steam turbines.

Engineers concerned with the design and maintenance of power generating machines should have a basic knowledge of the working substances which are used in the process of conversion of heat into work. A sound knowledge and understanding of the basic laws of thermodynamics is necessary for the design of efficient boilers, engines, turbines, compressors, refrigerators and air-conditioning systems.

Though the study of thermodynamics started with the analysis of heat engine processes with the aim of improving the efficiency of heat engines, today the scope has widened and there are many important applications of thermodynamic principles outside the field of heat engines.

1.2 WORKING SUBSTANCE

In heat engines, a fluid is always used to receive heat, expand and produce work output. In refrigerators and heat pumps also, a fluid is used to receive heat at a low temperature and after an increase of pressure rejects heat at a higher temperature. Such a fluid with convenient properties is known as a working substance.

The common working substances used are in the form of either gas or vapour. Air, steam and refrigerants are commonly used in work developing (engines) and work absorbing (compressor and refrigerator) devices. It is essential that the properties of the working fluids should be known in order to understand their behaviour under different pressure and temperature conditions. Extensive data of properties are available for air, steam and refrigerants like ammonia and freons.

A mixture of air and fuel is used as working substance in internal combustion engines which are used to drive scooters, motorcycles, automobiles, locomotives and ships. Steam is used as working substance in steam power plants for producing power. Ammonia is used as working substance in ice plants and Freon-12 is used as working substance in house-hold refrigerator.

Pure Substance : A pure substance has a homogeneous and invariable chemical composition, irrespective of its phase as solid, liquid and vapour. Water is considered as a pure substance as its chemical composition (H_2O) is same either it remains in the form of ice, water or steam or mixture of any two.

Dry air or liquid air separately can be considered as pure substance, but mixture of dry air and liquid air cannot be considered as pure substance as the percentages of O_2 and N_2 in dry air and liquid air are different.

1.3 THERMODYNAMIC SYSTEM AND SURROUNDINGS

A thermodynamic system may be considered as a quantity of working substance with which heat and work interactions are studied. The concept of thermodynamic system is useful for the study of either power generation equipments like engines and turbines or power absorbing equipments (like compressors used for compressing gases and refrigerators used for producing low temperature conditions). It may also be used to analyse combustion problems. The envelope enclosing the system, which may be real or hypothetical, is known as boundary of the system. The boundary may be rigid or flexible. The region outside the system is known as surroundings. The transfer of mass and energy takes place between the system and **surroundings.** The system and surroundings together is known as Universe. Thermodynamic systems are classified as (a) Closed, (b) Open and (c) Isolated.

(a) Closed System : This is a system of fixed mass of working substance and its boundary is determined by the envelope of the space occupied by the working substance.

A good example of closed system is a piston and cylinder as shown in Fig. 1.1. No mass can flow in or out, only heat or work or both may flow into or out of a closed system. If heat is supplied to the cylinder from external source, the volume of the gas increases and the piston moves. Work transfer occurs due to the movement of the boundary of the system. In other words, heat and work cross the boundary of the system during this process but there is no addition or loss of the original mass of the working substance.

Very often the closed system concept is used in thermodynamic analysis of various equipments.

(b) Open System : In open system, the working substance used crosses the boundary of the system. Heat and work also crosses the boundary.

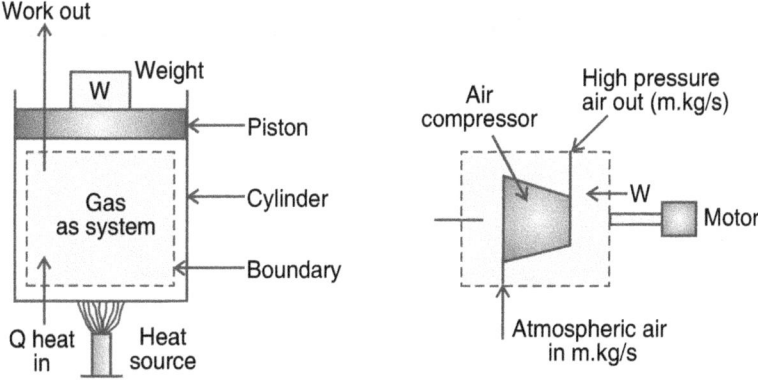

Fig. 1.1 : Closed system   Fig. 1.2 : Open system

The steam turbine, gas turbine and rotary compressor are good examples of open system. Fig. 1.2 shows the diagram of an air compressor which illustrates the open system.

Matter crosses the system boundary as low pressure air coming in and high pressure air leaving the unit. Work crosses the boundary through the driving shaft and heat is transferred across the boundary from the compressor surfaces due to cooling of the compressed air.

(c) Isolated System : An isolated system has no mass or energy interactions with the surroundings. Though such a system has no practical interest, it is a useful concept in the study and analysis of thermodynamic principles.

1.4 THERMODYNAMIC EQUILIBRIUM

The properties of the working substance (pressure, temperature, volume) in the system should be measured in order to fix the state of the system. The state of the system defines the condition of the system. As the system goes through a process (change of state), the state of the system at each instant should be known in order to define the process. The state of the system can be fixed only if the system is in equilibrium.

A system is said to be in thermodynamic equilibrium if no spontaneous change in the properties of the system can occur. Such a system is in complete balance with the restraints offered by the surroundings.

1.5 PROPERTY, STATE AND PROCESS

The state of the working fluid in a system at any equilibrium condition is described by properties like temperature, pressure and specific volume. The state of a system can be represented by a point on a diagram whose co-ordinates are properties. When the system goes from one equilibrium state to another equilibrium state due to energy or work transfer, the new state is represented by another point on the property diagram as shown in Fig. 1.3.

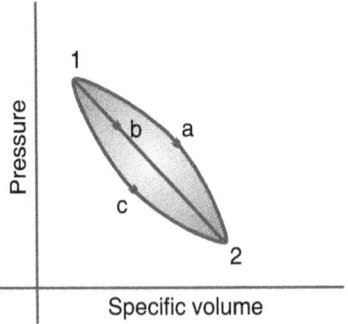

Fig. 1.3

The change in the property when the system goes from state-1 to state-2 (the new state as shown in fig. 1.3) is obtained from the difference between the co-ordinates of the two points 2 and 1 representing the equilibrium states. The properties do not depend on the path followed in reaching the state but only on, the equilibrium state itself. The change in the property, say pressure, between the states 1 and 2 is the same irrespective of the path a, b or c followed by the system in reaching condition 2 from condition 1.

The properties like internal energy and volume proportional to the mass in the system are called extensive properties. Temperature and pressure are not dependent on the mass of the system and are called intensive properties.

A process is said to occur when the system undergoes a change in state. If the process occurs at a very fast rate, the intermediate equilibrium conditions are not definable. For convenience, the process is assumed to occur at such a rate that intermediate equilibrium conditions can be described. This helps in fixing the path followed by the process as shown in Fig. 1.4.

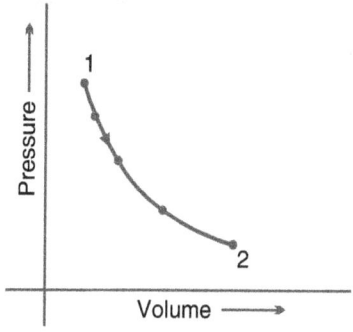

Fig. 1.4

1.5.1 Cyclic Process

If the number of processes in sequence bring the system back to its initial state, the system is said to execute a cycle or cyclic process. The cyclic process plays an important role in the study of thermodynamics. Because, the effect of a cyclic process may be conversion of part of the heat received into work (engine) or maintaining a system at lower temperature than the surroundings (refrigerator) by means of work input.

Cyclic processes are classified as closed cycles and open cycles. In a closed cyclic process, the same working substance is used again and again and only heat and work transfers take place between system and surroundings. The steam power plant and refrigeration system work on closed cycle. In an open cycle system, the working fluid once used during that cyclic process is thrown out and new mass of working fluid is taken during the next cyclic process. Internal combustion engines and gas turbines work on open cycle.

Different ideal closed cyclic processes are shown in Fig. 1.5. The cyclic processes (a) and (b) are used for power development using engines. The cyclic process (c) is used for producing a low temperature with the help of air refrigeration machine.

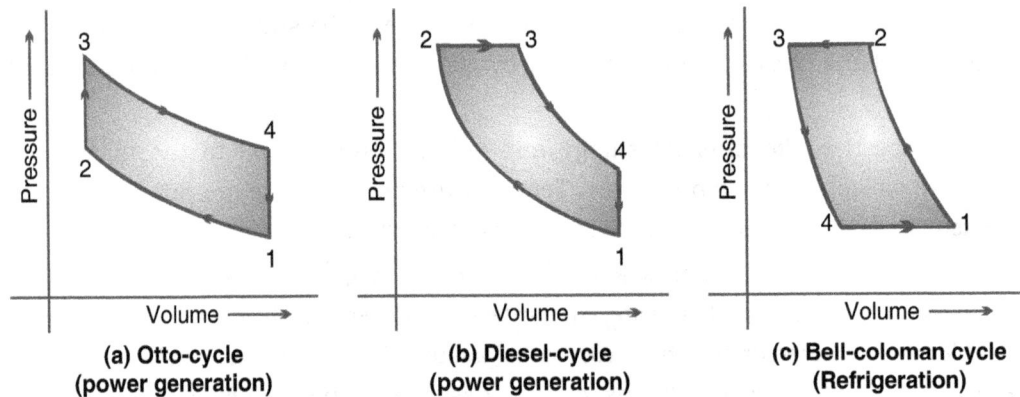

(a) Otto-cycle
(power generation)

(b) Diesel-cycle
(power generation)

(c) Bell-coloman cycle
(Refrigeration)

Fig. 1.5 : Different Cycles

1.5.2 Reversible and Irreversible Processes

A process is said to be reversible if the reversal of the process does not leave any trace on the system and the surroundings. For example, if during a process from state 1 to 2, as shown in Fig. 1.6, the work and heat transfers are W and Q and if by supplying back W and Q to the system, the state of the system can be brought back from 2 to 1, the process is said to be reversible.

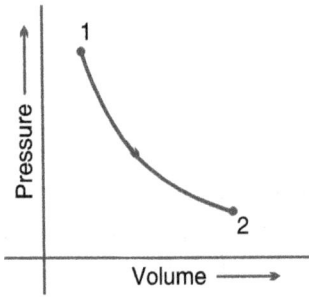

Fig. 1.6

If there is any change in the requirement of work and heat to bring back the system from state 2 and 1, this process is known as irreversible process. The processes used in practice are mostly irreversible due to friction, heat transfer and mixing, but in many cases idealisation is used for analysis.

A cycle which consists of processes, all of which are reversible, is known as a reversible cycle. In the analysis of thermodynamic processes, it is generally assumed that the processes are reversible, because only then the state of the system and path followed during the process can be represented on property diagram.

When a system changes its state in such a way that at any instant during the process, the state point can be located on the diagram, then the process is said to be reversible. The fluid undergoing such a process passes through a continuous series of equilibrium states. Therefore, a reversible process between two states can be drawn as a line on any diagram of properties as shown in Fig. 1.7. In practice, the fluid undergoing a process cannot be kept in equilibrium in its intermediate states and a continuous path cannot be traced on a diagram of properties. Such real processes are called irreversible processes. An irreversible process is usually represented on a property diagram by a dotted line as shown in Fig. 1.7 joining the end states to indicate that the intermediate states are indeterminate.

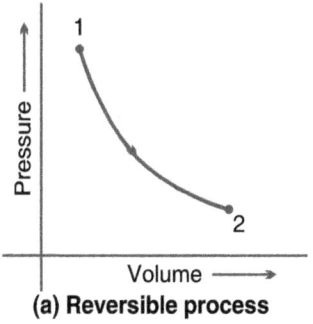
(a) Reversible process

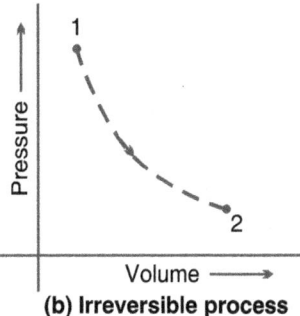
(b) Irreversible process

Fig. 1.7

1.6 WORK, POWER AND ENERGY

(a) Mechanical Work : Work is said to be done when a force acts upon a body causing that body to move along the direction of the force. The work done is given by the product of force and distance travelled by the body along the direction of force.

$$W = F \cdot S$$

This work done is known as mechanical work.

(c) Thermodynamic Work : Thermodynamic work is an interaction between the system and the surroundings. The work is said to be done by the system on surrounding, if the total external effect is lifting the body up.

Consider a system consisting of a battery and motor as shown in Fig. 1.8 (a). The fan is driven by a motor. The system is doing work on the surroundings.

When the fan is replaced by a pulley and a weight W as shown in Fig. 1.8 (b), then the weight is raised up as the pulley is driven by the motor. Therefore, the net external effect is raising the weight W up. Therefore. the system is doing thermodynamic work.

When the work is done by the system, then it is taken as positive and when the work is done on the system, then it is taken as negative.

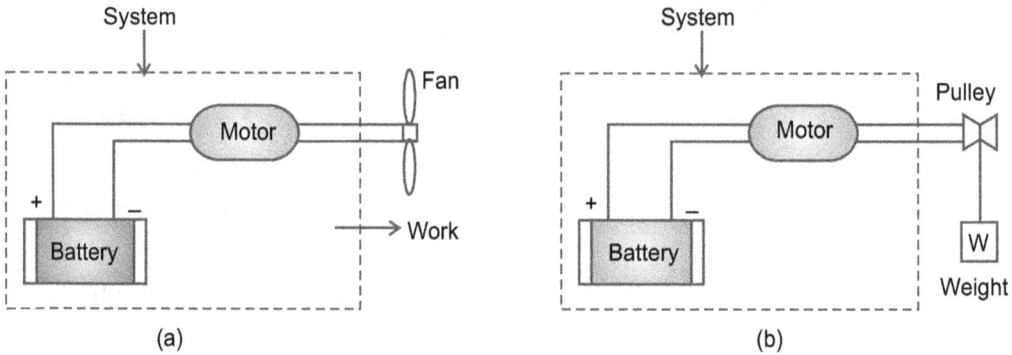

Fig. 1.8

(c) Work of Expansion : Consider a closed system of a piston and cylinder as shown in Fig. 1.9. The net pressure of the gas in the system acts on the piston and causes the piston to move in the forward direction. The force acting on the piston is p·A where A is the area of the piston. If the piston moves through a small distance dx, the work done by the gas on the piston = pA · dx = p·dv as A·dx is the change in the volume of the gas. If the gas expands from state 1 to 2 as shown in Fig. 1.9, the work done is given by,

$$W = \int_{V_1}^{V_2} p \cdot dv \quad \ldots (1.1)$$

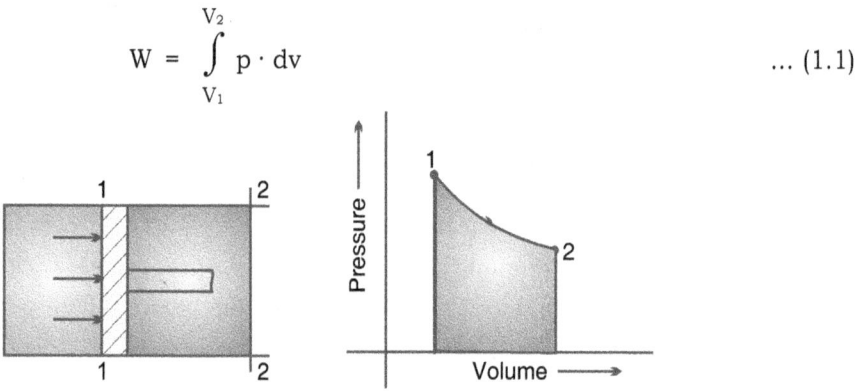

Fig. 1.9

This integral is the area below the curve 1-2. This expansion cannot be integrated unless the path followed is specified. Therefore, it becomes necessary that the system should be in equilibrium at all the intermediate states between 1 and 2, as only then the path can be defined. The work done depends upon the path followed by the system during the process 1-2 and not on the end conditions only. The work given by the above expression is known as work of expansion.

Comparison between Work and Heat :

Similarities :

1. Both work and heat are path functions.
2. Both are recognized at the boundaries of the system.
3. Both are associated with the process only.

Dissimilarities :

1. In heat transfer, temperature difference is essential which is not the case with work.
2. There is no work transfer with stable system, however, there is no restriction for the heat transfer.

Power : Power is the rate at which work is done. The common unit of power is H.P. (horse power) which is defined as 75 kgf-m/sec or 4500 kgf-m/min.

In S.I. system, common unit of power is kW (kilowatt) which is generally used for electrical equivalent of mechanical power.

$$1 \text{ kW} = 1.36 \text{ H.P}$$
$$= 101.9 \text{ kgf-m/sec}$$

If one kW capacity unit is allowed to operate for one hour, the energy coming out in the form of heat or work is given by

$$1 \text{kW} = 1000 \text{ Nm/sec} = 1000 \text{ J/sec} = 1 \text{ kJ/sec}$$

In S.I. units,
$$1 \text{kWh} = 1000 \times 3600 = 36 \times 10^5 \text{ J or Nm}$$
$$= 3600 \text{ kJ}$$

Energy : Energy is defined as the capacity, a body possesses for doing work. The energy may exist in the form of potential energy, kinetic energy, mechanical work or heat. Energy may exist in the form of stored energy or energy in transition. Potential energy can be considered as stored energy, whereas heat and work are identifiable only during transition.

Stored energy of a system remains constant until such time, when work or heat transfer takes place between the system and surroundings. Stored energy in a system can be increased or decreased by adding or removing heat or by doing work on the system or allowing system to perform work. The unit of energy is kgf-m or kcal in Metric units and Nm or J in S.I. units.

HEAT AS A SOURCE OF ENERGY

Heat is defined as the energy transferred without transfer of mass across the boundary of a system due to a temperature difference between the system and surroundings.

The amount of heat transferred during a process or work done by the system during the same process is dependent on the path followed during the process. Though the end conditions are same as shown in Fig. 1.10, the heat exchange and work done during the processes will be different for the two different paths. Thus heat and work are said to be path functions and not point functions (like properties).

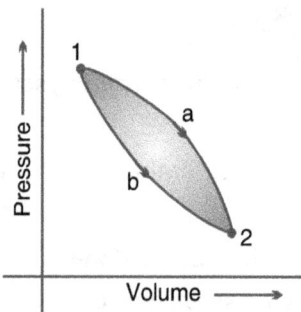

Fig. 1.10

The unit of heat in MKS system is kcal, which is defined as a quantity of heat required to raise the temperature of 1 kg water through 1°C. The unit of heat in S.I. system is joule which is equivalent to 1 Nm.

Most of the energy stored in fuels is evolved as heat and the heat has to be transferred through the system boundaries during various processes.

Heat energy is generally transferred in three ways, namely conduction, convection and radiation in the direction of lower temperature in all the three modes.

Conduction : If one end of a metal rod is heated to higher temperature, energy flows from the hot end to the cold end and the temperature of the cold end continues to rise. The transfer of energy takes place from the hot end to the cold end by molecular activity. The molecular activity at the hot end increases the molecular activity of an adjacent section and heat is transferred through the molecular activity. This mode of heat transfer without change of position of the molecules is known as conduction.

Convection : The transfer of heat by convection only occurs in fluids, since in this mode, the energy is exchanged between the molecules of hotter fluid and those of the cooler fluid when the former move in amongst the later. The molecules of the hotter fluid moving in amongst those of the cooler fluid will collide with the latter and impart energy to them through these collisions. This mode of heat transfer by the hotter molecules colliding with the cooler molecules is known as convection.

Radiation : The transfer of heat by electromagnetic wave propagation from one body (hot) to other body (cold) is known as radiation. No medium is necessary between bodies for a transfer of heat by this mode to take place. For heat transfer by radiation there should be a visual path between the bodies.

In actual practice, heat transfer takes place by one of the modes or simultaneously through all the three modes. Consider the generation of steam in the boiler. The transfer of heat of combustion from the gases to the boiler takes place through radiation and convection. The heat is further conducted through the boiler shell and finally it is passed on to the water through convection leading to the generation of steam.

Limitations of Expansion Work :
1. The process must be reversible.
2. It is applicable for closed system only.
3. The exact relation between pressure and volume during expansion or compression must be known.

All the above mentioned conditions must be satisfied simultaneously.

1.7 TOTAL INTERNAL ENERGY

Energy that remains within the boundary of a system is called its total internal energy. The energy is associated with the matter in the form of potential energy, kinetic energy, internal energy as well as magnetic, electrical, chemical and many other forms of energy. In the absence of other forms of energy except potential, kinetic and internal, the energy possessed by the mass is known as total energy

$$e_t = u + PE + KE \qquad ...(1.2)$$

where e_t is known as total internal energy.

The energy directly associated with matter is termed as its internal energy and is unrelated to its position or velocity (and hence the potential and kinetic energy). Although the internal energy is not associated with potential or kinetic energy of the mass, the same is not true for the atoms of which the mass is comprised. A significant portion of the internal energy is associated with the kinetic energy of its atoms. The internal energy of the mass is present in the form of translational energy, rotational energy and vibrational energy of the individual atom.

Different Forms of Energy :

Potential Energy : The potential energy possessed by a body is due to its position or elevation relative to some datum plane. Therefore, the potential energy of a substance is equal to the work that can be done by allowing the substance to fall from the given position to the surface of the earth, as the surface of the earth is taken as the datum. The potential energy of a body of W newtons weight at a height Z metres is equal to WZ (Nm) = $\frac{mgZ}{g_c}$ (Nm).

Kinetic Energy : The kinetic energy possessed by a body is due to the reason of its motion. A body of mass m kg moving with a velocity V (m/sec) possesses an amount of kinetic energy = $\frac{1}{2}$ mV² (Nm).

Internal Energy : Matter is composed of molecules which move continuously and randomly. In gases, the movement of the molecules is more pronounced than in solids and liquids. Matter possesses internal kinetic energy due to the motion of its molecules. In addition to this internal kinetic energy, matter has internal potential energy due to the relative position of their molecules. The sum of these two energies is known as internal energy and it is denoted by u, the unit commonly used being J/kg or kJ/kg. If the temperature of a gas is increased by adding heat, the molecular activity increases. Therefore, the internal energy of a gas is a function of its temperature and its value can be increased or decreased by adding or removing heat from the gases which are commonly used as working fluids.

The total stored energy of a substance per kg is given by

$$\left(u + \frac{Z}{J}\frac{g}{g_c} + \frac{1}{2}\frac{V^2}{g_c J}\right) \text{J/kg}. \qquad \ldots (1.3)$$

where J is a conversion factor which converts work units into heat units and it has value of 1 Nm/joule in SI units and the value of $g_c = 1$

Specific heat of a substance is the joules of heat that must be added to unit mass of the substance to raise the temperature through one degree centigrade. The unit is J/kg-°C.

When the heat is added to a body, the heat energy is used to speed-up the molecular activity (motion) and also to expand its volume. The amount of expansion in solids and liquids is very small but it is considerable in the case of gases. We have seen that when gas expands, the amount of work done during expansion is given by $\int_1^2 p.dv$.

Therefore, when heat is added to gases, part of the heat is used up to expand the gas and the remaining is used to increase the molecular activity or internal energy or temperature except when the volume is not constant. Therefore, gases have two specific heats, namely specific heat at constant volume and specific heat at constant pressure.

Specific Heat at Constant Volume (C_v) : The amount of heat required in J to raise the temperature of 1 kg of the gas through 1°C at constant volume, as shown in Fig. 1.11 (a), is known as specific heat at constant volume. There is no work of expansion as the gas volume remains constant and, therefore, all the heat supplied is used to increase its internal energy.

Specific Heat at Constant Pressure (C_p) : The amount of heat required in J to raise the temperature of one kg of the gas through 1°C at constant pressure, (as shown in Fig. 1.11 (b)), is known as specific heat at constant pressure.

When the gas is heated at constant pressure, it expands and moves the piston through a distance L, therefore, in addition to the heat required to increase the kinetic energy of the molecules, further heat must be added to perform the work of moving the piston through a distance L. Therefore, the specific heat of a gas at constant pressure is always greater than the specific heat of the gas at constant volume by an amount equivalent to expansion work. The values of C_v and C_p for air are 0.71 and 1.005 kJ/kg-K, respectively.

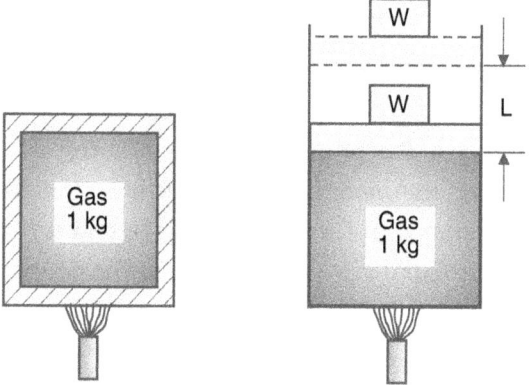

(a) Heating at constant volume   **(b)** Heating at constant pressure

Fig. 1.11

Flow Work or Flow Energy :

In case of flow process, certain amount of work is required to push the fluid into and out of the system. This work is known as flow work or flow energy.

Consider a flow process as shown in Fig. 1.12.

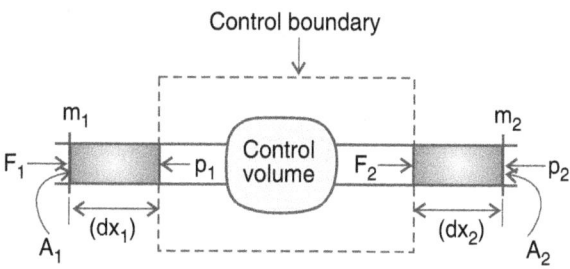

Fig. 1.12

Let F_1 is the force required to push the mass m, through a cross-sectional area A_1, into the system against the pressure p_1 and pushing through a distance dx_1.

Work done on the system, $dW = - F_1 \cdot dx_1$

(– ve sign indicates that the work is done on the system)

$= - p_1 A_1 \cdot dx_1$

$= -p_1 \cdot dv_1$ as $A_1 \cdot dx_1 = dv_1$

∴ Total flow work, $W = p_1 v_1$

Similarly, the work done by the system to force the fluid out of the system = $p_2 v_2$.

∴   Net flow work = $(p_2 v_2 - p_1 v_1)$ ... (1.4)

Enthalpy :

We come across many times the summation of the terms $(u + pv_s)$ which is known as enthalpy and denoted by h. u is internal energy and p and v_s are the pressure and specific volume of the fluid taking part in the heat and work reactions.

In the previous chapter, the term pv was shown to be equal to the flow energy or flow work.

The reason for introducing the property enthalpy at this stage is that most steam tables and other tables of thermodynamic properties of (NH_3, CO_2) give values of enthalpy but not internal energy. In these cases, it is necessary to calculate the internal energy at a state using the tabulated values and using the equation

$$u = h - pv \qquad \ldots (1.5)$$

In the superheat region of most thermodynamic tables, values of the specific internal energy u are not given. These can be readily calculated by using the above relation.

1.8 ZEROTH LAW OF THERMODYNAMICS

Consider body A is in thermal equilibrium with body B (respective of their sizes) and body A is also in thermal equilibrium with body C as shown in Fig. 1.13 (a) and (b).

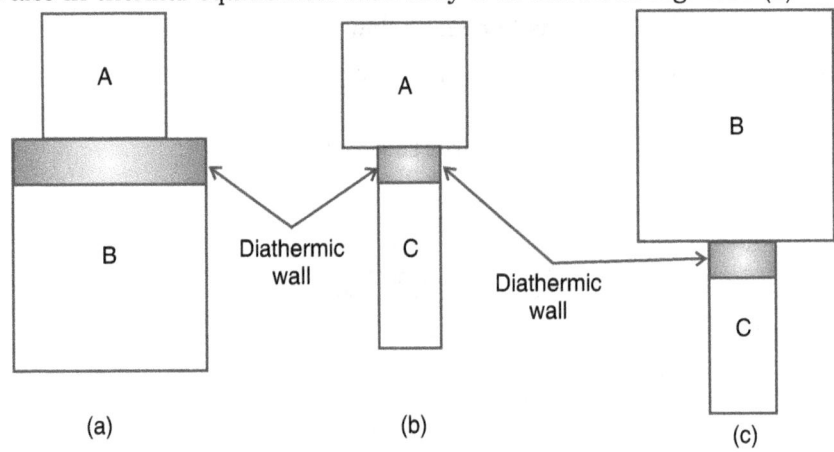

Fig. 1.13

The body C will be in thermal equilibrium with body B. This statement is known as Zeroth law of thermodynamics. This forms the basis for temperature measurement.

1.9 LAW OF CONSERVATION OF ENERGY AND JOULES LAW

1.9.1 Law of conservation of energy

The law of conservation of energy states that energy can neither be created nor destroyed. Whenever there is a change in the state of a system, there is only transformation of one form of energy into another.

Consider the following changes in the system :

(a) The water is passing down a vertical pipe. The potential energy of water is converted into kinetic energy.

(b) A brake is applied to a moving automobile. The kinetic energy of automobile is converted into heat energy through friction.

(c) A. current is passing through an electric heater. The electrical energy is converted into heat energy.

The above examples show that one form of energy is simply converted into another form and there is no change in the total energy of the system and surroundings.

1.9.2 Joule's Experiment and Relation Between Work and Heat

In 1844-1854, the English Scientist J. P. Joule conducted experiments which were the first step in the quantitative analysis of thermodynamic systems, and which led to the first law of thermodynamics.

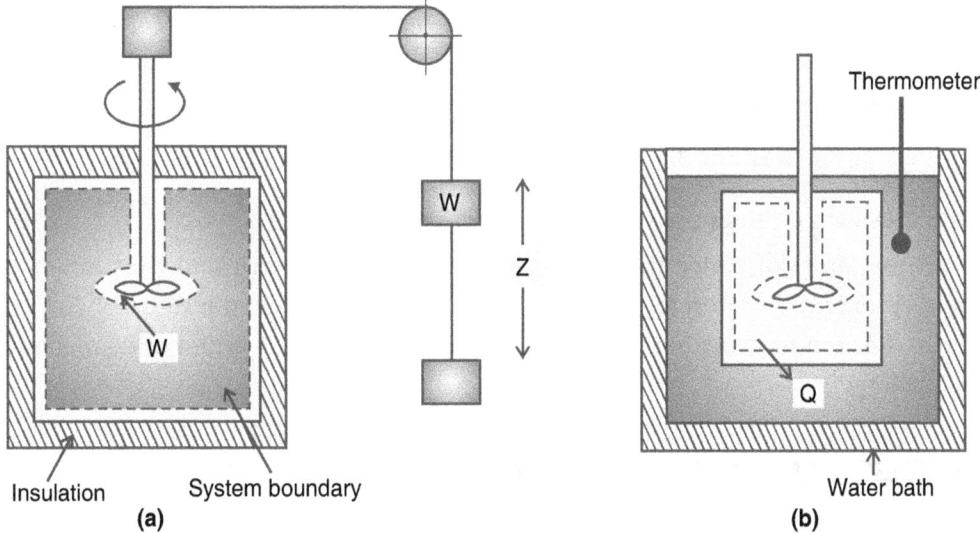

Fig. 1.14

The experiment conducted by Joule is shown in Fig. 1.14. In this experiment, work was done on the fluid by means of a paddle wheel. This work caused a rise in temperature of the fluid. The amount of work done was measured by the change in potential energy as the weight W fell through a height Z. Then the system was placed in the water bath, so that the heat was transferred from the fluid to the water until the original state of the liquid was re-established (as indicated by the pressure and temperature of the fluid). In this way, the system was taken through a cycle. It was observed that the amount of heat rejected by the fluid to the water was proportional to the increase of energy of the water bath which could be easily determined by measuring the rise in temperature of the water bath. With this experiment, Joule found that the net work input W to the system was always proportional to the net heat Q transferred by the system, regardless of the rate at which the work was done and the scheme used for transforming it into heat. As the system at the end of the cycle does not experience any change, the transfer of heat and work across the boundary of the system can be represented mathematically as

$$\oint \frac{dW}{J} + \oint dQ = 0 \qquad \ldots (1.6)$$

where dW and dQ are infinitesimal amount of work and heat transfer and the symbol $\oint$ denotes cyclic summation or integration.

The magnitude of $\oint dW$ is always equal to the magnitude of $\oint dQ$ if the work and heat both are measured in same units. If work is measured in work units and heat in heat units, then a proportionality factor relating work and heat, was found to exist and this was called as the mechanical equivalent of heat (J). It is the ratio of work done to the heat transferred from a system during a cycle and denoted by J_c, which is known as Joule's constant. It is only a unit conversion factor.

$$J_c = \frac{\text{Work}}{\text{Heat}}$$

In S.I. system of units the value J_c is unity, i.e. 1 Nm = 1 J.

The equation (1.6) states that the algebraic sum of the work and heat interactions during a cycle or cycles is zero. Heat and work can be represented in the same units (as Joules or Newton-metres) but this does not mean that heat and work are identical forms of energy.

1.10 FIRST LAW OF THERMODYNAMICS

This law based on a Joule's experiment states that if a system executes a cycle transferring work and heat through its boundary, then the net work transfer is equivalent to the net heat transfer.

or $\qquad \oint dW = \oint dQ$

The first law of thermodynamics cannot be proved mathematically, but experimental evidences have repeatedly confirmed its validity. Also, no phenomenon has been shown to contradict it and therefore it is accepted as a law of nature. No restriction was imposed which limited the application of first law to reversible energy transformations. Hence, the first law of thermodynamics applies to reversible as well as to irreversible transformations.

Application of First Law to a Process : When a system executes a process, the change in stored energy of the system is numerically equal to the net heat interactions minus the net work interaction during the process.

$\therefore \qquad E_2 - E_1 = Q - W$

$\therefore \qquad \Delta E = Q - W$

or $\qquad \Delta E = (E_2 - E_1) = \int_1^2 d(Q - W) \qquad \ldots (1.7)$

where E represents the total internal energy. In the absence of electric, magnetic and chemical energy, and neglecting the changes in potential and kinetic energy for a closed system, the above equation can be written as

$$\Delta U = (U_2 - U_1) = \int_1^2 d(Q - W) \qquad \ldots (1.8)$$

$\therefore \qquad \Delta U = U_2 - U_2 - U_1 = Q - W \qquad \ldots (1.9)$

In the above equation, the mass of the system is taken as unity. The above equation can be written as

$$m(\Delta U) = m(U_2 - U_1) = Q_t - W_t \qquad \ldots (1.10)$$

In general, the addition of heat to a system results in a rise in temperature of the system and external work is performed due to increase in volume of the system. The rise in temperature is an indication of increase in internal energy. Heat added to the system will be considered positive and the heat rejected by the system will be considered negative.

1.11 APPLICATIONS OF FIRST LAW OF THERMODYNAMICS

(A) Closed Systems :

1. Reversible Constant Volume Process : The system and the states before and after heat addition at constant volume are shown in Fig. 1.15.

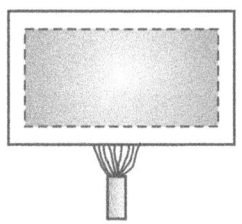 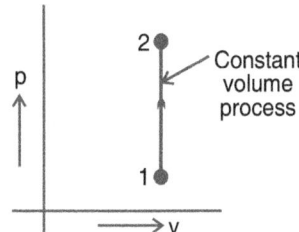

Fig. 1.15

Considering the mass of the system as unity and applying the first law to the process.

$$q = w + (u_2 - u_1) \qquad \ldots (1.11)$$

The work done, $\qquad w = \int_1^2 p \cdot dv = 0 \text{ as } dv = 0$

$$Q = (u_2 - u_1) = C_v (T_2 - T_1) \quad \ldots (1.12)$$

where C_v is known as specific heat at constant volume.

∴ $C_v = (\Delta u/dT)$, change in internal energy per degree change in temperature per kg mass.

2. Reversible Constant Pressure Process : The system and the states before and after heat addition are shown in Fig. 1.16.

Considering the mass of the system as unity and applying the first law to the process,

$$*q = w + (u_2 - u_1)$$

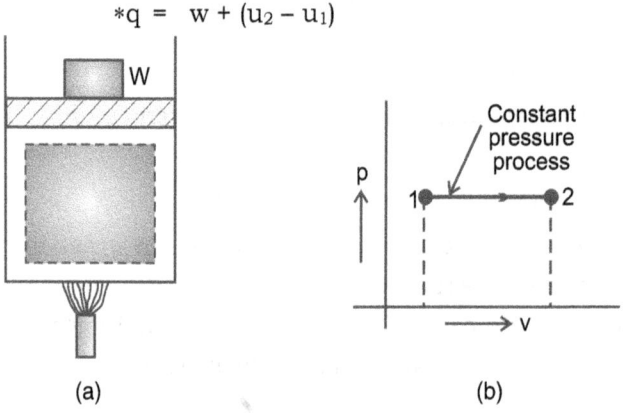

Fig. 1.16

The work done, $w = \int_1^2 p \cdot dv = (v_2 - v_1)$ as p is constant and v_1 and v_2 are specific volumes.

∴ $$q = \frac{p(v_2 - v_1)}{J_c} + (u_2 - u_1) \quad \ldots (1.13)$$

where J_c is conversation factor which is unity in S.I. system.

$$q = (u_2 + pv_2) - (u_1 + pv_1) = h_2 - h_1 = C_p (T_2 - T_1) \quad \ldots (1.14)$$

w**here h is the enthalpy and C_p is known as the specific heat at constant pressure.

∴ $C_p = \Delta h/dT$, change in enthalpy per degree change in temperature per kg mass.

Also, $q = C_p(T_2 - T_1) = (p_2 v_2 - p_1 v_1) + (u_2 - u_1)$

$= R(T_2 - T_1) + C_v(T_2 - T_1)$

$$\boxed{C_p = R + C_v} \quad \ldots (1.15)$$

(*q, w are used for heat and work when mass in the system is unity and Q and W are used when the mass is m and in that case $U_2 - U_1 = m(u_2 - u_1)$.

3. Reversible isothermal process : The system and the states before and after heat addition at constant temperature are shown in Fig. 1.17.

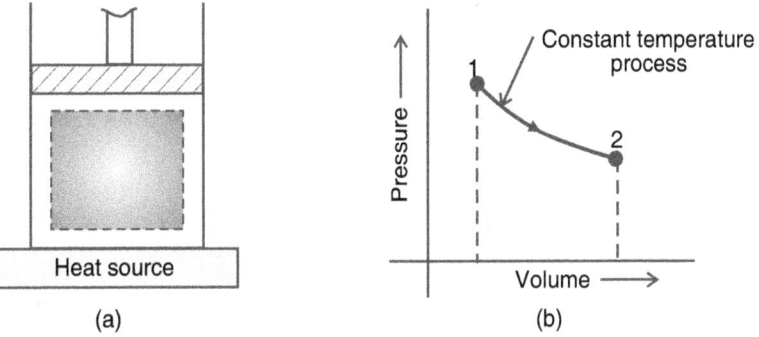

Fig. 1.17

Considering the mass of the system as unity and applying the first law to the process,

$$q = w + (u_2 - u_1) = w + C_v (T_2 - T_1)$$
$$= w + 0 \text{ as } T_2 = T_1 \text{ (condition required for isothermal process)}$$
$$= \int_1^2 p \cdot dv \qquad \ldots (1.16)$$

4. Reversible adiabatic process : The system and the states before and after execution of the process are shown in Fig. 1.18.

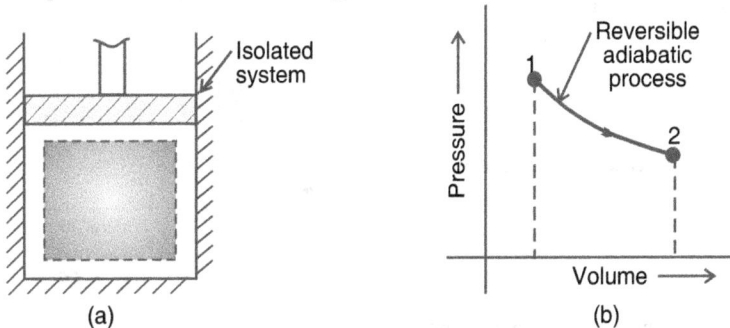

Fig. 1.18

Considering the mass of the system as unity and applying the first law to the process,

$$q = w + u_2 - u_1$$
$$0 = w + u_2 - u_1 \text{ as } Q = 0$$

(Condition required for adiabatic process)

$$\therefore \qquad w = u_1 - u_2 = C_v (T_1 - T_2) \qquad \ldots (1.17)$$

It is obvious from the above equation that the system develops work at the expense of its internal energy.

5. Irreversible Process : The work done in the previous processes is given by $W = \int_1^2 p \cdot dv$, but this cannot be applied to processes such as free expansion and when paddle work is done on the system, keeping the system boundary fixed.

(i) Free expansion : In this case, the work done W = 0 as the boundary of the system is fixed, but

$$\int_1^2 p \cdot dv \neq 0$$

(ii) Addition of Paddle Work : Referring to Fig. 1.14, the work developed by the system $\int_1^2 p \cdot dv = 0$ as the boundary is fixed but $W \neq 0$ as the work is fed to the system.

All the processes in practice are irreversible, (internally) to some extent due to turbulence, friction and temperature gradient in the system. Applying the first law to an irreversible process,

$$q = w_n + (u_2 - u_1)$$

where,
$$w_n = \int_1^2 p \cdot dv - w_l \qquad \ldots (1.18)$$

where w_n is the net work done and w_l is the work lost due to internal irreversibility of the system. To calculate w_l is always difficult as it is not possible to predict the sources of irreversibility and their exact magnitudes. In the above analysis, the mass is considered as unity.

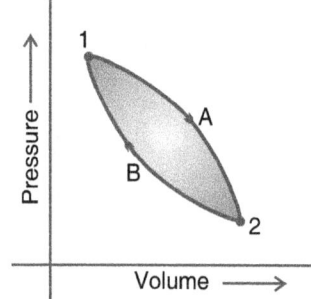

Fig. 1.19

6. Cyclic Process : A cyclic process is shown in Fig. 1.19.

In a cyclic process, the change in internal energy becomes zero as the system reaches to its original condition.

Application of first law to this cyclic process, yields,

$$\oint dQ = \oint dW \qquad \ldots (1.19)$$

(B) Open systems :

Application of First Law to Steady Flow Process:

Consider a steady flow system as shown in Fig. 1.20. The following assumptions are made in the system analysis:

1. The mass flow through the system remains constant.
2. There is no change in chemical composition of the fluid or there is no chemical reaction.
3. The state of fluid at any point remains constant with time.
4. Fluid is uniform in composition.
5. The potential, kinetic, internal and flow energies are only considered in the analysis. Other forms of energy (electrical, chemical, magnetic etc.) are not considered in most of the thermodynamic systems discussed in this text.
6. The only interactions between the system and surroundings are work and heat.

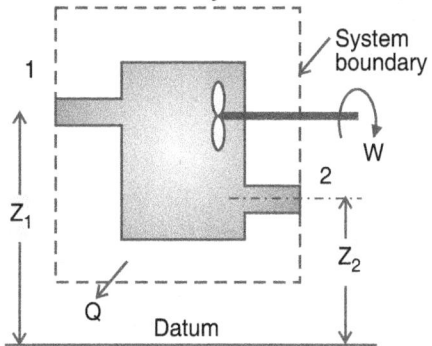

Fig. 1.20: Steady flow current

It is considered that the working fluid enters in the system at state 1 and leaves the system at state 2. Therefore, the energy at entry and exit are subscripted by 1 and 2.

As per the law of conservation of energy,

$$E_1 \pm W \pm Q = E_2$$

where E represents the sum of all the energies associated with the fluid.

For thermodynamic system, the above equation can be written as

$$m\left[\frac{Z_1}{J_c} \cdot \frac{g}{g_c} + \frac{V_1^2}{2g_c J_c} + u_1 + \frac{p_1 v_{s_1}}{J_c}\right] \pm W \pm Q = m\left[\frac{Z_2}{J_c} \cdot \frac{g}{g_c} + \frac{V_2^2}{2g_c J_c} + u_2 + \frac{p_2 v_{s_2}}{J_c}\right] \quad \ldots (1.20)$$

where Z and V are elevation in metres and velocity in metre/sec, u is internal energy in J/kg respectively. W and Q are work and heat interactions between the system and surroundings.

g = Acceleration due to gravity (m/s²)

g_c = Force unit conversion constant (1 kg-m/Ns²)

J_c = Joule constant to convert work unit into heat unit (J_c = 1 N/m)

(a) The term $\dfrac{Z}{J_c} \dfrac{g}{g_c}$ is the potential energy per unit mass in joule/kg, where Z is in metres.

(b) The term $\dfrac{1}{2} \dfrac{V^2}{g_c J_c}$ is the kinetic energy per unit mass in joule/kg, where V is in m/s.

(c) The term u is the internal energy per unit mass in joules/kg.

(d) The term $\dfrac{pv_s}{J_c}$ is the flow work per unit mass in joules/kg where p is in N/m² and v_s is specific volume in m³/kg.

Now substituting the values of $J_c = 1$ and $g_c = 1$ in the above equation,

$$m\left[Z_1 g + \dfrac{V_1^2}{2} + u_1 + p_1 v_{s_1}\right] \pm W \pm Q = m\left[Z_2 g + \dfrac{V_2^2}{2} + u_2 + p_2 v_{s_2}\right] \quad \ldots (1.21)$$

By definition, $h = u + \dfrac{pv_s}{J_c} = u + pv_s$ as $J_c = 1$.

Substituting this value in the above equation,

$$m\left[Z_1 g + \dfrac{V_1^2}{2} + h_1\right] \pm W \pm Q = m\left[Z_2 g + \dfrac{V_2^2}{2} + h_2\right] \quad \ldots (1.22)$$

The above two equations can also be written as

$$\left[m \cdot Z_1 g + \dfrac{mV_1^2}{2} + U_1 + p_1 v_1\right] \pm W \pm Q = \left[mZ_2 g + \dfrac{mV_1^2}{2} + U_2 + p_2 v_2\right] \quad \ldots (1.23)$$

where, $U_1 = mu_1$ and $U_2 = mu_2$
$V_1 = mv_{s_1}$ and $v_2 = mv_{s_2}$

$$\left[mZ_1 g + \dfrac{mV_1^2}{2} + H_1\right] \pm W \pm Q = \left[mZ_2 g + \dfrac{mV_1^2}{2} + H_2\right] \quad \ldots (1.24)$$

where, $H_1 = mh_1$ and $H_2 = mh_2$

The typical systems are shown in Fig. 1.21, where work and heat reactions are shown.

(a) In this system, work and heat both are coming out of the system, so for substituting in the energy equation, these should be taken as – Q and – W.

(b) In this system work and heat both are supplied to the system, so for substituting in the energy equation, these should be taken as + Q and + W.

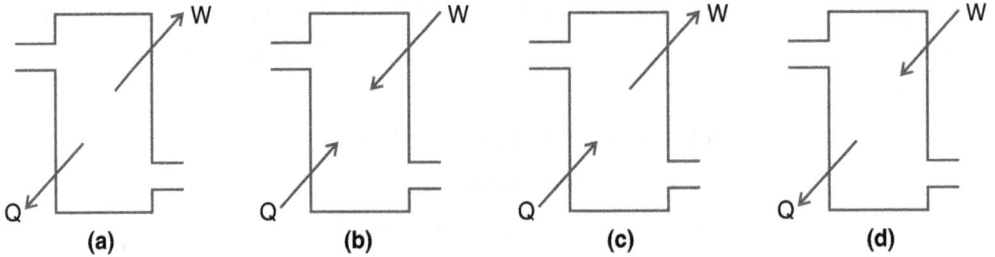

Fig. 1.21: Different possible systems

(c) In this system heat is supplied and work comes out of the system, so for substituting in the energy equation, these should be taken as +Q and –W.

(d) In this system work is supplied and heat comes out of the system, so for substituting in the energy equation, these should be taken as $-Q$ and $+W$.

Engineering Applications of Steady Flow Energy Equation :

Systems which are commonly used in engineering are classified as :

1. Work developing systems (engines and turbines).
2. Work absorbing systems (pumps, compressors and refrigerators).
3. Neither work developing nor work absorbing systems (nozzle and heat exchangers).

In the present analysis, the mass flow rate is considered as unity.

1. Work Developing Systems :

(a) Water Turbine : In a water turbine, water is supplied from a height to a turbine. Potential energy of water is converted into kinetic energy when it enters into the turbine and part of it is converted into useful work which is used to generate electricity as shown in Fig. 1.22. Considering the centre of the shaft of turbine as datum, we can write energy equation as

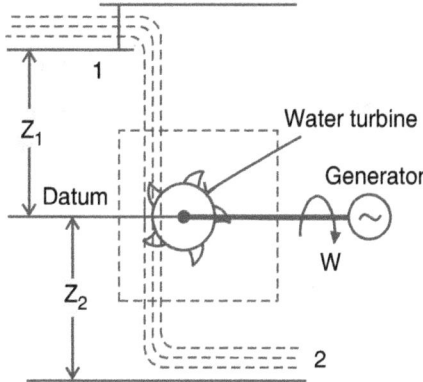

Fig. 1.22: Water turbine

$$\left[u_1 + p_1 v_{s_1} + Z_1 g + \frac{V_1^2}{g}\right] \pm q \pm w = \left[u_2 + p_2 v_{s_2} + Z_2 g + \frac{V_2^2}{2}\right]$$

In this case, $q = 0$, $\Delta u = u_2 - u_1 = 0$ and $v_{s_1} = v_{s_2} = v_s$

The work is coming out of the system,

$$\therefore \quad \left[Z_1 g + \frac{V_1^2}{2}\right] - w = \left[Z_2 g + \frac{V_2^2}{2}\right] + v_s (p_2 - p_1) \quad \ldots (1.25)$$

The value of Z_2 will be negative as it is measured from the axis of the turbine.

If it is assumed $p_1 = p_2$, then

$$w = (Z_1 + Z_2) g + \left(\frac{V_1^2 - V_2^2}{2}\right)$$

Note : Z_1 and Z_2 can also be measured from ground level.

(b) Steam or Gas Turbine : The steam or gas turbine is a mechanical system for developing power. High pressure, high temperature steam or gas is passed through the turbine and part of its energy is converted into work in the turbine and is fed to run the generator as shown in Fig. 1.23. The steam or gas leaves the turbine at lower pressure and temperature.

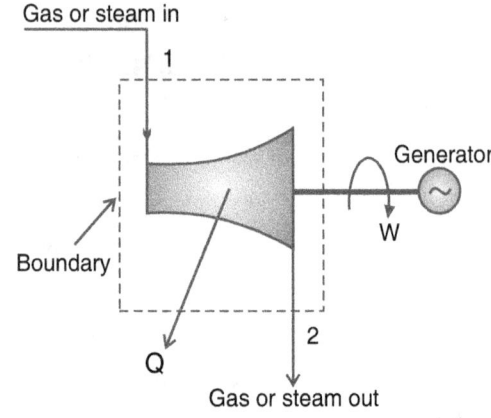

Fig. 1.23: Steam turbine

Applying energy equation to the system

$\Delta Z = 0$ for these systems

$$\therefore \quad \left[h_1 + \frac{V_1^2}{2}\right] - q - w = \left[h_2 + \frac{V_2^2}{2}\right]$$

The signs of q and w are taken negative as both come out of the boundary. As the temperature of the system is less than surroundings, heat is lost to the surroundings.

$$\left[h_1 + \frac{V_1^2}{2}\right] - q = \left[h_2 + \frac{V_2^2}{2}\right] + w \qquad \ldots (1.26)$$

or $\quad w = (h_1 - h_2) + \dfrac{V_1^2 - V_2^2}{2} - q$

2. Work Absorbing Systems :

(a) Centrifugal Water Pump : The water pump takes the water from a lower level and pumps to higher level as shown in Fig. 1.24. The work required to run the pump is supplied from external source as electric motor or diesel engine.

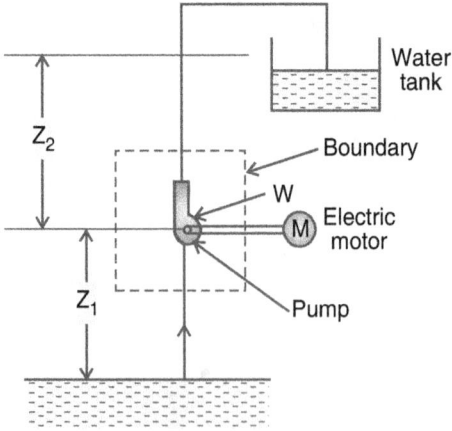

Fig. 1.24: Centrifugal water pump

In this system q = 0 and Δu = 0 as there is no change in temperature of the water.
Applying the energy equation to the system,

$$\left[Z_1 g + \frac{V_1^2}{2} + p_1 v_{s_1}\right] + w = \left[Z_2 g + \frac{V_2^2}{2} + p_2 v_{s_2}\right]$$

The w is taken as positive as the work enters the system.
As $v_{s_1} = v_{s_2} = v_s$

$$\therefore \quad \left[-Z_1 g + \frac{V_1^2}{2}\right] + w = \left[Z_2 g + \frac{V_2^2}{2}\right] + v_s (p_2 - p_1) \quad \ldots (1.27)$$

$$\therefore \quad w = (Z_2 + Z_1) \cdot g + \frac{V_2^2 - V_1^2}{2} + v_s (p_2 - p_1)$$

The vertical distances are measured from the centre of the pump.

(b) Centrifugal Compressor : The purpose of the centrifugal compressor is to compress the air and supply the same at moderate pressure and large in quality.

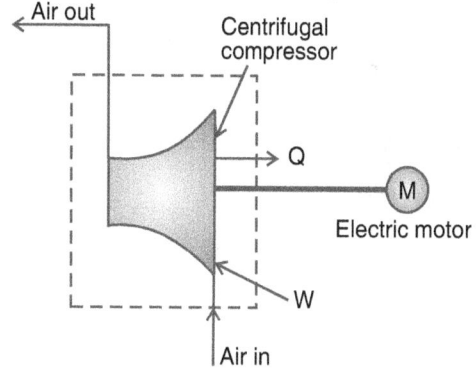

Fig. 1.25 : Centrifugal compressor

The system is shown in Fig. 1.25. For this system, ΔZ = 0 is generally taken, therefore, the energy equation becomes

$$\left[\frac{V_1^2}{2} + h_1\right] - q + w = \left[\frac{V_2^2}{2 + h_2}\right] \quad \ldots (1.28)$$

The q is taken negative as heat is lost from the system and w is taken as positive as work is supplied to the system.

(c) Blowers : The function of the blower is to supply air without much increase in pressure. Ceiling fans and exhaust fans can also be considered as blowers.

The energy equation for the blower can be written as

$$\left[\frac{V_1^2}{2} + u_1\right] - q + w = \left[\frac{V_2^2}{2} + u_2\right] \quad \ldots (1.29)$$

as $\quad p_1 v_{s_1} = p_2 v_{s_2}$

Generally q is taken as zero for small fans and rise in temperature is also negligible.

$$\therefore \quad \Delta u = 0$$

$$\therefore \quad w = \frac{V_2^2 - V_1^2}{2}$$

But $w = \frac{V_2^2}{2}$ for household fans as $V_1 = 0$ ... (1.30)

3. Some Other Systems :

(a) Steam Nozzle : In a nozzle, the flow of fluid is accelerated while the enthalpy of the fluid is diminished and pressure drops at the same time. This is generally used to convert the part of the heat energy of steam into kinetic energy of the steam supplied to the turbine.

A convergent-divergent nozzle commonly used is shown in Fig. 1.26.

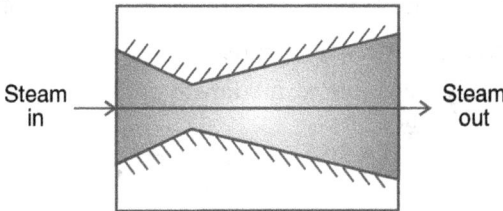

Fig. 1.26 : Flow through a convergent-divergent nozzle

For the above system, $\Delta PE = 0$, $w = 0$, $q = 0$.

Now, applying the energy equation to the system,

$$h_1 + \frac{V_1^2}{2} = h_2 + \frac{V_2^2}{2}$$

$$\therefore \quad V_2^2 = V_1^2 + 2(h_1 - h_2)$$

$$\therefore \quad V_2 = \sqrt{V_1^2 + 2(h_1 - h_2)} \quad \ldots (1.31)$$

where, velocity is in m/s and enthalpy (h) is in joules.

If $V_1 \ll V_2$, then $V_2 = \sqrt{2(h_1 - h_2)} = \sqrt{2(\Delta h)}$ ... (1.32)

1.12 LIMITATIONS OF FIRST LAW OF THERMODYNAMICS

The first law of thermodynamics states the equivalence of different forms of energy and makes no distinction between the forms of energy. If one form of energy disappears (say work), it appears in another form in equal amount and that means energy is neither created nor destroyed. First law is silent about the possibility or otherwise of any energy conversion.

If a closed system executes a cycle, then according to first law of thermodynamics,

$$\oint dW = \oint dQ$$

As per the above equation, the first law merely states that the work transfer during the cycle is equal to the heat transfer and does not place any restriction on the direction of heat and work transfer. According to this law, it is assumed that the energy transfer can take place in either direction. It does not specify the direction of the energy transfer.

With experiences, we know that non-violation of the first law by a proposed cycle does not ensure that the cycle will actually occur. Such experimental evidence has led to the formulation of the second law of thermodynamics. Thus, a cycle can occur only if it satisfies both the first and second laws of thermodynamics.

The second law states whether it is possible for energy transfer to proceed along a particular direction or not. Many day-to-day experiences indicate that the transfer process can proceed along one direction, but reverse is impossible.

The following few examples will illustrate the statement made above.

1. A hot cup of tea cools by virtue of heat transfer to the cooler surrounding; but once it is cooled, it can never be heated by addition of heat from the cooler surroundings.

2. Gasoline is used as the vehicle drives up the hill; but on coming down the hill, the fuel level in the gasoline tank cannot be restored to its original level.

3. When a moving car is stopped by mechanical braking action, brake gets hot and internal energy of the brake increases by an amount equal to the decrease in kinetic energy of the car. To satisfy the first law, the hot brake should cool off and give back its increase in internal energy to the wheels of the car causing it to resume its speed. This is never seen to happen.

4. As per the Joule's experiment, it has been found that when the free expansion takes place with a gas, there is no change in temperature, but the volume increases and pressure decreases without doing any work. If the above process has to take place in opposite direction, then the gas at low pressure should rush back through the valve and compress itself to its original pressure. It is found in practice that such process is impossible.

5. Take H_2 and O_2 in proper proportions in a rigid insulated vessel and ignite with the help of a spark. A chemical reaction takes place converting H_2 and O_2 into water vapour at high pressure and temperature. The water vapour formed will never spontaneously dissociate into H_2 and O_2 at lower temperature and pressure.

In all the above mentioned examples, it is obvious that the energy transfer or the process can proceed along a particular direction while it is impossible in the opposite direction even if the first law is satisfied.

It is obvious that the first law of thermodynamics is not sufficient to predict whether a system will or will not undergo a particular change, as no restriction has been imposed on the possibility of conservation of energy from one form to another by the first law of thermodynamics.

It is also obvious from the above practical examples that additional restrictions do exist and all forms of energy are not equally amenable to transformation into work.

The first law of thermodynamics is a necessary but not sufficient condition for a process to take place. Therefore, it becomes necessary to study the laws which give more information about the restriction in designing the various devices involving transformation of heat (or any other form of energy as potential, kinetic or chemical) into useful work.

1.13 HEAT ENGINE AND HEAT PUMP

Heat Engine : Heat engine is a device which is working in a cycle converts energy received in the form of heat into work. Only heat and work cross the boundary of the system during the execution of cyclic process.

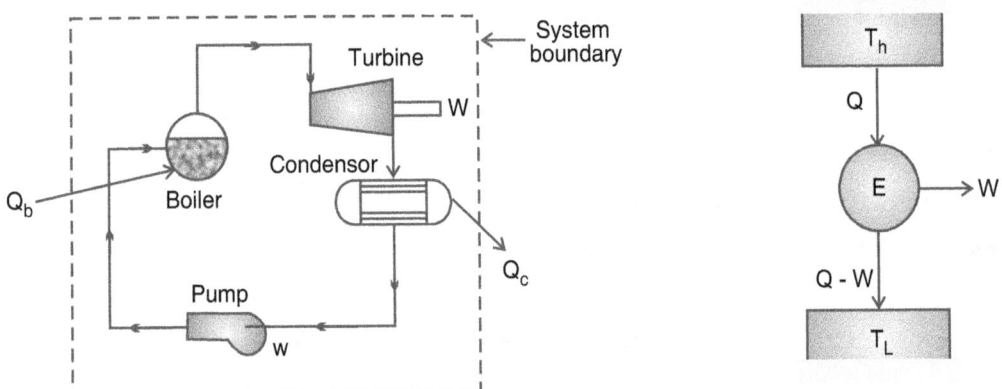

Fig. 1.27 : Heat engine system

A heat engine using a cyclic process is shown in Fig. 1.27. Steam is generated from water in the boiler and is used to develop useful work in the steam turbine. The steam coming out of the turbine is condensed in the condenser and fed back to the boiler with the help of the pump to complete the cycle. All the four units of the system, boiler, turbine, condenser and pump constitute a heat engine and the input to the system is heat supplied to the boiler and net output is work given out by the turbine.

The only interaction between the system and surrounding is work and heat as shown in figure. W is the work output from the turbine and w is the work supplied to the pump. Therefore, the net work output from the system during cyclic process is (W − w),

The net heat interaction between the system and surroundings is ($Q_b - Q_c$) as shown in the figure as the system completes the cycle, where Q_b is the heat supplied to the boiler and Q_c is the heat rejected by steam in the condenser.

As per the first law of thermodynamics,

$$\oint dw = \oint dQ$$

∴ $\quad (W - w) = Q_b - Q_c \quad \ldots (1.33)$

The efficiency of the engine is defined as

$$\eta = \frac{\text{Output work}}{\text{Input heat}} = \frac{W - w}{Q_b} = \frac{Q_b - Q_c}{Q_b} = 1 - \frac{Q_c}{Q_b} \quad \ldots (1.34)$$

It has been found in practice that Q_c is about 60% to 70% of Q_b and therefore the maximum efficiency of the heat engine of this type lies between 30% to 40%.

As per the first law of thermodynamics for a cyclic operation, the efficiency can be as high as 100% because it states that complete conversion of Q_b into useful work without rejecting any part of it is possible. Then the question arises in mind why it is not possible to obtain 100% efficiency as per the first law of thermodynamics. This question is answered by the second law of thermodynamics.

Heat Pump : Heat pump is a device which is working in a cycle delivers energy from a low temperature system to a high temperature system. Usually work is required as input.

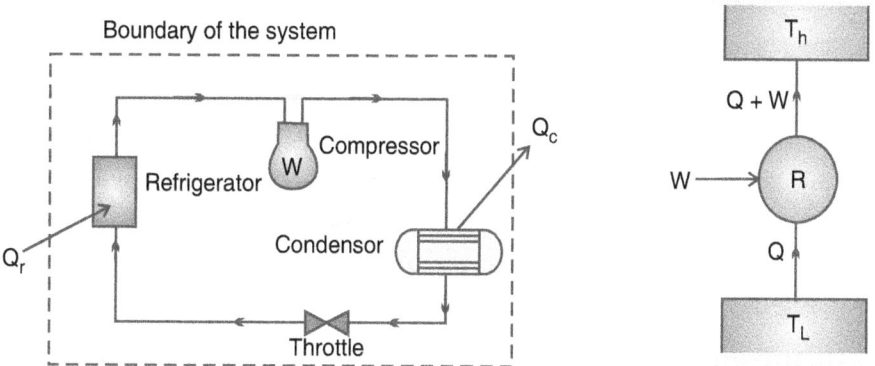

Fig. 1.28 : Refrigeration plant

In a household refrigerator, the energy from the refrigerator, at lower temperature is delivered to atmosphere which is at a higher temperature with the help of heat pump, thus maintaining a low temperature in the refrigerator.

During cold weather, the energy from the atmosphere at lower temperature is supplied to the heated houses at a higher temperature with the help of heat pump. In this way it is possible to maintain a comfortable temperature level in heated houses.

The arrangement of the heat pump system is shown in Fig. 1.28.

In this system of operation, as the refrigerator is maintained at a lower temperature than the surroundings, heat naturally flows into the refrigerator and this heat is removed with the help of the system as shown in Fig. 1.28. The four units compressor, condenser, throttle valve and refrigerator forms a system and this system is known as a refrigeration system. When this system works in a cyclic process, according to first law of thermodynamics,

$$\oint dW = \oint dQ$$

$$W = Q_c - Q_b$$

In the system described above the purpose is to maintain a lower temperature in the refrigerator by removing the heat coming in and discharge the same to the atmosphere which is at higher temperature than the refrigerator. The performance of this system is calculated in terms of C.O.P. (coefficient of performance) which is defined as

$$\text{C.O.P.} = \frac{\text{Heat removed from refrigerator}}{\text{Work supplied}} = \frac{Q_r}{W} = \frac{Q_r}{Q_c - Q_r} \quad \ldots(1.35)$$

The same plant can be used to heat the house during cold winter when the surrounding is at a lower temperature. In this case, the refrigerator takes the heat from the surroundings (may be river, lake, sea or atmospheric air) whose temperature will be at a lower level (say $-5°C$) and this energy is rejected at an elevated temperature (say $30°C$) and supplied to the house where the temperature is to be maintained at say $25°C$. In this case Q_r is taken from the atmosphere and Q_c supplied is to the house. As the purpose of this system is to supply Q_r to the house, the C.O.P. of the system is given by

$$\text{C.O.P.} = \frac{\text{Heat supplied to house or rejected by condenser}}{\text{Work supplied}}$$

$$= \frac{Q_c}{W} = \frac{Q_c}{Q_c - Q_r} \quad \ldots(1.36)$$

It may be noted that the C.O.P. of the heat pump is the reciprocal of the efficiency of a heat engine working between the same sources.

The engine, refrigerator and heat pump system are also shown in Fig. 1.29 mentioning the temperature levels.

The whole object of the study of thermodynamics is to design a more efficient engine which will develop maximum power for a given supply of heat energy and a more efficient refrigeration system which will remove maximum heat for a given amount of work or minimum work for the required quantity of heat to be removed.

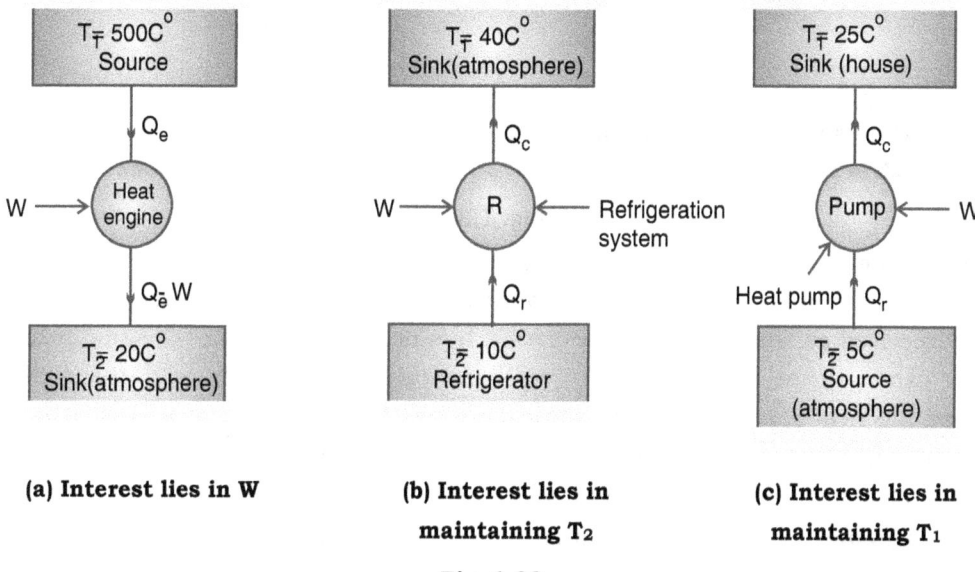

(a) Interest lies in W (b) Interest lies in maintaining T_2 (c) Interest lies in maintaining T_1

Fig. 1.29

1.14 STATEMENTS OF SECOND LAW OF THERMODYNAMICS

Based on the observations cited, many statements of Second Law are available. Few of them are listed below and discussed.

1. Kelvin Plank Statement : The Kelvin Plank statement of second law of thermodynamics states that "no system, whose working fluid undergoes a cycle, can receive heat from a single source** and produce work without rejecting heat to a lower temperature sink[††]" OR "it is impossible to construct an engine working in a cyclic process whose sole effect is the conversion of all the heat energy supplied to it by a source into an equivalent amount of work".

The system which is impossible as per the above statement is shown in Fig. 1.30 (a).

[††] Sink is also a source of infinite energy capacity but at lower temperature. The facts which are true for source are also true for sink.

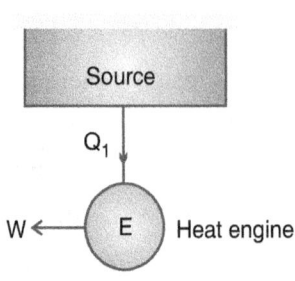
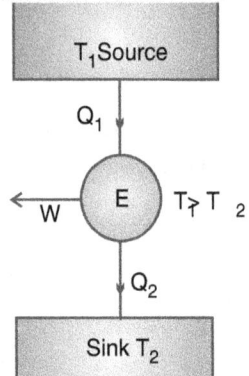

(a) **Impossible heat engine as per Kelvin Plank statement**

(b) **Possible heat engine as per Kelvin-Plank statement**

Fig. 1.30

Since, the system executes a cycle, no energy can be stored in the system. As all the heat received cannot be converted to work and nothing can be stored, some of the energy received as heat has to be rejected. If this heat is rejected to the same reservoir, then it can again be supplied to the engine for conversion to work. So, the difference between the heat received and the work done has to be rejected to a sink at a lower temperature, compared to the source. Such an arrangement which is not contrary to Kelvin Planck statement is shown in Fig. 1.30 (b).

2. Clausius Statement : Clausius statement tells that, "it is impossible to construct a device working in a cyclic process whose sole effect is the transfer of energy in the form of heat from a body at a lower temperature (sink) to a body at a higher temperature (source)". OR "it is impossible for energy in the form of heat to flow from a body at a lower temperature to a body at higher temperature without the aid of external work".

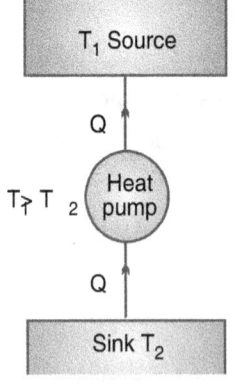
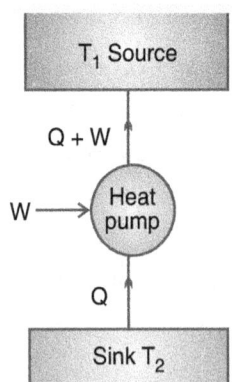

(a) **Impossible system**

(b) **Possible system**

Fig. 1.31

The impossible system and possible system as per the Clausius statement of second law of thermodynamics are shown in Figs. 1.31 (a) and (b).

At first sight, the Kelvin Plank and Clausius statements do appear different and unconnected but in fact, they are equivalent in all respects. It is impossible to have a system which satisfies one of the statements and violates the other.

It can be proved that a system which violates one statement, also violates second statement. For further analysis refer the book Thermal Energy by the same author.

IMPORTANT FORMULAE

The following formulae are used for solving the problems :

1. $\oint dW = \oint dQ$ (for cycle).
2. $Q = W + \Delta U$ (for process) when mass is m kg. (For closed system)
3. $m\left[\dfrac{V_1^2}{2} + Z_1 g + u_1 + p_1 v_{s1}\right] \pm W \pm Q = m\left[\dfrac{V_2^2}{2} + Z_2 g + u_2 + p_2 v_{s2}\right]$

   (a) If W is going out (work developing system) then –W should be taken and if W is coming in (work absorbing system), then +W should be taken. Similarly, Q should be taken –ve if going out and +ve if coming in.

   (b) If m is the mass flow in kg per second, then W and Q should be per second basis and P (power) = W as W directly gives power.

   (c) If m = 1 kg then W and Q should be on the basis of 1 kg and P = W × m.

SOLVED PROBLEMS

First Law of Thermodynamics

Problem 1.1 : (a) A certain reversible cycle is completed during the following given processes. The changes in q, w and u for each process are tabulated below :

If the work done per kg of fluid is 40 kJ/kg, complete the table.

Process	q (kJ/kg)	w (kJ/kg)	Δu (kJ/kg)
1-2	52	–	22
2-3	–32	–42	–
3-1	–	–	–32

(b) Find the power developed by the system if the mass of the system is 0.15 kg and system executes 300 cycles/min.

Solution :

(a) Mass given is one kg. in the given table

Applying first law of thermodynamics,

(1) Process 1-2 :

$$q = w_{12} + \Delta u$$
$$52 = w_{12} + 22 \quad \therefore \quad w_{12} = \mathbf{30 \text{ kJ/kg}}$$

(2) Process 2-3 :

$$q = w + \Delta u$$
$$-32 = -42 + \Delta u \quad \therefore \quad \Delta u = \mathbf{10 \text{ kJ/kg}}$$

For cyclic process,

$$w_{12} + w_{23} + w_{31} = 40 \text{ (given)}$$
$$30 + (-32) + w_{31} = 40 \quad \therefore \quad w_{31} = \mathbf{42 \text{ kJ/kg}}$$

(3) Process 3-1 :

$$q = w + \Delta u$$
$$q = 42 + (-32) \quad \therefore \quad q = \mathbf{10 \text{ kJ/kg}}$$

(b) Power developed = Work done per second
= [(Work done/kg) × Mass of system × Cycles /sec]
= $(40 \times 0.15) \times \dfrac{300}{60}$ = **30 kW**

Problem 1.2 : A cycle of operation for a piston and cylinder system is completed during four processes. The net heat transfer during the cycle is −200 kJ/cycle. Complete the following table and find out the net work done in kW if the system completes 100 cycles per minute.

Process	Q (kJ/min)	W (kJ/min)	ΔU (kJ/min)
1-2	0.0	2500	–
2-3	20000	0.0	–
3-4	−1800	–	−35000
4-1	–	–	–

Solution :

Process 1-2 :

$$Q = W + \Delta u$$
$$0 = 2500 + \Delta U \quad \therefore \quad \Delta U = \mathbf{2500 \text{ kJ/min}}$$

Process 2-3 :

$$Q = W + \Delta U$$

$$20000 = 0 + \Delta U \qquad \therefore \quad \Delta U = \textbf{20000 kJ/min}$$

Process 3-4 : $\qquad Q = W + \Delta U$

$$-1800 = W + (-35000) \qquad \therefore \quad W = \textbf{17000 kJ/min}$$

For the cycle

$$\Sigma Q = \oint dQ = (-200 \text{ kJ/cycle}) \times \frac{\text{Cycle}}{\text{Min}} = -200 \times \frac{100}{\text{Min}}$$

$$= -20{,}000 \text{ kJ/min}$$

$$\therefore \quad Q_{12} + Q_{23} + Q_{34} + Q_{41} = -20000$$

$$0 + 20000 - 1800 + Q_{41} = -20000$$

$$\therefore \qquad Q_{41} = -38200 \text{ kJ/min}$$

$$\Sigma U = \oint dU = U_{12} + U_{23} + U_{34} + U_{41} = 0 \text{ (as U is a property)}$$

$$\therefore \quad -2500 + 20000 - 35000 + U_{41} = 0$$

$$\therefore \qquad U_{41} = \textbf{17500 kJ/min}$$

Process 4-1 : $\qquad Q = W + \Delta U$

$$-38200 = W + 17500 \qquad \therefore \quad W = \textbf{-55700 kJ/min}$$

Now U_{12}, U_{23}, U_{41}, W_{34}, W_{41} and Q_{41} are calculated and table is completed.

As per first law of thermodynamics,

$$\Sigma W = \Sigma Q = -20000 \text{ kJ/min}$$

$$\therefore \qquad \text{Power} = -\frac{20000}{60} \text{ kW}$$

$$= \textbf{-333.3 kW}$$

The –ve sign indicates that the system is work absorbing system.

Problem 1.3 : A stone of 10 kg mass and tank containing 100 kg water are initially at the same temperature. The stone is 100 m above the water level falls into the water. Considering stone and water as a system.

Determine ΔU, ΔPE, ΔKE, Q and W when

(a) the stone is about to enter the water,

(b) the stone has come to rest in the water bucket, and

(c) the heat is transferred to the surroundings in such an amount that the stone and water come to their initial temperature.

Solution :

Applying the first law of thermodynamics,

$$Q = (U_2 - U_1) + m\left[\frac{V_2^2 - V_1^2}{2}\right] + mg(Z_2 - Z_1) + W$$

$$= \Delta U + \Delta KE + \Delta PE + W \qquad \ldots (1)$$

Here Q is the heat going out from system boundary.

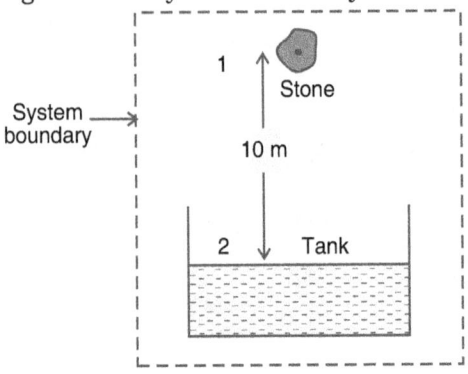

Prob 1.3

(a) When the stone just reaches the water surface,

$$Q = 0, W = 0, \Delta U = 0 \quad \therefore -\Delta KE = \Delta PE$$
$$= mg(Z_2 - Z_1)$$
$$= 10 \times 9.81 \times (0 - 10)$$
$$= -981 \text{ J}$$

$\therefore \quad \Delta KE = 981 \text{ J} \qquad \therefore \quad \Delta PE = -981 \text{ J}$

(b) When the stone dips into the tank and comes to rest,

$$Q = 0, W = 0, \Delta KE = 0.$$

Putting these values in equation (1),

$$0 = \Delta U + 0 + \Delta PE + 0 \quad \therefore \quad \Delta U = -\Delta PE = -(-981) = 981 \text{ J}$$

This shows that the internal energy (temperature) of the system increases.

(c) When the water and stone come to their initial temperature,

$$W = 0, \Delta KE = 0$$

Substituting these values in equation (1),

$$\therefore \qquad Q = -\Delta U = -981 \text{ J}$$

The –ve sign indicates that the hat is lost by the system to the surroundings.

First Law for Processes

Problem 1.4 : A gas of 0.5 m³ at 1 bar is compressed reversibly at constant pressure till its volume becomes 0.2m³. During compression, 40 kJ of heat is rejected. Find the change in internal energy of the gas.

Solution :

$$W = \int_1^2 p \cdot dv = p \int_1^2 dv = p(v_2 - v_1)$$
$$= 1 \times 10^5 \times (0.2 - 0.4) = -0.2 \times 10^5 \text{ J} = \mathbf{-20 \text{ kJ}}$$

As per the first law of thermodynamics,

$$Q = W + \Delta U$$

∴ $\quad -40 = -20 + \Delta U$

∴ $\quad \Delta U = -20 \text{ kJ}$

The −ve sign indicates decrease in internal energy.

Problem 1.5 : The work and heat transfer per centigrade temperature change for a steady state reversible non-flow system is given by

$$\frac{dW}{dT} = \frac{1}{8} \text{ kJ/°C and } \frac{dQ}{dT} = 0.4 \text{ kJ/°C}$$

Find the change in internal energy when the temperature change is from 100°C to 260°C.

Solution :

$$W = \int_{100}^{260} \frac{dT}{8} = \frac{1}{8} \times (260 - 100) = \mathbf{20 \text{ kJ}}$$

$$Q = \int_{100}^{260} 0.4 \times dT = 0.4 \times (260 - 100) = \mathbf{64 \text{ kJ}}$$

Applying the first law of thermodynamics,

$$Q = W + \Delta U$$

∴ $\quad \Delta U = Q - W = 64 - 20 = \mathbf{44 \text{ kJ}}$

This indicates that the internal energy of the system is increased.

Problem 1.6 : A fluid at 5 bar and with specific volume of 0.2 m³/kg expands in an engine reversibly to a pressure of 1.2 bar following the law.

$$P = \frac{C}{v^2} \text{ where C is constant.}$$

Find the work done during the process.

Solution :

$$\text{Work done, } W = \int_1^2 p \cdot dv$$

$$= \int_1^2 \frac{C}{v^2} \cdot dv = C\left[\frac{1}{v_1} - \frac{1}{v_2}\right] \quad \ldots(a)$$

As per the given law,

$$C = p_1 v_1^2 = p_2 v_2^2 \quad \ldots(b)$$

∴ $\quad C = 5 \times 10^5 \times (0.2)^2 = 0.2 \times 10^5$

Using the equation (b),

$$5 \times (0.2)^2 = 1.2 \times (v_2)^2$$

$$\therefore \quad v_2 = \sqrt{\frac{5}{1.2}} \times 0.2 = 0.408 \text{ m}^3/\text{kg}$$

Substituting the values in equation (a), we get

$$W = 0.2 \times 10^5 \times \left[\frac{1}{0.2} - \frac{1}{0.408}\right] = 0.2 \times 10^5 (5 - 2.45)$$

$$= 0.51 \times 10^5 \text{ Nm/kg} = 51000 \text{ J/kg} = \mathbf{51 \text{ kJ/kg}}$$

Problem 1.7 : In a non-flow reversible process, the pressure and volume are related by

$$p = v^2 + \frac{10}{v} \text{ where p is in bar and v is in m}^3.$$

During the process, the volume changes form 1.2 m³ to 4.5 m³. The heat added during the process is 10 MJ. Find the change in internal energy during the process.

Solution : The work done during the process is given by

$$W = \int_1^2 p \cdot dv$$

$$= \int_1^2 \left(v^2 + \frac{10}{v}\right) \times 10^5 \cdot dv$$

$$= 10^5 \times \left[\frac{v^3}{3} + 10 \log_e (v)\right]_{1.2}^{1.5}$$

$$= 10^5 \times \left[\frac{1}{3}[(4.5)^3 - (1.2)^3] + 10 \log_e \left(\frac{4.5}{1.2}\right)\right] \text{ Nm or J}$$

$$= 100 \times [29.8 + 13.22] \text{ kJ} = \mathbf{4302 \text{ kJ}}$$

Using the first law of thermodynamics to the process,

$$Q = W + \Delta U$$

$$\therefore \quad 10000 = 4302 + \Delta U$$

$$\Delta U = \mathbf{5698 \text{ kJ}}$$

Problem 1.8 : A fluid system undergoes a non-flow frictionless process following the pressure-volume relation as $p = \frac{4.5}{v} + 2$ where p is in bar and v is in m³. During the process, the volume changes from 0.12 m³ to 0.04 m³ and the system rejected 40 kJ of heat. Determine the change in internal energy and enthalpy.

Solution : Work done is given by

$$W = \int_1^2 p \cdot dv = \int_{v_1}^{v_2} \left(\frac{4.5}{v} + 2\right) \cdot dv$$

$$= \left[4.5 \log_e \left(\frac{v_2}{v_1}\right) + 2(v_2 - v_1)\right] \times 10^5 \text{ Nm}$$

$$= 10^5 \times \left[4.5 \log_e \left(\frac{0.04}{0.12} \right) + 2 \,(0.04 - 0.12) \right]$$

$$= 10^5 \times [(4.5 \times (-1.1)) - 2 \times 0.08)] \text{ Nm}$$

$$= 10^5 \times (-5.11) \text{ Nm} = -511 \times 10^3 \text{ Nm} = -511 \times 10^3 \text{ J} = \mathbf{-511 \text{ kJ}}$$

Applying the first law of energy equation,

$$Q = W + \Delta U$$

$$\therefore \quad \Delta U = Q - W = -40 - (-511) = \mathbf{471 \text{ kJ}}$$

This indicates that the internal energy is increased.

$$\Delta h = \Delta U + \Delta (pv) = 471 \times 10^3 + [p_2 v_2 - p_1 v_1]$$

$$p_1 = \frac{4.5}{v_1} + 2 = \frac{4.5}{0.12} + 2 = 49.5 \text{ bar} = 49.5 \times 10^5 \text{ N/m}^2$$

$$p_2 = \frac{45}{0.04} + 2 = 144.5 \text{ bar} = 144.5 \times 10^5 \text{ N/m}^2$$

$$\therefore \quad \Delta h = 471 \times 10^3 + [144.5 \times 10^5 \times 0.04 - 49.2 \times 10^5 \times 0.12]$$

$$= 471 \times 10^3 + 10^3 \times [144.5 \times 4 - 49.5 \times 12]$$

$$= 10^3 \times [471 + 578 - 594] = 10^3 \times 455 \text{ J} = \mathbf{455 \text{ kJ}}$$

Problem 1.9 : During a reversible constant pressure non-flow process with p = 1.5 bar, the properties of the system change from v_{s1} = 0.25 m^3/kg, T_1 = 10°C to v_{s2} = 0.45 m^3/kg, T_2 = 240°C. The specific heat of the fluid is given by

$$C_p = \left(1.6 + \frac{80}{T + 40} \right) \text{ kJ/kg where T is in °C}$$

Find (a) q, (b) w, (c) Δu and (d) Δh.

Solution : The heat added per kg of fluid is given by,

$$q = \int_{T_1}^{T_2} C_p \cdot dT = \int_{10}^{240} \left(1.6 + \frac{80}{T + 40} \right) dT$$

$$= 1.6 \times (240 - 10) + 80 \log_e \left(\frac{240 + 40}{10 + 40} \right)$$

$$= 368 + 80 \log_e (5.6) = 368 + 137.5 = \mathbf{505.5 \text{ kJ/kg}}$$

The work done per kg of fluid is given by

$$w = \int_{v_1}^{v_2} p \cdot dv = p \,(v_{s2} - v_{s1})$$

$$= 1.5 \times 10^5 \times (0.45 - 0.25) = 30 \times 10^3 \text{ Nm} = 30 \times 10^3 \text{ J} = \mathbf{30 \text{ kJ/kg}}$$

Applying the first law energy equation.

$$q = w + \Delta u$$

$$\therefore \quad \Delta u = 505.5 - 30 = \mathbf{475.5 \text{ kJ/kg}}$$

For steady flow process, $\Delta h = q = \mathbf{505.5 \text{ kJ/kg}}$.

First Law for Work Developing Systems

Problem 1.10 : Steam enters the turbine at 20 m/sec and h_1 = 3 MJ/kg and leaves at 40 m/sec and h_2 = 2.5 MJ/kg. Heat lost to the surrounding is 25 kJ/kg of steam flow. If the steam flow is 6000 kg/min, find out the power developed by the turbine in MW.

Solution :

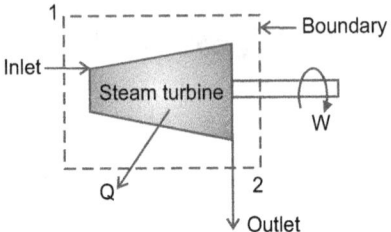

Prob 1.10

We can write the energy equation on the basis of 1 kg of steam as

$$\left(\frac{V_1^2}{2} + h_1\right) - q - w = \left(\frac{V_2^2}{2} + h_2\right) \text{ As } Z_1 = Z_2$$

$$\therefore w = (h_1 - h_2) + \left(\frac{V_1^2 - V_2^2}{2}\right) - q$$

$$= (3000 - 2500) \times 10^3 + \frac{(20)^2 - (40)^2}{2} - 25 \times 10^3$$

$$= 500 \times 10^3 - 600 - 25 \times 10^3$$

$$= 10^3 \times (500 - 0.6 - 25) = 474.4 \times 10^3 \text{ J/kg}$$

Power, P $= w \times m \text{ (kg/sec)}$

$$= 474.4 \times 10^3 \times \frac{6000}{60}$$

$$= 47.44 \times 10^6 \text{ watts} \qquad = \mathbf{47.44 \text{ MW}}$$

Problem 1.11 : Steam enters a steam turbine with a velocity of 40 m/s and enthalpy of 2500 kJ/kg and leaves with a velocity of 90 m/s and enthalpy of 2030 kJ/kg. The heat lost from the turbine to the surrounding is 240 kJ/min. Find the power developed by the turbine if the steam flow rate is 6000 kg/hr.

Solution :

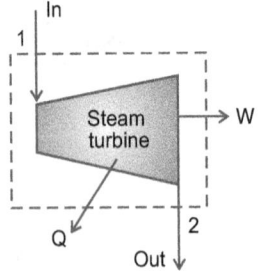

Prob 1.11

The energy equation for the given system on sec basis can be written as

$$m\left(\frac{V_1^2}{2}+h_1\right)-W-Q = m\left(\frac{V_2^2}{2}+h_2\right)$$

where m is mass of steam flow per second.

$$= \frac{6000}{3600} = 1.67 \text{ kg/s}$$

∴ $$W = m\left[(h_1-h_2)+\frac{V_1^2-V_2^2}{2}\right]-Q$$

where Q is heat lost per second.

∴ $$W = 1.67\times\left[(2500-2030)\times 10^3+\left(\frac{(40)^2-(90)^2}{2}\right)\right]-\frac{240\times 10^3}{60}$$

$$= 1.67\times[470\times 10^3-3250]-4\times 10^3$$

$$= 1.67\times 466.75\times 10^3-4\times 10^3$$

$$= 775.5\times 10^3 \text{ J/sec} = 775.5 \text{ kJ/sec}$$

∴ Power, P = **775.5 kW**

Problem 1.12 : A stream of gases at 7.5 bar, 800°C and 150 m/s enters into a gas turbine of jet engine and comes out at 2 bar, 600°C and 300 m/s. Find the power developing capacity of the turbine if the gas flow rate is 5 kg/sec. Assume the process passing through the turbine is reversible adiabatic. Take C_p = 1.05 kJ/kg°C for the gas.

Solution :

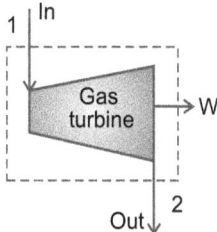

Prob 1.12

We can write the flow energy equation for the system on the basis of 1 kg mass.

$$\left(\frac{V_1^2}{2}+h_1\right)-w\pm q = \left(\frac{V_2^2}{2}+h_2\right)$$

$$q = 0.0 \text{ as the process is adiabatic}$$

∴ $$w = (h_1-h_2)+\left(\frac{V_1^2-V_2^2}{2}\right)$$

$$= C_p(T_1-T_2)+\left(\frac{V_1^2-V_2^2}{2}\right)$$

$$= 1.05 \times 10^3 \times (800 - 600) + \left(\frac{(150)^2 - (300)^2}{2}\right)$$

$$= 2.1 \times 10^3 - 33750$$

$$= 1.7625 \times 10^5 \text{ J/kg}$$

$$P = w \times \text{Mass flow in kg/sec}$$

$$= 1.7625 \times 10^5 \times 5 \text{ watts}$$

$$= \mathbf{881.25 \text{ kW}}$$

Problem 1.13 : The gas at 5 bar, 500°C enters the gas turbine with a velocity of 200 m/s and comes out at 1.2 bar and 40 m/s. Assuming the flow thorough the turbine is reversible adiabatic, find out the power developed by the turbine if the gas flow is 100 kg/min. Take C_p = 1.05 kJ/kg°C and γ = 1.38 for gas.

Solution :

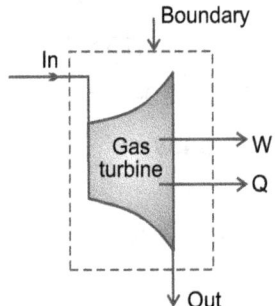

Prob 1.13

We can use the flow energy equation as

$$m\left(\frac{V_1^2}{2} + gZ_1 + h_1\right) \pm W \pm Q = \left(\frac{V_2^2}{2} + gZ_2 + h_2\right)$$

As the flow is reversible adiabatic :

$$Q = 0.0$$

$$Z_1 = Z_2 \text{ (for gas turbine)}$$

As gas turbine is work developing system,

$$\therefore \quad -W + 0 = m\left[\frac{V_2^2 - V_1^2}{2} + (h_2 - h_1)\right]$$

$$\therefore \quad W = m\left[\frac{V_1^2 - V_2^2}{2} + (h_1 - h_2)\right]$$

$$= m\left[\frac{V_1^2 - V_2^2}{2} + C_p(T_1 - T_2)\right]$$

As the flow through the turbine is isentropic,

$$\frac{T_2}{T_1} = \left(\frac{P_2}{P_1}\right)^{\frac{\gamma-1}{\gamma}}$$

$$T_2 = (500 + 273)\left(\frac{1.2}{5}\right)^{\frac{0.38}{1.38}} = 773 \times 0.675 = 522 \text{ K} = 249°C$$

$$\text{Power, P} = \frac{100}{60} \times \left[\frac{(200)^2 - (40)^2}{2} + 1.05 \times 1000 \times (500 - 249)\right]$$

$$= 1.67 \times [19200 + 263.55 \times 1000]$$

$$= 1.67 \times 10^3 \times [19.2 + 263.55] = 460.9 \times 10^3 \text{ J/s or watts}$$

$$= \textbf{460.9 kW}$$

Problem 1.14 : A water turbine is supplied water from a dam whose water height is 1500 m above the centre of the turbine. The water from the turbine is discharges 3 m below the centre of the turbine. The velocity of water at the discharge point is 10 m/s. Find the power developed by the turbine if the water flow rate is 200 m³/sec.

Solution :

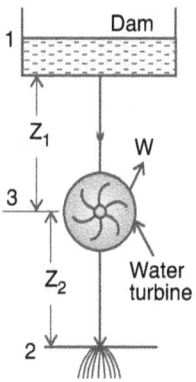

Prob 1.14

As the temperature of water at inlet and outlet is same and q = 0 in the hydraulic system. We can write flow energy equation for the water turbine as

$$\left(\frac{V_1^2}{2} + Z_1 g\right) - w = \frac{V_2^2}{2} + Z_2 g$$

when $\quad m = 1$ kg

where the energies are measured form the centre of turbine.

$$\therefore \quad w = g(Z_1 - Z_2) - \frac{V_2^2}{2} \text{ as } V_1 = 0 \text{ (in the dam)}$$

$$= 9.81 \times [1500 - (-3)] - \frac{10^2}{2}$$

$$= 9.81 \times 1503 - 50 = 14694.4 \text{ Nm/kg}$$

$\therefore \quad$ Power, $P = 14694.4 \times (200 \times 1000)$ Nm or J/sec

$$= 2938.9 \times 10^6 \text{ watts} = \textbf{2938.9 MW}$$

Problem 1.15 : A water turbine develops 10 MW power when the supply head of water is 400 m. The water is discharged 5 m below the centre of turbine. The velocity of water at the discharge point is 5 m/sec. Find the quantity of water supplied to the turbine in m³/min.

Solution :

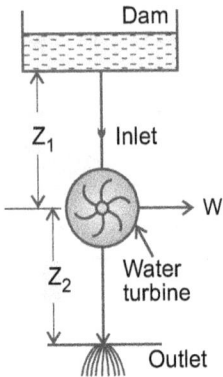

Prob 1.15

The energy equation for the water turbine can be written as

$$m\left(\frac{V_1^2}{2} + Z_1 g\right) - W = m\left(\frac{V_2^2}{2} + Z_2 g\right)$$

$$\therefore \quad m\left[g(Z_1 - Z_2) - \frac{V_2^2}{2}\right] = W \text{ as } V_1 = 0$$

where m is water flow in kg/sec and W is the work output per second (watts).

$$\therefore \quad m\left[9.81\,[400 - (-5)] - \frac{5^2}{2}\right] = 10 \times 10^6$$

$$\therefore \quad m\,(3960.55) = 10 \times 10^6$$

$$m = \frac{10 \times 10^6}{3960.55} = 2525.25 \text{ kg/sec}$$

$$= \frac{2525.25 \times 60}{1000} = \mathbf{151.5 \text{ m}^3/\text{min}} \text{ as } 1 \text{ m}^3 = 1000 \text{ kg}$$

Problem 1.16 : The conditions of the working fluid entering and leaving the power developing system are

$V_1 = 300$ m/s, $p_1 = 6.2$ bar, $u_1 = 2100$ kJ/kg, $V_{s1} = 0.37$ m³/kg and

$V_2 = 150$ m/s, $p_2 = 1.3$ bar, $u_2 = 1500$ m/kg, $V_{s2} = 1.2$ m³/kg

The fluid rejects heat at the rate of 120 kW. If the flow rate is 4 kg/s, find the power developed by the system.

Solution : We can write the energy equation for the given flow system as

$$\left[\frac{V_1^2}{2} + Z_1 g + p_1 V_{s1} + u_1\right] - q - w = \left[\frac{V_2^2}{2} + Z_2 g + p_2 V_{s2} + u_2\right]$$

Assume $Z_1 = Z_2$ (as nothing is mentioned in the example).

$$\therefore \left[\frac{V_1^2}{2} + u_1 + p_1 v_{s1}\right] - q - w = \left[\frac{V_2^2}{2} + u_2 + p_2 v_{s2}\right]$$

As q and w are the quantities per kg of fluid.

$$Q = \frac{120 \times 10^3 \text{ J}}{\text{sec}}$$

$$\therefore \quad q = \frac{120 \times 10^3}{4}$$

$$= 30 \times 10^3 \text{ J/kg}$$

$$\therefore \quad w = \left[\frac{V_1^2 - V_2^2}{2} + (u_1 - u_2) + (p_1 v_{s1} - p_2 v_{s2})\right] - q$$

$$= \frac{(300)^2 - (150)^2}{2} + (2100 - 1500) \times 10^3 + (6.2 \times 0.37 - 1.3 \times 1.2) \times 10^5] - 30 \times 10^3$$

All the above quantities are in J per kg of fluid.

$$w = \frac{67500}{2} + 600 \times 10^3 + 0.734 \times 10^5 - 0.3 \times 10^5$$

$$= (0.3375 + 6 + 0.734 - 0.3) \times 10^5 \text{ J/kg}$$

$$= 6.7715 \times 10^5 \text{ J/kg}$$

$$\therefore \quad \text{Power, } P = w \times m \text{ (kg/sec)}$$

$$= 6.7715 \times 10^5 \times 4 \text{ watts}$$

$$= \mathbf{2708.6 \text{ kW}}$$

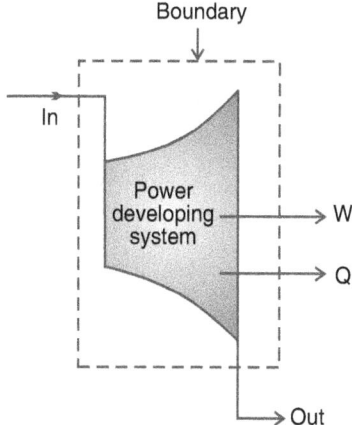

Prob 1.16

First Law for Work Absorbing Systems

Problem 1.17 : A fluid flows through a work absorbing system is 5 kg/sec. The inlet conditions of the fluid are $V_1 = 50$ m/s, $h_1 = 4000$ kJ/kg, and outlet conditions are $V_2 = 20$ m/s, $h_2 = 4100$ kJ/kg. The inlet is 40 m above the outlet and heat transferred to the system is 200 kJ/s. Find the power supplied to the system.

Solution :

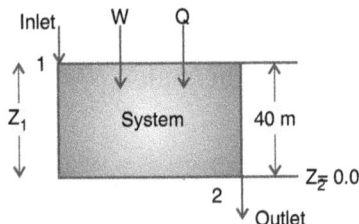

Prob 1.17

The energy equation on the basis of one sec for the given system can be written as

$$m\left[\frac{V_1^2}{2} + Z_1 g + h_1\right] + Q + W = m\left[\frac{V_2^2}{2} + Z_2 g + h_2\right]$$

where m is in kg/sec and Q is also in J/sec.

$$\therefore\ W = m\left[\frac{V_2^2 - V_1^2}{2} + g(Z_2 - Z_1) + (h_2 - h_1)\right] - Q$$

$$= 5 \times \left[\frac{(20)^2 - (50)^2}{2} + 9.81(-40) + (4100 - 4000) \times 10^3\right] - 200 \times 10^3 \text{ as } Z_2 - Z_1 = -40 \text{ given}$$

$$= 5\,[-1050 - 392.4 + 100 \times 10^3] - 200 \times 10^3$$

$$= 5 \times 10^3 \times [-1.05 - 0.3924 + 100] - 200 + 10^3$$

$$= 5 \times 10^3 \times 98.5576 - 200 \times 10^3 = 292.8 \times 10^3 \text{ J/sec}$$

$\therefore$ P = **292.8 kW.**

This is power supplied to the system

Problem 1.18 : A centrifugal air compressor supplying air to a gas turbine, receives air at 1 bar and 27°C and discharges at 4 bar and 227°C. The velocity of air leaving the compressor is 100 m/s. Neglecting the velocity at the entry of the compressor, find out the power required to run the compressor if the mass flow rate is 15 kg/sec. Take C_p = 1 kJ/kg –°C and neglect the heat transfer from the compressor to the surrounding.

Solution :

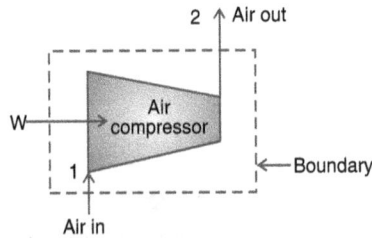

Prob 1.18

The energy equation can be written as

$$m\left[\frac{V_1^2}{2} + Z_1 g + h_1\right] + W \pm Q = m\left[\frac{V_2^2}{2} + Z_2 g + h_2\right]$$

$V_1 = 0.0$, $Q = 0.0$ (given) and $Z_1 = Z_2$

$$\therefore \quad m(h_1) + W = m\left[\frac{V_2^2}{2} + h_2\right]$$

$$\therefore \quad = m\left[(h_2 - h_1) + \frac{V_2^2}{2}\right]$$

$$= m\left[C_p(T_2 - T_1) + \frac{V_2^2}{2}\right]$$

$$= 15 \times \left[1 \times 10^3 \times (227 - 27) + \frac{(100)^2}{2}\right] J/s$$

$$\therefore \quad \text{Power} = 15 \times 10^3 \times [200 + 5]$$

$$= 15 \times 205 \times 10^3 \, J/s$$

$$= \mathbf{3075 \text{ kW}}$$

Problem 1.19 : A centrifugal air compressor delivers 15 kg of air per minute. The inlet and outlet conditions of air are $V_1 = 10$ m/s, $p_1 = 1$ bar, $v_{s1} = 0.5$ m³/kg and $V_2 = 80$ m/s, $p_2 = 7$ bar, $v_{s2} = 0.15$ m³/kg. The increase in enthalpy passing through the compressor is 160 kJ/kg and heat loss to the surrounding is 720 kJ/min.

(a) Find the power required to run the compressor and

(b) Ratio of inlet to outlet pipe diameter.

Solution :

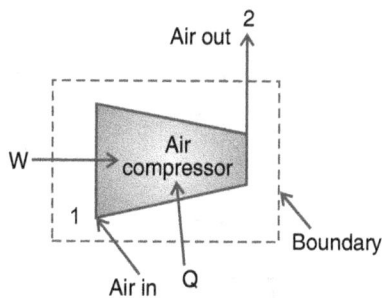

Prob 1.19

The energy equation for unit mass flow is given by

$$\left[\frac{V_1^2}{2} + h_1\right] - w - q = \left[\frac{V_2^2}{2} + h_2\right]$$

$$\therefore \quad w = (h_2 - h_1) + \left(\frac{V_2^2 - V_1^2}{2}\right) + q$$

$$q = \frac{720}{15} = 48 \text{ kJ/kg}$$

$$\therefore \quad w = (160 \times 10^3) + \frac{(80)^2 - (10)^2}{2} + 48 \times 10^3$$

$$= 10^3 \times (160 + 3.15 + 48) = 211.15 \times 10^3 \text{ J/kg}$$

$\therefore \quad$ Power, $P = w \times m$ (mass flow per second)

$$= 211.15 \times 10^3 \times \frac{15}{60} \text{ J/s} = 52.8 \times 10^3 \text{ watts} = \mathbf{52.8 \text{ kW}}$$

The mass flow through the compressor is given by

$$m = \frac{A_1 V_1}{v_{s1}} = \frac{A_2 V_2}{v_{s2}}$$

$\therefore \quad \frac{\pi}{4} D_1^2 \cdot \frac{V_1}{v_{s1}} = \frac{\pi}{4} D_2^2 \cdot \frac{V_2}{v_{s2}}$

$\therefore \quad \frac{D_1}{D_2} = \sqrt{\frac{V_2}{V_1} \times \frac{v_{s1}}{v_{s2}}} = \sqrt{\frac{80}{10} \times \frac{0.5}{0.15}} = \mathbf{5.16}$

Problem 1.20 : A centrifugal pump delivers 60 kg of water per second. The inlet and outlet pressures are 1 bar and 4 bar respectively. The suction is 2 m below and delivery is 8 m above the centre of the pump. The suction and delivery pipe diameters are 20 cm and 10 cm respectively. Find the power required to run the pump in kW.

Solution :

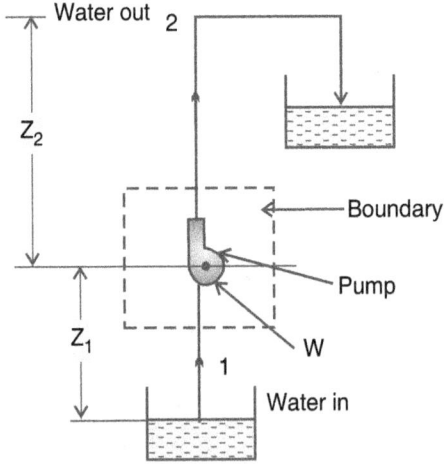

Prob 1.20

The energy equation for the pump for the given conditions can be written as when mass flow per second is given.

$$m \left[\frac{V_1^2}{2} + Z_1 g + p_1 v_{s1} \right] + W = m \left[\frac{V_2^2}{2} + Z_2 g + p_2 v_{s2} \right] \text{ as } Q = 0.0 \text{ (for pump)}$$

$\therefore \quad W = m \left[\frac{V_2^2 - V_1^2}{2} + g(Z_2 - Z_1) + (p_2 v_{s2} - p_1 v_{s1}) \right] \quad \ldots(a)$

$$m = \frac{\pi}{4} d_1^2 \, V_1 \, \rho = \frac{\pi}{4} d_2^2 \, V_2 \, \rho \text{ as } \rho_1 = \rho_2 = \rho \text{ (for water)}$$

$$\therefore \quad V_1 = 1.91 \text{ m/sec and } V_2 = 7.64 \text{ m/sec}$$

$$\therefore \quad 60 = \frac{\pi}{4}\left(\frac{20}{100}\right)^2 \times V_1 \times 1000 = \frac{\pi}{4}\left(\frac{10}{100}\right)^2 V_2 \times 1000$$

$$\therefore \quad V_1 = 1.91 \text{ m/s and } V_2 = 7.64 \text{ m/s}$$

Considering the centre of pump is datum and substituting the values in equation (a), we get,

$$\therefore \quad W = 60\left[\frac{(7.64)^2 - (1.91)^2}{2} + 9.81 \times [8 - (-2)] + 10^5 \times \left(4 \times \frac{1}{1000} - 1 \times \frac{1}{1000}\right)\right]$$

as $Z_1 = -2$ as it is below centre and $v_{s1} = v_{s2} = \frac{1}{1000}$

$$\therefore \quad W = 60 \times [27.4 + 98.1 + 100 \times 3] = 25530 \text{ J/s} = 25530 \text{ watts}$$

$$\therefore \quad \text{Power} = \mathbf{25.53 \text{ kW}}$$

Problem 1.21 : A centrifugal pump delivers water at a rate if 3000 kg/min. The suction and delivery pressures are 80 kPa and 300kPa respectively. The suction and delivery pipe diameters are 15 cm and 10 cm respectively. Assuming the suction and discharge are at same level. Find the capacity of an electric motor in kW if the mechanical efficiency between the pump and motor is 90%.

Solution :

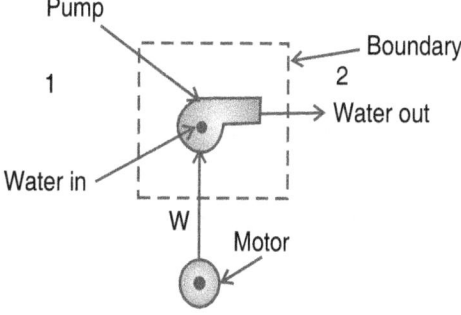

Prob 1.21

The energy equation for the given pump on per sec basis can be written as

$$m\left[\frac{V_1^2}{2} + p_1 v_{s1}\right] + W = m\left[\frac{V_2^2}{2} + p_2 v_{s2}\right]$$

As $Q = 0.0$, $Z_1 = Z_2$ (given) and $u_1 = u_2$ (for water system)

$$\therefore \quad W = m\left[(p_2 v_{s2} - p_1 v_{s1}) + \left(\frac{V_2^2 - V_1^2}{2}\right)\right]$$

$$= m\left[v_s(p_2 - p_1) + \left(\frac{V_2^2 - V_1^2}{2}\right)\right] \text{ as } v_{s1} = v_{s2} = v_s \text{ (for water)} = \frac{1}{1000} \text{ m}^3/\text{kg}$$

The mass flow is given by,

$$m = \frac{\pi}{4} d_1^2 V_1 \rho = \frac{\pi}{4} d_2^2 V_2 \rho_2 \text{ where } \rho_1 = \rho_2 = 1000 \text{ kg/m}^3 \text{ (for water)}$$

∴ $$\frac{3000}{60} = \frac{\pi}{4} \left(\frac{15}{100}\right)^2 \times V_1 \times 1000 = \frac{\pi}{4} \left(\frac{10}{100}\right)^2 V_2 \times 1000$$

∴ $V_1 = 2.83 \text{ m/s}$ and $V_2 = 6.37 \text{ m/s}$

Now, substituting the values in the above equation, we get

∴ $$W = \frac{3000}{60} \left[\frac{1}{1000} \times 10^3 \times (300 - 80) + \frac{(6.37)^2 - (2.83)^2}{2}\right] \text{J/s}$$

∴ Power = $50 \times (220 + 16.25) = 11812.5$ watts = **11.82 kW**

∴ Power of motor, $P_e = \dfrac{11.82}{0.9} = $ **13.13 kW**

Problem 1.22 : A centrifugal pump delivers water increasing its pressure from 0.8 bar to 2.8 bar. The suction is 2 m below and 5 m above the centre of the pump. The power required to run the pump is 13.9 kW. The suction and delivery pipe diameters are 15 cm and 10 cm respectively. Find the quantity of water delivered in m³/min. The inlet and outlet velocities of water are 2.6 m/s and 5.8 m/s respectively.

Solution :

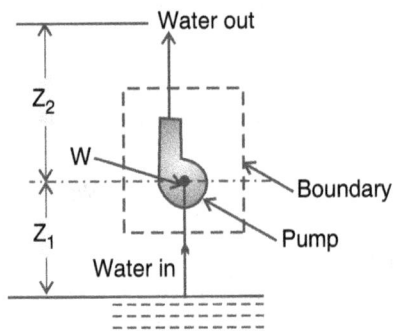

Prob 1.22

The energy equation for the pump for the given conditions, assuming m kg of water is delivered per second can be written as

$$m\left[\frac{V_1^2}{2} + Z_1 g + p_1 v_{s1}\right] + W = m\left[\frac{V_2^2}{2} + Z_2 g + p_2 v_{s2}\right]$$

∴ $$m\left[\frac{V_2^2 - V_1^2}{2} + g(Z_2 - Z_1) + v_s(p_2 - p_1)\right] = W \text{ as } v_{s1} = v_{s2} = v_s$$

∴ $$m\left[\frac{(5.8)^2 - (2.6)^2}{2} + 9.81 \times [5 - (-2)] + \frac{1}{1000} \times 10^5 \times (2.8 - 0.8)\right] = 13.9 \times 10^3$$

∴ $m [13.14 + 68.67 + 200] = 13.9 \times 10^3$

∴ $m = \dfrac{13.9 \times 10^3}{282.11} = $ **49.3 kg/s**

$$= \frac{49.3 \times 60}{1000} \text{ m}^3/\text{min} = \mathbf{2.96 \text{ m}^3/\text{min}}.$$

Nozzles

Problem 1.23 : A steam at the rate of 40 kg/min at 15 bar is passed through a nozzle. The inlet and outlet conditions of the steam are V_1 = 30 m/s, v_{s1} = 0.15 m³/kg, u_1 = 2600 kJ, and p_2 = 1 bar, v_{s2} = 1.7 m³/kg, u_2 = 2500 kJ/kg. Find the velocity of steam at the exit of the nozzle.

Solution :

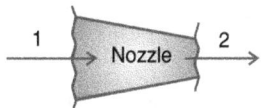

Prob 1.23

The energy equation for the nozzle can be written as,

$$\frac{V_1^2}{2} + u_1 + p_1 v_{s1} = \frac{V_2^2}{2} + u_2 + p_2 v_{s2}$$

$$\therefore \quad \frac{V_2^2}{2} = \frac{V_1^2}{2} + (u_1 - u_2) + (p_1 v_{s1} - p_2 v_{s2})$$

$$= \frac{(30)^2}{2} + 10^3 \times (2600 - 2500) + 10^5 \times (15 \times 0.15 - 1 \times 1.7)$$

$$= 450 + 10^5 + 10^5 \times 0.55 = 10^5 \times (0.0045 + 1 + 0.55) = 1.5545 \times 10^5$$

$$\therefore \quad V_2 = 100 \sqrt{2 \times 15.545} = 100 \times 5.58 = \mathbf{558 \text{ m/s}}$$

Problem 1.24 : The inlet and exit conditions of steam passing through a nozzle are h_1 = 2880 kJ/kg, V_1 = 60 m/s and h_2 = 2770 kJ/kg. Neglecting heat loss from the nozzle and assuming nozzle is horizontal, find exit velocity of the steam, mass flow rate if its inlet area is 1000 cm² and specific volume at inlet is 0.187 m³/kg. Also find out exit area of nozzle if specific volume is 0.5 m³/kg.

Solution :

Prob 1.24

The energy equation for the nozzle can be written as

$$\frac{V_1^2}{2} + h_1 = \frac{V_2^2}{2} + h_2$$

$$\therefore \quad V_2 = \sqrt{2(h_1 - h_2) + V_1^2}$$

$$= \sqrt{2(2880 - 2770) \times 10^3 + (60)^2} = 473 \text{ m/s}$$

$$m = \frac{A_1 V_1}{V_{s1}}$$

$$= \frac{1000 \times 10^{-4} \times 60}{0.187} = \mathbf{32 \text{ kg/s}}$$

But

$$m = \frac{A_2 V_2}{V_{s2}}$$

$$A_2 = \frac{32 \times 0.5}{473} = 0.034 \text{ m}^2 = \mathbf{340 \text{ cm}^2}$$

EXERCISES

1.1 Define the terms "system", "surrounding" and "boundary" of a system.

1.2 Discuss briefly giving suitable examples about closed system and open system.

1.3 Define state, property and process. Explain their importance in thermodynamics.

1.4 With a suitable example, explain the concept of "cyclic process". Indicate its importance in thermodynamics. Differentiate between closed cycle and open cycle giving examples.

1.5 Define "pressure due to a fluid" and describe different methods used for measuring pressure.

1.6 What do you understand by vacuum ? How is it measured ? Explain when mercury and water manometers are used.

1.7 Define "temperature". Differentiate between heat and temperature. Mention different methods used for measuring temperature.

1.8 Explain the difference between a point function and path function.

1.9 Define thermodynamic work and prove that work is a path function.

1.10 Define work, energy and power. List the different units used for measuring work, energy and power.

1.11 State the first law of thermodynamics and prove that for non-flow process, it leads to $Q = W + \Delta U$.

1.12 Define "internal energy" and prove that it is a property (point function) of the system.

1.13 Define "enthalpy" of a system and prove that the change in enthalpy for a non-flow constant pressure process is equal to the heat exchange.

First Law of Thermodynamics

1.14 A rice bag of 100 kg is lifted to the third-storey whose height is 15 m. Determine the work done and its heat equivalent.

1.15 One kg of oil can produce 40000 kJ of heat. If 40% of this heat is transformed into work, determine the work done in kNm. If this work is used for lifting a mass of 50 kg, against standard gravity, to what distance could the load be lifted ?

1.16 Determine the energy produced in kNm and kJ when 0.8 kW engine runs for 40 minutes.

1.17 A car of 1500 kg moving with a velocity of 100 km/hr is brought to rest by the application of brakes. Determine the heat generated in kJ.

1.18 What will be the weight of man on Mercury and Jupiter if he weighs 500 N on the earth ? The relative gravitational accelerations are 2.65 m/s² on Jupiter and 0.36 m/s² on Mercury.

1.19 200 kg of water is heated by means of 1 kW capacity heater. Determine the time required to increase the temperature of water by 40°C.

1.20 A cage of 2000 N can carry 10 persons of average weight of 500 N. It is driven by a winding rope attached to a drum of 100 cm diameter. It is driven by an electric motor at 60 rpm through a gearing. Determine the power required in kW to drive the cage. Neglect the losses.

1.21 The value of the ratio of specific heats (γ) for a certain gas is 1.67 and its specific heat at constant volume is 0.28 kJ/kg°C. Determine the heat given out by the gas per kg when it is cooled from 100°C to 20°C (a) at constant pressure, and (b) at constant volume.

1.22 A motor cycle with two persons has to run at 40 km/hr. Determine the capacity of the engine in kW to run the motor cycle if the resistance for movement is 80 N at this speed.

1.23 A small hydro-electric power plant supplies 10 m³ of water per second at a head of 60 metres. Determine the maximum possible power generating capacity in kW.

1.24 The steam supplied to a steam turbine has an enthalpy of 2720 kJ/kg. When it comes out of the turbine, the enthalpy of the steam is 2480 kJ/kg. If the flow rate of steam through the turbine is 20 kg/sec, determine the power generating capacity of the turbine in kW.

1.25 0.1 m³ of a gas at a pressure of 8 bar expands reversibly. Calculate the work done if the expansion takes place (a) at constant pressure to a final volume of 0.25 m³, (b) according to the law pv = constant to a final volume of 0.2 m³, (c) according to the law $pv^{1.2}$ = constant to a final volume of 0.15 m³.

1.26 0.2 m³ of a gas at 10 bar expands reversibly in a cylinder behind a piston according to the law $pv^{1.25}$ = constant until the volume becomes 0.3 m³. Calculate the work done in kNm.

1.27 In a compression stroke of a gas engine, the work done on the gas by the piston is 32 kNm and heat rejected to the cooling water is 18 kJ. Determine the change in internal energy stating whether it is a gain or loss.

1.28 The gases in the cylinder of an internal combustion engine have an internal energy of 720 kJ/kg, and a specific volume of 0.06 m³/kg at the beginning of expansion. The reversible expansion follows the law $pv^{1.3}$ = constant from 75 bar to 1.25 bar. The internal energy after expansion is 280 kJ/kg. Calculate the heat rejected to the cylinder cooling water per kg of gases during the expansion.

1.29 A gas undergoes a non-flow frictionless process from V_1 = 0.128 m³ to V_2 = 0.048 m³ following the relation

$$p = \left(\frac{42}{V} + 21\right) N/cm^2$$

where V is in m³. During the process, the system rejects 50 kJ of heat. Determine the work done (whether supplied to or developed by the system) and change in internal energy.

1.30 What are the limitations of the first law of thermodynamics ? Illustrate with examples.

1.31 What are the principle reasons for irreversibility ? Give five examples of irreversibility.

1.32 What are the conditions to be satisfied for a process or a cycle to be reversible ? Give few examples of both reversible and irreversible processes. Also give two examples each of non-flow and steady flow reversible process.

1.33 Explain mechanical reversibility differs from thermodynamic reversibility ? What is the difference between internal and external reversibility ? Give examples.

1.34 Write down the general steady flow energy equation. Derive the simplified forms when used for the following system.

(1) Centrifugal water pump, (2) Steam turbine, (3) Table fan, (4) Water turbine, (5) Centrifugal compressor, (6) Flow through an inclined diverging pipe, (7) Steam nozzle.

1.35 During the execution of a reversible non-flow process the pressure the work done is – 160 kJ. If v_1 = 0.85 m³ and the pressure during the process varies as p = (–3v + 7) bar where v is in cu.m, find the final volume.

1.36 A fluid system undergoes a non-flow frictionless process from v_1 = 0.1281 m³ to v_2 = 0.0427 cu.m following the relation p = (4.2/v + 2.1) bar where v is in cu.m. During the process the system rejects 50 kJ of heat. Find the work done and change in internal energy.

1.37 The specific heat at constant pressure of a non-flow thermodynamic system. Whose mass is 1 kg, may be expressed as C_p = 6.4 + $\dfrac{280}{(T + 40)}$ kJ/kg-°C where T is in °C. During a reversible constant pressure process with p = 1.5 bar, the system changes from v_1 = 0.25 cu.m and T_1 = 10°C to v_2 = 0.45 cu.m and T_2 = 240°C. Determine the work done, change in internal energy and enthalpy.

1.38 The internal energy of a certain system is a function of temperature only and is given by u = 25 + 0.25 T, where T is the temperature in °C. When this executes a certain process, the work done per degree temperature change is given by $\dfrac{dW}{dT}$ = 350 $\sqrt{T}$ N-m.

Find the heat transferred when the temperature of the system changes form 100°C to 260°C.

1.39 A fluid system undergoes a non-flow frictionless process from v_1 = 0.197 m³ to v_2 = 0.057 m³ in accordance with

$$v = \dfrac{1.05}{p-1} \text{ where p is in bar.}$$

During the process, the fluid system rejects 12 kJ of heat. Determine the change in enthalpy.

First Law for Power Generation and Power Absorbing Systems

1.40 A 150 kW steam turbine receives steam at a pressure of 14 bar with u_1 = 2600 kJ/kg, v_{s1} = 0.166 m³/kg and V_1 = 120 m/sec. The steam is exhausted at 0.07 bar with u_2 = 2080 kJ/kg, v_{s2} = 18.6 m³/kg and V_2 = 330 m/sec. The heat loss from the steam in the turbine is 20 kJ/kg. Neglecting change in potential energy, find (a) work developed per kg of steam and (b) steam flow in kg per hour.

1.41 A steam turbine operating under steady flow condition receives 4500 kg of steam per hour. The steam enters the turbine at a velocity of 2500 m/min at an elevation of 4 m and a specific enthalpy of 2790 kJ/kg. It leaves the turbine at a velocity of 560 m/min, at an elevation of 1 m and specific enthalpy of 2270 kJ/kg. The heat losses from turbine to the surrounding amounts to 16000 kJ/hr. Determine the power output of the machine in kW.

1.42 The turbine of a jet engine receives a steady flow of gases at 7 bar, 860°C and 160 m/s. Its discharges the gases at 2 bar, 640°C and 330 m/s. Evaluate the work output of the turbine. Assume C_p = 1.1 kJ/kg-K and enthalpy to be a function of temperature only.

1.43 Im a air turbine, air at a pressure of 2.1 bar and a temperature of 57°C flows steadily into turbine with a velocity of 45 m/s. Air leaves the turbine at 1.1 bar, a temperature of 2°C and a velocity of 150 m/s. Shaft work delivered by the turbine is 5400 Nm per kg of air. Neglecting changes in elevation, determine the magnitude and sign of the heat transfer per unit mass of air flow.

For air, take C_p = 1 kJ/kg-K and assume enthalpy of air to be a function of temperature only.

1.44 The gas flows into a turbine with an initial pressure of 7 bar, specific volume of 0.085 m³/kg and velocity of 150 m/sec. The corresponding values of pressure, specific volume and velocity at exit are 4 bar, 0.1113 m³/kg and 300 m/sec respectively. The internal energy of the gas decreases by 90 kJ per kg in passing through the turbine and loss due to radiation is 5 kJ/kg. What amount of shift work is developed per kg of gas flow ? If the gas flow is 20 kg/sec, find the power developed by the machine in kW.

1.45 In an centrifugal air compressor, air enters steadily at 1 bar and 15°C with a velocity of 100 m/sec. The cross-sectional area of the intake is 25 cm². At discharge, the air has a temperature of 65°C and a velocity of 130 m/sec. Neglecting all losses, determine (a) the rate of air flow in kg/sec and (b) power required to run the machine in kW.

Take R = 287 Nm/kg-K for air.

1.46 Air at 1 bar having a specific volume of 0.6 m³/kg flows into a centrifugal compressor and it is discharged at 7 bar with a specific volume of 0.015 m³/kg. During the process, the internal energy of air is increased by 90 kJ/kg and mechanical work required by the compressor is 160 kJ/kg. Neglecting changes in KE and PE, find the heat transfer from the system per kg of air.

1.47 During a steady flow process, 5000 kg/hr of fluid passes through a system in which the exit pipe is 3 m below the inlet connection. Taking the following data,

(a) Pressure decreases from 7 to 1.2 bar.

(b) Velocity increases from 60 to 400 m/sec.

(c) Internal energy decreases by 50 kJ/kg.

(d) Specific volume increases from 0.03 to 0.2 m³/kg.

(e) Heat lost by the system is 100 MJ/hr.

Find the power developed by the system in kW.

1.48 300 kg of working fluid enters a steady flow system with p_1 = 8 bar, ρ_1 = 3.25 kg/cu.m, V_1 = 35 m/sec, u_1 = 2520 kJ/kg and leaves with p_2 = 2 bar, ρ_2 = 0.75 kg/cu.m, V_2 = 150 m/sec and u_2 = 2430 kJ/kg. During the passage through the open system, each kg of fluid rejects 25 kJ of heat. Find the work done by the fluid.

1.49 An insulated constant volume system containing 2 kg of air at 80°C is churned by stirrer and receives 120 kJ of energy from external work. Determine (a) change in temperature, (b) change in internal energy, and (c) change in enthalpy. Take C_p = 1005 J/kg-K and C_v = 715 J/kg-K for air.

1.50 A pump raises the pressure of water in a line by 300 kN/m². The pump exit is 5 m above in the inlet. Neglecting the changes in KE and PE, compute the shaft work required to drive the pump if the flow of water is 5 kg/s.

1.51 A water pump takes water from a well of 5 m below the pump and discharges to the tank which is 50 m above. The pressure of the water at the inlet and exit are 95 kPa and 120 kPa respectively. The water velocity is 2 m/s at exit. Find the power required to run the pump if the discharge from the pump is 2.5 m³/sec.

1.52 Steam at a rate of 3000 kg/hr is passed through a nozzle. The conditions of steam at inlet and exit are given as p_1 = 15 bar, V_1 = 50 m/s, v_{s1} = 0.15 m³, u_1 = 2600 kJ/kg and p_2 = 1 bar, v_{s2} = 1.7 m³/kg, u_2 = 2500 kJ/kg. Determine the velocity of steam at the nozzle exit.

1.53 Steam enters the nozzle of turbine with a low velocity at a pressure of 3 MPa, 350°C and leaves the nozzle at 1.6 MPa at velocity of 550 m/s. The flow rate of steam is 0.5 kg/s. Calculate the quality or temperature of the steam leaving the nozzle. Also determine the exit area of nozzle.

2

INTRODUCTION TO I C ENGINE

2.1 Introduction
2.2 Classification of I.C. Engines
2.3 Parts of I.C. Engine and their Functions
2.4 Terminology used with I.C. Engines
2.5 Working of 4-Stroke Petrol Engine
2.6 Working of 4-Stroke Diesel Engine
2.7 Working of 2-Stroke Petrol Engine
2.8 Working of 2-Stroke Diesel Engine
2.9 Comparison between Petrol and Diesel Engine
2.10 Comparison between 4-Stroke and 2-Stroke Engines
2.11 Air standard Cycles
2.12 Carnot Cycle
2.13 Joules Cycle
2.14 Otto-Cycle and its Analysis
2.15 Diesel Cycle and its Analysis
     Solved Problems
     Exercises

2.1 INTRODUCTION

Any machine which derives heat energy from the combustion of fuel and converts part of this energy into mechanical work is known as **heat engine**. Heat engines are mainly divided into two groups as : external combustion engines and internal combustion engines.

Steam engines fall under the category of external combustion engines whereas internal combustion engines (popularly written as I.C. Engines) are those engines in which the combustion of fuel takes place inside the engine cylinder. These are commonly used in trucks and buses, scooters and cars, ships and locomotives, agricultural and earth moving machinery, many industrial applications and for power generation.

The I.C. engines offer some special advantages over external combustion engines (steam engines) as listed below :

1. The thermal efficiency of the engines (35% to 45%) is much higher than steam engine (30 % to 35%).
2. The power developed by the I.C. engine per kg weight of engine is higher, therefore, it is lighter and occupies less space.

3. The I.C. engine can be started quickly whereas a steam engine requires much more time as the steam has to be generated in the boiler.
4. It offers greater mechanical simplicity.
5. The I.C. engine being more compact, practically it has no competitor for small and portable power range.

The temperatures in I.C. engines are very high (2000°C) as the combustion takes place inside the engine cylinder, therefore, a cooling arrangement is necessary to prevent the overheating of the cylinder. It is to be noted here that the steam engines are heated by providing fresh steam to prevent the condensation and power loss. I.C. engines are commonly single acting as temperature encountered is high whereas reciprocating steam engines are commonly double acting.

I.C. engine is adopted universally as a best prime mover in small capacity power range and its replacement in near future is not possible.

2.2 CLASSIFICATION OF I.C. ENGINES

The I.C. engines may be classified as follows :

1. According to the Type of Fuel Used : On this basis, they are classified as petrol engines, diesel engines and gas engines. This classification is based on the type of fuel used in the engine.

2. According to the Number of Strokes Required to Complete the Cycle : They are classified as four strokes and two strokes engines. In four strokes engine, there is one power stroke in every four strokes or one during two revolutions of the crank. In two strokes engine, there is one power stroke in every two strokes or one during each revolution of the crank. The petrol, diesel or gas engines may be operated on two stroke cycle or four stroke cycle.

3. According to the Cycle of Operation : They are classified mainly as Otto-cycle and Diesel cycle engines. In Otto cycle, the combustion of fuel takes place at constant volume. In Diesel cycle, the combustion of fuel takes place at constant pressure. The petrol and gas engines work on Otto cycle.

4. According to the Method of Ignition : They are classified as spark ignition (S.I.) engines and compression ignition (C.I.) engines. In spark ignition system, the mixture of fuel and air is ignited with the help of an electric spark. Petrol engines work on this system. In compression ignition system, the fuel is ignited as it comes in contact with hot air in the cylinder due to high compression ratio. The diesel engines work on this system.

5. According to the Method of Cooling : They are classified as air cooled and water cooled engines. Small capacity engines (car, scooter and motor cycle) are cooled with the help of air whereas large capacity engines (car, bus, trucks) are cooled with the use of water.

6. According to the Method of Governing Used : They are classified as quality governing and quantity governing. In quantity governing method, the quantity of mixture of air and fuel is changed maintaining the air fuel ratio of the supplied mixture constant. The petrol engines are governed by this method. In quality governing method, the quantity of fuel supplied is changed as per requirement and the air-fuel ratio cannot remain constant. Diesel engines are governed by using this method.

7. According to Speed of the Engine : They are classified as low speed, medium speed and high speed engines. Petrol engines are generally high speed engines (5000 to 7000 RPM) whereas diesel engines fall under low or medium speed (500-2000 RPM).

8. According to the Arrangement of Cylinders : They are classified as horizontal, vertical, inline, V-type and radial engines. This classification is based as per the arrangement of the cylinders. The scooter and motor cycle engines are the examples of vertical arrangement. The engine used in car and bus is a multi-cylinder inline engine. The engines earlier used in aeroplane were of radial arrangement of the cylinders as its balancing is good and requires minimum space.

2.3 PARTS OF I.C. ENGINES AND THEIR FUNCTIONS

Sectional view of 4-stroke diesel engine is shown in Fig. 2.1. The top end of the engine cylinder is closed by means of a cover known as cylinder head and it contains inlet and exhaust valves. The fuel injector is also fitted in this cover. The two valves are kept closed with the help of springs and are opened mechanically by means of rocker arms, and cams which are fitted on cam shaft. The cam shaft is driven by the crank shaft through a gear.

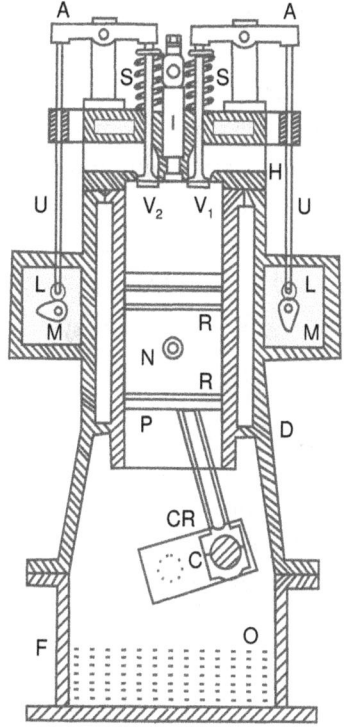

Where,
- D – Cylinder block
- P – Piston
- N – Piston pin or gudgeon pin
- R – Piston ring
- J – Water jacket
- M – Cam
- L – Cam follower
- U – Push rod
- A – Rocker arm
- S – Spring
- V_1, V_2 – Valve
- I – Atomiser
- H – Cylinder head
- CR – Connecting rod
- C – Crank
- F – Frame
- O – Lubricating oil

Fig. 2.1 : General Outline of I.C. Engine

The functions of different parts are outlined below :

1. Frame : It generally consists of bed plate, crank case and it also supports the different moving parts. The bed plates are rigidly fixed with the foundations of the floor. The lower part of the crank case contains oil for lubricating purposes.

2. Cylinder and Cylinder Block : Single cylinder engine has a single cylinder. Multi-cylinder engine has a cylinder block which contains cylinder bores and openings for the valves. To avoid the wear of cylinder block, cylinder liners are provided. It may contain the passage for the flow of cooling water. A separated cylinder head is fitted over the cylinder block with studs and nuts. The cylinder block is made of cast iron.

3. Piston : It is a gas tight movable cylindrical disc which moves up and down in the cylinder against which the hot gases act to cause the rotation of crank shaft through connecting rod. The small end of the connecting rod is fitted to the piston with the help of a pin known as Gudgeon pin. Piston rings are provided over the piston to prevent the leakage of hot high pressure gases around the piston. Pistons are generally made of aluminium alloys.

4. Connecting Rod and Crank Shaft : One end of the connecting rod is fitted to the piston through a pin known as Gudgeon pin or piston pin and other end is connected to the crank pin. It transmits the reciprocating motion of the piston to the crank pin and causes the crank to rotate. They are usually made of steel forging.

Crank-shaft is the principal rotating part of the engine. The part of the crank-shaft to which the big end of connecting rod is fitted is called crank pin. It is also generally made from a steel forging.

5. Valve Gear : The combination of parts which control the admission of fresh charge into the cylinder and discharge of exhaust gases from the cylinder is termed as valve gear. The combination of cam and cam shaft, follower, push rod, rocker arm, spring and valves is known as valve gear. The inlet valve controls the admission of fresh charge whereas the exhaust valve controls the discharge of exhaust gases. Valves are made of nickel steel or chrome steel as they are subjected to high temperatures.

The other important parts like carburetter, fuel pump, ignition system will be described in this chapter in more details.

2.4 TERMINOLOGY USED WITH I.C. ENGINES

1. TDC and BDC : When the piston travels in the cylinder towards top stop, that point is known as **Top Dead Centre** position and denoted by TDC. When the piston travel towards bottom in the cylinder stop, that point is known as **Bottom Dead Centre** and denoted by BDC.

2. Diameter of the Cylinder : The diameter of the cylinder in which piston reciprocates is known as diameter of the cylinder. This is used for calculating the power developed by the engine in the cylinder.

3. Length of the Stroke : The travel of the piston along one direction from BDC to TDC or TDC to BDC is known as the **stroke of the engine**.

4. Clearance Volume : The volume occupied by the fluid when the piston reaches to TDC as shown in Fig. 2.2. This is denoted by v_c and it is given by

$$v_c = \frac{\pi}{4} D^2 \cdot \delta$$

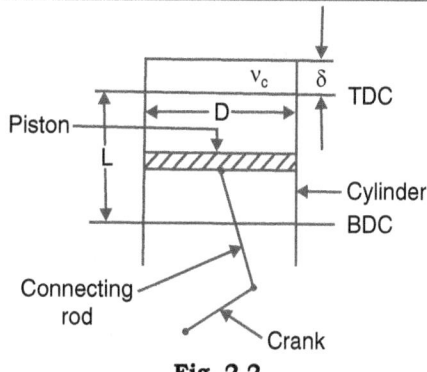

Fig. 2.2

Where, δ is clearance between TDC and top of the cylinder.

5. Swept or Stroke Volume : The volume occupied by the fluid in between BDC and TDC is known as swept or stroke volume.

This is denoted by v_s and it is given by

$$v_s = \frac{\pi}{4} D^2 \cdot L$$

The addition of v_c and v_s is known as total volume of the engine cylinder.

The clearance volume is always given as a percentage of stroke volume.

6. Compression Ratio : This is defined as a ratio of fluid volume in the cylinder when the piston is at BDC [this is equal to $(v_c + v_s)$] to the volume occupied by the fluid when the piston is at TDC (this is equal to v_c).

$$\therefore \quad R_c = \frac{v_s + v_c}{v_c} = 1 + \frac{v_s}{v_c}$$

2.5 WORKING OF 4-STROKE PETROL (S.I.) ENGINE

There are distinctly 4-strokes for different operations in the cycle and each stroke is identified as per the function.

1. Suction or Induction Stroke : During this stroke, the inlet valve remains open and air and fuel vapour mixture is taken in. The piston moves from TDC (top dead centre position) to BDC (bottom dead centre position).

2. Compression Stroke : The mixture of air and fuel is compressed during this stroke and the pressure and temperature are increased due to compression. Both the valves remain closed during this stroke. The piston moves from BDC to TDC during this stroke.

3. Expansion Stroke : During this stroke, both the valves remain closed. The gases are burned with the help of an electric spark at the beginning of the expansion stroke and its temperature and pressure suddenly increase. The high pressure, high temperature gases push the piston downward under the force from TDC to BDC. It is called working stroke as work is done by the expansion of hot gases. At the end of expansion, the exhaust valve opens and the pressure of the exhaust gases suddenly falls to atmospheric pressure.

4. Exhaust Stroke : During the operation of this stroke, the exhaust gases are pushed out through the exhaust valve. The exhaust valve remains open during this stroke. The piston moves from BDC to TDC.

Again the inlet valve opens and the same operations are repeated. The cycle is completed during four strokes and the fuel used is petrol therefore it is known as 4-stroke petrol engine.

The operations during the four strokes are shown in Fig. 2.3.

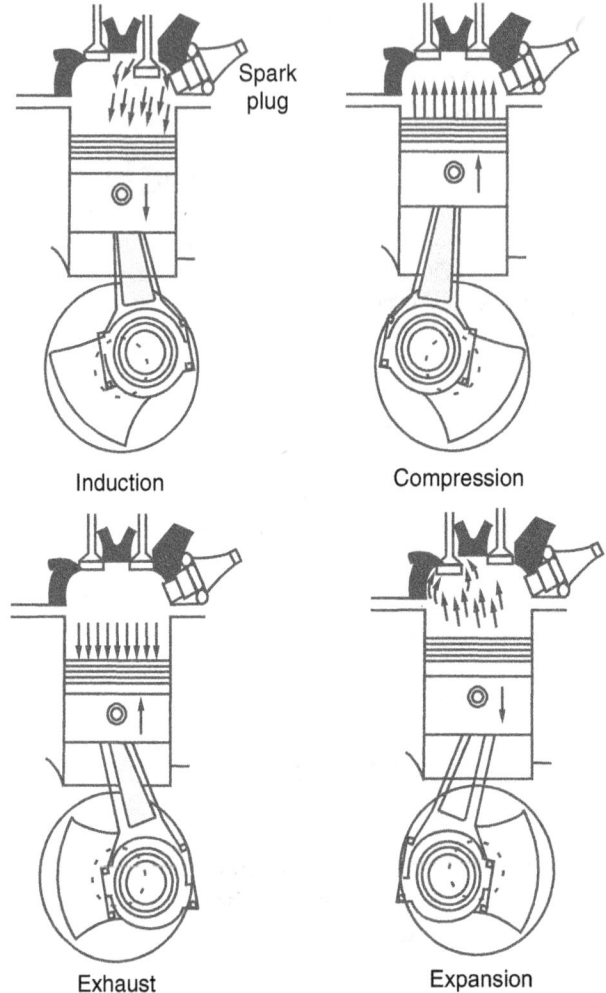

Fig. 2.3 : **Working Positions of 4-stroke Petrol Engine**

2.6 WORKING OF 4-STROKE DIESEL (C.I.) ENGINE

All working operations such as suction, compression, expansion and exhaust are also completed in 4-strokes and diesel is used as fuel instead of petrol. Therefore, it is known as 4-stroke diesel engine. The liquid fuel like diesel which cannot be vapourised is injected into the engine cylinder in the form of fine spray with the help of fuel pump and injector. The working of the 4-stroke diesel engine is described as given below :

1. Suction Stroke : The inlet valve remains open during this operation. The only air is taken in through the inlet valve as the piston moves from TDC to BDC.

2. Compression Stroke : During this stroke, the inlet and exhaust valves remain closed. The piston moves from BDC to TDC and compresses the air with an increase in pressure and temperature and decrease in volume.

3. Expansion Stroke : Just before completing the compression stroke, the fuel injector opens and injects the diesel fuel in the form of fine spray inside the cylinder. The injected fuel starts burning due to the high temperature inside the cylinder as *compression ratio of diesel engine is high (20). The supply of fuel is cut off after 20% of the expansion stroke, and the hot gases expand pushing the piston towards BDC. During this stroke, the piston moves from TDC to BDC. At the end of the stroke, exhaust valve opens and the pressure inside the cylinder falls to just above the atmospheric pressure.

4. Exhaust Stroke : The hot gases in the cylinder are driven out through the exhaust valve from the cylinder as the piston moves from BDC to TDC. The exhaust valve is closed at the end of the stroke. Again the inlet valve opens and the same operations are repeated. The cycle is completed during 4-strokes and the fuel used is diesel, therefore, the engine is known as 4-stroke diesel engine.

The operations during the four strokes are shown in Fig. 2.4.

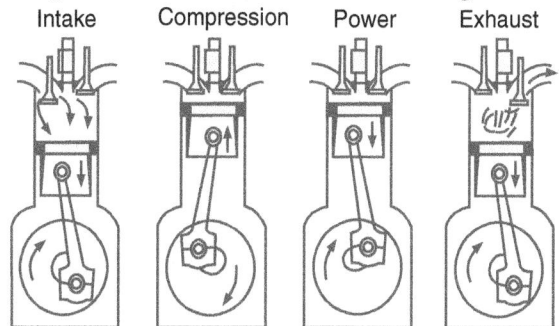

Fig. 2.4 : Working Positions of 4-stroke Diesel Engine

The cyclic operation is completed within 4 strokes in both petrol and diesel engines. The basic difference between the two is in the method of fuel supply. A mixture of air and fuel is taken during suction stroke in petrol engine whereas only air is taken during suction stroke in diesel engine and fuel is supplied at the end of compression stroke. The charge is ignited by spark in petrol engine whereas the ignition takes place due to high temperature as compression ratio used in diesel engine is considerably high.

2.7 WORKING OF 2-STROKE PETROL (S.I.) ENGINE

In two-stroke engines, the cycle is completed in two-strokes of the piston or one revolution of crank-shaft. In two stroke engines, the valves are replaced by the ports and the exhaust gases are removed from the cylinder with the help of fresh compressed charge. This process of removing exhaust gases is called the scavenging. A specific shape is given to the piston which helps to prevent the loss of incoming charge and helps for exhausting the hot gases effectively.

In case of single cylinder engines as used in scooter and motor cycle, three ports are provided as exhaust, transfer and inlet. Through the exhaust port, the hot gases are pushed out. Through the transfer port, the fresh charge from the bottom of the engine piston is supplied to the cylinder and also helps for exhaust. Through the inlet ports, fresh charge from the carburettor is taken into the cylinder crank case.

---

* Compression ratio is defined as the volume before compression to the volume at the end of compression. The compression ratio is 6 to 10 in petrol engine and 14 to 22 in diesel engine.

It will be easier to describe the working cycle, beginning at the point when the piston has reached to TDC completing the compression stroke.

First Stroke : The position of the piston at the end of compression is shown in Fig. 2.5 (a). The spark is produced by the spark plug as the piston reaches TDC. The pressure and temperature of the gases increase and push the piston downward producing the power stroke. When the piston uncovers (opens) the exhaust port as shown in Fig. 2.5 (b), during the downward stroke, the burned gases leave the cylinder through the exhaust port.

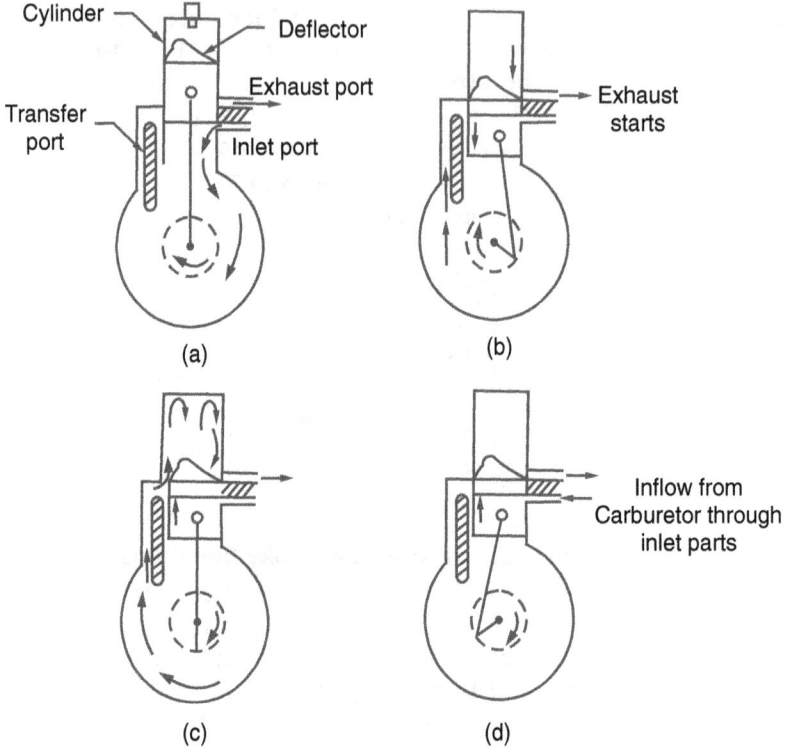

Fig. 2.5 : Working Positions of 2-stroke Petrol Engine

A little later, the piston uncovers the transfer port as shown in Fig. 2.5 (c). In this position, the crank case is directly connected to the cylinder through transfer port. During the downward stroke of the piston, the charge in the crank case is compressed by the underside of the piston to 1.2 bar. At the position shown in Fig. 11.5 (c), the compressed mixture of petrol and air is transferred through transfer port to the upper part of the cylinder. The exhaust gases are pushed out with the help of fresh charge. This is also known as scavenging. This is continued until the piston reaches BDC.

During this stroke, power is developed, the exhaust gases are removed and the charge is compressed in the crank case with the help of underside of the piston.

Second Stroke : As the piston starts moving upward, it covers the transfer ports and stops the flow of fresh charge into the cylinder. A little later, the piston covers the exhaust ports and actual compression of the charge starts. This position of the piston is shown in Fig. 11.5 (d). The upward motion of the piston during this stroke lowers the pressure in the crank case through the inlet ports as they are uncovered by the piston. The compression of the charge is continued until the piston reaches to its original position (TDC) and the cycle is completed as shown in Fig. 2.5 (a).

During this stroke, partly exhaust gases are removed, the fresh charge is taken into the crank case through the carburetter and the compression of the charge is completed.

In this way, the cyclic operation is completed within two strokes, therefore, they are known as two-stroke engines.

2.8 WORKING OF 2-STROKE DIESEL (C.I.) ENGINE

First Stroke : The position of the piston at the end of compression is shown in Fig. 2.6 (a). The diesel fuel is injected just before completing the compression and it starts burning at the end of compression as the pressure and temperature inside the cylinder are sufficient to burn. The supply of fuel is also continued. The high pressure, high temperature gases push the piston downward producing the power stroke. As the piston moves little down, then supply of fuel stops and the piston is pushed further due to expansion of gases. When the piston uncovers the exhaust port as shown in Fig. 2.6 (b) during the downward stroke, the burnt gases leave the cylinder through the exhaust port. A little later, the piston uncovers the transfer port as shown in Fig. 2.6 (c). In this position, the crank case is directly connected to the cylinder through the transfer port. During the downward stroke of the piston, the air in the crank case is compressed by underside of the piston to 1.2 to 1.4 bars. At the position shown in Fig. 2.6 (c), the compressed air is transferred through transfer port to the upper part of the cylinder. The exhaust gases are pushed out with the help of fresh air similar to 2-stroke petrol engine. This is continued until the piston reaches BDC.

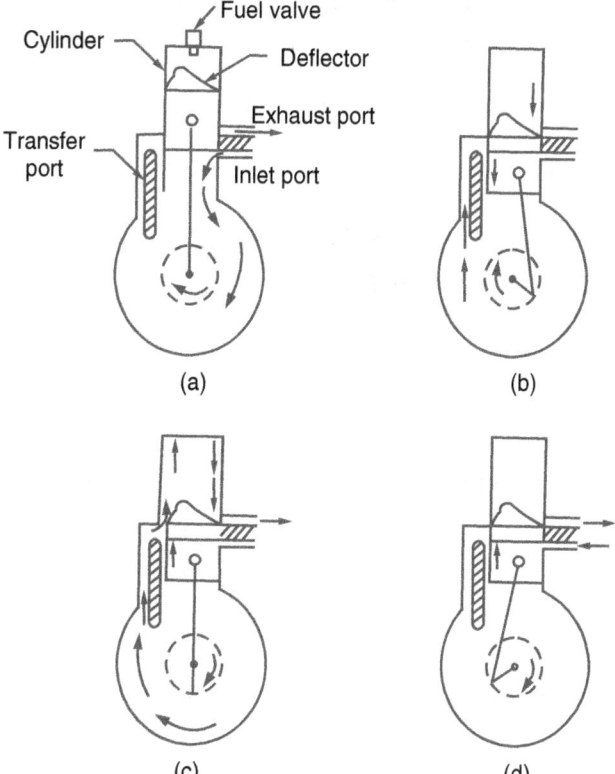

Fig. 2.6 : Working Positions of 2-stroke Diesel Engine

During this stroke, power is developed, the exhaust gases are removed and the fresh air in the crank-case is compressed with the help of underside of the piston.

Second Stroke : As the piston starts moving upward, it first covers the transfer port and stops the flow of high pressure (1.4 bar) fresh air into the cylinder. A little later, the piston covers the exhaust port and actual compression of the air starts. The upward motion of the piston during this stroke lowers the pressure in the crank case below atmosphere and fresh air is induced in the crank case through the inlet port as it is uncovered. The compression of the air is continued until the piston reaches to its original position (TDC). The fuel supply starts just before the piston reaches TDC and the cycle is completed as shown in Fig. 2.6 (a).

During this stroke, partly exhaust gases are removed, the fresh air is taken in the crank case and the compression of the air in the cylinder is completed.

The basic differences between two stroke petrol and two stroke diesel engines are listed below :

1. Only air is taken in the engine cylinder during the suction stroke of the diesel engine whereas the fresh charge is taken in case of petrol engine.
2. The fuel is injected in the air at the end of compression in case of diesel engine where petrol and air mixture is compressed in petrol engine.
3. The compression ratio of petrol engine lies between 5 to 9 whereas the compression ratio of diesel engine lies between 14 to 22.
4. As the compression ratio of diesel engine is high, the temperature in the cylinder at the end of compression is sufficient to burn the fuel itself whereas electric spark is provided for burning the charge in petrol engine. The petrol engines are also known as S.I. (spark ignited) engines and diesel engines are known as C.I. (compression ignited) engines.

The highest pressure after compression in the petrol engine is nearly 25 bar and 60 bar in case of diesel engine irrespective of whether it is two stroke engine or four stroke engine.

2.9 COMPARISON BETWEEN PETROL (S.I.) ENGINE AND DIESEL (C.I.) ENGINE

Petrol Engine	Diesel Engine
1. Engine cost is less.	1. Engine cost is more.
2. More fuel consumption.	2. Less fuel consumption.
3. Engine is lighter in weight.	3. Engine is heavy.
4. Engine requires regular maintenance of ignition system.	4. Fuel injection does not require that frequent maintenance.
5. Engine requires change of spark plug after few thousand km.	5. No spark plugs are fitted.
6. Engine overhaul life is less.	6. Engine requires overhaul after long time. i.e., life of the engine is more.
7. Spares required for overhauling are less costly.	7. Spares required for overhauling an engine are costly.

(Contd.....)

8. Engine is flexible due to higher governed speed.	8. Due to lower governed speed, engine is not that flexible.
9. Due to low engine torque, the transmission is not made for heavy duty.	9. Due to high engine torque. It is generally used for heavy duty engines.
10. At idle speed. engine does not run effectively.	10. It runs good even at idling speed also.
11. Engine starting is good even in cold weather.	11. Engine starting is difficult in cold weather and requires heating coil.
12. Engine requires small capacity battery as starting engine torque is less.	12. Engine requires high capacity battery as engine starting torque is more.
13. Costly machines are not required for adjusting or testing of carburettor or ignition system.	13. For testing, calibrating or phasing, injection pump and repairing, costly machines are required.
14. Mechanics, familiar with repair of petrol engines, are available easily and everywhere.	14. Diesel testing machines are not available at all places. Facility for testing of injection pump is not available at all stations.
15. Engine runs without vibration.	15. Engine runs without vibrations.
16. Due to less weight of engine and smooth working, vehicle chassis is not made very strong.	16. Due to heavy weight of engines and more vibration in the engine, chassis is made extra strong.
17. While running, engine does not produce much sound.	17. Engines produce more sound while running.
18. Radiators used in the engine are light in weight.	18. Radiators uses in these engines are heavy duty.
19. Engine running cost is more.	19. Engine running cost is less.

2.10 COMPARISON BETWEEN FOUR AND TWO STROKE ENGINES

The advantages and disadvantages of two-stroke engines over four-stroke engines are discussed below :

Advantages of Two-Stroke Engine Over Four-Stroke Engine :

1. A two-stroke engine develops twice the power of four-stroke engine of the same size at the same engine speed theoretically. But actually, it develops 1.7 to 1.8 times the power developed by four-stroke engines as some power is used for compressioning the charge in the crank case and due to scavenging.

2. Two-stroke engine is much lighter, less bulky and occupies less floor area compared with four-stroke engine.

3. The torque is more uniform in two-stroke engine compared with four-stroke engine, therefore, it requires lighter flywheel and lighter foundation.
4. It provides mechanical simplicity as valves, rocker arms, push rods, cams and cam shaft are not required.
5. The friction loss is less therefore it gives higher mechanical efficiency.
6. The starting of two-stroke engine is easy compared with four-stroke engine.
7. The weight per kW capacity of the two-stroke engine is less than four-stroke engine.
8. The capital cost is also less.

Disadvantages of Two-Stroke Engine Over Four-Stroke Engine :
1. The overall efficiency of two-stroke petrol engine is less than four-stroke petrol engine as some charge is lost to atmosphere during scavenging.
2. The fuel consumption per kilometre and the running cost of two-stroke petrol engine is higher than four-stroke petrol engine.
3. The engine is always overheated as power stroke exists after every revolution compared with after every two revolutions in case of four-stroke engines. Therefore, more effective cooling is necessary.
4. The consumption of lubricating oil is more as it is subjected to higher temperatures.
5. The exhaust of two-stroke engine is more noisy therefore more effective silencers are required.
6. The scavenging is not complete particularly in high speed engines as very short time is available for exhaust and hence fresh charge is polluted.

The two-stroke engines are preferred where the compactness of the engine and less space area requirement are the main considerations as in scooter and motor cycle engines. Its use is also limited to low capacity engines only (5 to 8 kw).

2.11 AIR STANDARD CYCLES

We have seen in the previous chapter, that a thermodynamic system has to work continuously in cyclic process. It is also necessary that the system should develop maximum work for the given heat input. Therefore, it is necessary to study the ideal theoretical cycles which can provide maximum efficiency.

Following are the considerations and assumptions for the study of ideal cycles.

1. The working fluid in the cycle is air and its thermodynamic properties remain constant during the processes in the cycle.

2. All the processes in the cycle are reversible because maximum work is developed in the reversible cycle.

3. The heat supplied to working fluid and rejected by the working fluid to the surrounding take place externally.

2.12 CARNOT CYCLE

The cycle is represented on p-v and T-s diagrams as shown in Fig. 2.7.

This cycle consists of four operations as shown in the figure. At point '1', the working fluid is first compressed at constant temperature rejecting the heat during compression to the heat sink at temperature T_2 till its volume is reduced to v_2.

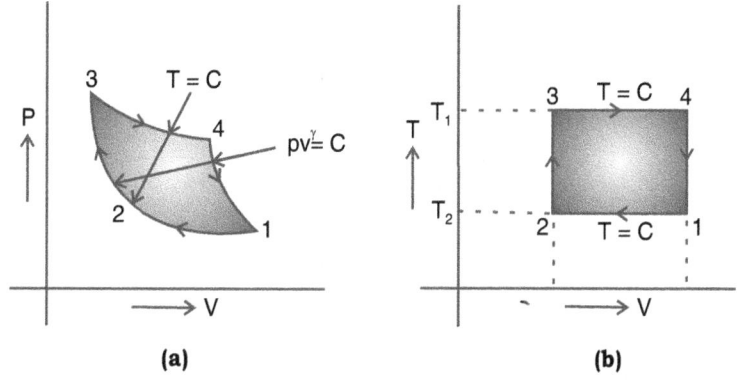

Fig. 2.7

At point 2, the sink is removed and the working substance is further compressed isentropically till the working fluid occupies the volume v_3. The temperature during this process increases from T_2 to T_1 ($T_1 > T_2$).

At point 3, heat is supplied to the working fluid at constant temperature T_1 with the help of heat source till the fluid occupies the volume v_4. Then the source is removed.

At point 4, the fluid is allowed to expand isentropically till it reaches to its initial condition '1', and completes the cycle.

Heat is supplied during the process 3-4 (Q_s) and it is rejected during the process 1-2 (Q_r) and there is no heat transfer during the other two processes 4-1 and 2-3.

According to the first law of thermodynamics,

$$\oint dW = \oint dQ$$

$$\therefore \quad \oint dW = W = (Q_s - Q_r)$$

The efficiency of the cycle is given by

$$\eta_c = \frac{W}{Q_s} = \frac{Q_s - Q_r}{Q_s} = 1 - \frac{Q_r}{Q_s} \qquad ...(2.1)$$

During the isothermal process, the heat transfer is equal to work done and during the isentropic process, the change in internal energy is equal to the work done.

Therefore, during the isothermal process 1-2, the work done on the engine per kg of working fluid is equal to heat rejected.

$$\therefore \quad Q_r = p_2 v_2 \log_e \left(\frac{v_1}{v_2}\right) \text{ N-m/kg}$$

$$= RT_2 \log_e \left(\frac{v_1}{v_2}\right) \text{ Joules/kg}$$

During the isentropic process 2-3, the increase in internal energy per kg of working fluid is equal to work done.

$$\therefore \quad \Delta u_1 = C_v (dT)_1 = \frac{p_3 v_3 - p_2 v_2}{(\gamma - 1) J} \text{ joules/kg}$$

$$= \frac{R (T_1 - T_2)}{(\gamma - 1)} \text{ joules/kg}$$

During the isothermal process 3-4, the work done by the engine per kg of working fluid is equal to heat supplied.

$$\therefore \quad Q_s = p_3 v_3 \log_e \left(\frac{v_4}{v_3}\right) \text{ N-m/kg}$$

$$= RT_1 \log_e \left(\frac{v_4}{v_3}\right) \text{ Joules/kg}$$

During the isentropic process 4-1, the decrease in internal energy per kg of working fluid is equal to work done.

$$\therefore \quad \Delta u_2 = C_v (dT)_2 = \frac{p_4 v_4 - p_1 v_1}{(\gamma - 1) J} \text{ joules/kg}$$

$$= \frac{R (T_1 - T_2)}{(\gamma - 1)} \text{ joules/kg}$$

Now, substituting the values of Q_r and Q_s in equation (3.17),

$$\eta_a = 1 - \frac{(RT_2/J) \cdot \log_e (v_1/v_2)}{(RT_1/J) \cdot \log_e (v_4/v_3)}$$

$$= 1 - \frac{T_2}{T_1} \cdot \frac{\log_e (v_1/v_2)}{\log_e (v_4/v_3)} \quad \ldots (2.2)$$

Applying the isentropic law to the processes 1-2 and 3-4, we can write

$$T_2 v_1^{\gamma-1} = T_1 v_2^{\gamma-1}$$

as temperature at point 1 is T_2 and at point 2 is T_1.

$$\therefore \quad \frac{v_1}{v_2} = \left(\frac{T_1}{T_2}\right)^{\frac{1}{(\gamma-1)}} \quad \ldots (2.3)$$

Similarly, $\quad T_1 v_3^{\gamma-1} = T_2 v_4^{\gamma-1}$

as temperature at point 3 is T_1 and at point 4 is T_2.

$$\therefore \quad \frac{v_4}{v_2} = \left(\frac{T_1}{T_2}\right)^{\frac{1}{(\gamma-1)}} \quad \ldots (2.4)$$

Comparing equations (2.3) and (2.4), we get

$$\frac{v_1}{v_2} = \frac{v_4}{v_3} \quad \ldots (2.5)$$

Substituting this value in equation (2.2),

$$\eta_c = 1 - \frac{T_2}{T_1} = \frac{T_1 - T_2}{T_1} \text{ Where, } T_1 > T_2 \quad \ldots (2.6)$$

From equation (2.5), $\dfrac{V_4}{V_1} = \dfrac{V_3}{V_2}$

The equation (2.5) and (2.6) indicate that the compression ratio and expansion ratio are same during isothermal compression and expansion and compression ratio and similarly, expansion ratio are also same during isentropic compression and expansion.

The equation (2.6) indicates that the efficiency of Carnot cycle is independent of the properties of working fluid and it is only dependent on the higher and lower temperatures of the cycle.

From the T-s diagram also, we can write

$$\eta_c = \dfrac{Q_s - Q_r}{Q_s} = 1 - \dfrac{Q_r}{Q_s} = 1 - \dfrac{T_2(s_1 - s_2)}{T_1(s_4 - s_3)} = 1 - \dfrac{T_2}{T_1} = \dfrac{T_1 - T_2}{T_1}$$

as $s_1 = s_4$ and $s_2 = s_3$ and area on T-s diagram gives heat supplied or rejected similar to p-v diagram, where area gives work done or work supplied.

Using the T-s diagram also, we get the same expression for the Carnot cycle.

This cycle was first presented in 1824 by a French engineer Sadi Carnot and it is named in his honour. This cycle theoretically permits the conversion of the maximum amount of heat at any temperature into mechanical work although no heat engine has ever been constructed to use this cycle. It gives the maximum efficiency under a given range of temperature that it is possible to obtain in a heat engine cycle. Hence, its usefulness lies in the comparison which it provides with other heat engines.

2.13 BRAYTON OR JOULE'S CYCLE

Dr. Joule proposed a cycle in 1851 in which heat is supplied at constant pressure and rejected also at constant pressure. This cycle is used in gas turbine plant.

The components of gas turbine plant are shown in Fig. 2.8 (a). The cycle of operation is represented on p-v and T-s diagrams in Fig. 2.8 (b) and 2.8 (c).

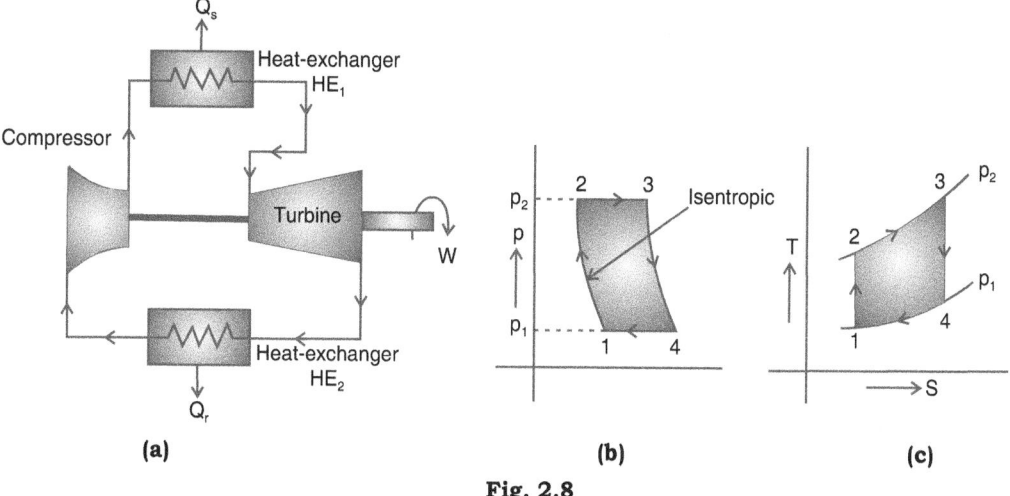

Fig. 2.8

Air at pressure p_1 and temperature T_1 is compressed using a centrifugal compressor isentropically as shown by the process 1-2. Then the air is heated with the help of the source at constant pressure in the heat exchange HE_1 till its temperature increases from T_2 to T_3. This is represented by the process 2-3. Then the air expands isentropically till its pressure falls to its original pressure p_1. This is represented by the process 3-4. Then the air is cooled at constant pressure rejecting heat to the sink. This is represented by the process 4-1. Thus, the cycle is completed.

According to the first law of thermodynamics,

$$\oint dW = \oint dQ$$

$$\therefore \quad W = \oint dQ = Q_s - Q_r$$

As the processes 1-2 and 3-4 are isentropic, therefore there are no heat transfers during these processes. The heat is supplied at constant pressure process 2-3 and rejected at constant pressure process 4-1.

$$\therefore \quad Q_s = C_p(T_3 - T_2) \text{ and } Q_r = C_p(T_4 - T_1)$$

$$\therefore \quad W = C_p[(T_3 - T_2) - (T_4 - T_1)]$$

The efficiency of the cycle is given by

$$\eta = \frac{W}{Q_s} = \frac{Q_s - Q_r}{Q_s} = 1 - \frac{Q_r}{Q_s}$$

$$= 1 - \frac{C_p(T_4 - T_1)}{C_p(T_3 - T_2)} = 1 - \left(\frac{T_4 - T_1}{T_3 - T_2}\right) \quad \ldots(2.7)$$

Applying isentropic law to the processes 1-2 and 3-4.

$$\frac{T_2}{T_1} = \left(\frac{p_2}{p_1}\right)^{\frac{\gamma-1}{\gamma}} = (R_p)^{\frac{\gamma-1}{\gamma}}$$

where $R_p = \frac{p_2}{p_1}$ (pressure ratio of the cycle)

$$\therefore \quad T_1 = \frac{T_2}{(R_p)^{\frac{\gamma-1}{\gamma}}}$$

Similarly,

$$\frac{T_3}{T_4} = \left(\frac{p_2}{p_n}\right)^{\frac{\gamma-1}{\gamma}} = (R_p)^{\frac{\gamma-1}{\gamma}}$$

$$\therefore \quad T_4 = \frac{T_3}{(R_p)^{\frac{\gamma-1}{\gamma}}}$$

Substituting the values of T_1 and T_4 in the equation (2.7) we get,

$$\eta = 1 - \frac{\dfrac{T_3}{(R_b)^{\frac{\gamma-1}{\gamma}}} - \dfrac{T_2}{(R_p)^{\frac{\gamma-1}{\gamma}}}}{(T_3 - T_2)} = 1 - \frac{1}{(R_b)^{\frac{\gamma-1}{\gamma}}} \quad \ldots(2.8)$$

Thus, this equation states that, the η increases with increasing the value of R_p but its value is limited to 5 to 8 for practical reasons.

2.14 ANALYSIS OF ENGINE CYCLES

The theoretical cycles on which the engines work are known as cycles of operation.

1. **Otto Cycle :** The cycle on which the petrol engine works is known as Otto-cycle. The four strokes of 4-stroke petrol engines are shown in Fig. 2.9 on p-v diagram. The 4-strokes are listed below :

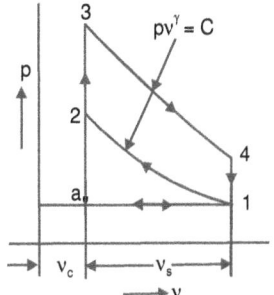

Fig. 2.9 : Otto-cycle

1. a-1 is the suction *stroke at atmospheric pressure.
2. 1-2 is the compression stroke.

    The process 2-3 represents the heat addition at constant volume so the pressure increases suddenly.
3. 3-4 is the expansion stroke.

    The process 4-1 is the cooling at constant volume so the pressure falls suddenly to atmospheric pressure.
4. 1-a represents the exhaust stroke.

    The suction and exhaust are considered at atmospheric pressure only.

The compression and expansion processes are considered isentropic.

Q_s (heat supplied) $= C_v (T_3 - T_2)$

Q_r (heat rejected) $= C_v (T_4 - T_1)$

In complete reversible cycle

W (Work done) $= (Q_s - Q_r) = C_v (T_3 - T_2) - (T_4 - T_1)$

The thermal efficiency of the cycle is given by

$$\eta_{th} = \frac{W}{Q_s} = \frac{C_v [(T_3 - T_2) - (T_4 - T_1)]}{C_v (T_3 - T_2)}$$

$$\eta_{th} = 1 - \frac{T_4 - T_1}{T_3 - T_2} \qquad .....(2.9)$$

Appling the isentropic law to the processes 1-2 and 3-4

$$\frac{T_2}{T_1} = \left(\frac{v_2}{v_1}\right)^{\gamma-1} \text{ and } \frac{T_3}{T_4} = \left(\frac{v_4}{v_3}\right)^{\gamma-1} = \left(\frac{v_1}{v_2}\right)^{\gamma-1} \text{ as } v_3 = v_2 \text{ and } v_4 = v_1$$

$$\frac{v_1}{v_2} = \frac{v_s + v_c}{v_c} = R_c$$

as $v_2 = v_c$ (clearance volume)

$v_1 = v_s + v_c$ (where v_s is the stroke volume)

This ratio $\left(\frac{v_1}{v_2}\right)$ is known as compression ratio and denoted by R_c.

---

* Stroke is the distance travelled by the piston when it moves from TDC to BDC or from BDC to TDC. The volume change during the stroke travel is v_s (stroke volume).

Substituting the values of T_2 and T_3 in equation (2.1), we get

$$\eta_h = 1 - \frac{T_3 \Big/\left(\frac{v_1}{v_2}\right)^{\gamma-1} - T_2 \Big/\left(\frac{v_1}{v_2}\right)^{\gamma-1}}{(T_3 - T_2)}$$

$$= 1 - \frac{1}{\left(\frac{v_1}{v_2}\right)^{\gamma-1}} = \frac{1}{(R_c)^{\gamma-1}} \quad\quad .....(2.10)$$

This indicates that the efficiency of the petrol engine working on Otto-cycle increases with an increase in compression ratio but its maximum value is limited to nine to ten for practical reasons.

The two-stroke petrol engine also works on Otto-cycle except the strokes are overlapped. The expansion and exhaust are overlapped and suction and compression are overlapped.

2.15 DIESEL CYCLE

The cycle on which the diesel engine works is known as Diesel cycle. The four strokes of 4-stroke diesel engine are shown in Fig. 2.10 on p-v diagram.

The four strokes are listed below :

1. a-1 is the suction stroke at atmospheric pressure.
2. 1-2 is the compression stroke which follows the isentropic law during compression.
3. 2-3-4 is the expansion stroke. The part 2-3 is the heat addition at constant pressure and 3-4 represents the isentropic expansion.
4. The process 4-1 is the removal of heat at constant volume.

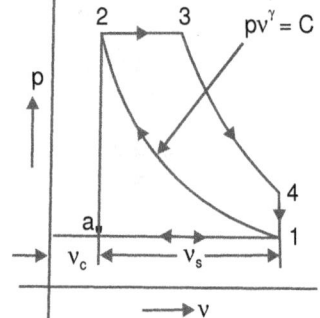

Fig. 2.10 : Diesel Cycle

For same cylinder dimensions (D & L), the compression stroke of 4-stroke engine is higher than the compression ratio of 2-stroke engine.

5. 1-a represents the exhaust at constant atmospheric pressure.

Q_s (heat supplied) = $C_p(T_3 - T_2)$

Q_r (heat rejected) = $C_v(T_4 - T_1)$

In complete reversible-cycle

W (Work done) = $(Q_s - Q_r) = C_p(T_3 - T_2) - C_v(T_4 - T_2)$

The efficiency of the cycle is given by

$$\eta_{th} = \frac{W}{Q_s} = \frac{Q_s - Q_r}{Q_s} = 1 - \frac{Q_r}{Q_s}$$

$$= 1 - \frac{C_v(T_4 - T_1)}{C_p(T_3 - T_2)} = 1 - \frac{(T_4 - T_1)}{\gamma(T_3 - T_2)} \quad \text{where } \gamma = \frac{C_p}{C_v}$$

The ratio $\left(\dfrac{v_1}{v_2}\right)$ is known as compression ratio and $\left(\dfrac{v_4}{v_3}\right)$ is known as expansion ratio.

The ratio $\left(\dfrac{v_3}{v_2}\right)$ is known as cut-off ratio and denoted by ρ.

$$R_c = \frac{v_1}{v_2} = \frac{v_s + v_c}{v_c} \qquad \rho = \frac{v_3}{v_2}$$

$$R_e = \frac{v_4}{v_3} = \frac{v_4}{\rho v_2} = \frac{v_s + v_c}{\rho v_c} = \frac{R_c}{\rho}$$

Applying the isentropic law to the processes 1-2 and 3-4

$$\frac{T_2}{T_1} = \left(\frac{v_2}{v_1}\right)^{\gamma-1} = (R_e)^{\gamma-1}$$

$$\therefore \quad T_1 = \frac{T_2}{(R_e)^{\gamma-1}}$$

$$\frac{T_3}{T_4} = \left(\frac{v_4}{v_3}\right)^{\gamma-1} = (R_e)^{\gamma-1} = \left(\frac{R_c}{\rho}\right)^{\gamma-1}$$

$$\therefore \quad T_4 = \frac{T_3}{\left(\dfrac{R_c}{\rho}\right)^{\gamma-1}}$$

Substituting the values of T_1 and T_4 in the efficiency expression.

$$\eta_{th} = 1 - \frac{T_3 \Big/ \left(\dfrac{R_c}{\rho}\right)^{\gamma-1} - T_2 \Big/ (R_c)^{\gamma-1}}{\gamma(T_3 - T_2)} \quad \ldots(2.11)$$

Applying the constant pressure law to the process 2-3.

$$\frac{v_2}{T_2} = \frac{v_3}{T_3}$$

$$\therefore \quad T_3 = T_2 \left(\frac{v_3}{v_2}\right) = T_2 \rho$$

Substituting this value in the above efficiency equation

$$\eta_{th} = 1 - \frac{\rho T_2 \Big/ \left(\dfrac{R_c}{\rho}\right)^{\gamma-1} - T_2 \Big/ (R_c)^{\gamma-1}}{\gamma(\rho T_2 - T_2)}$$

$$= 1 - \frac{\dfrac{\rho \rho^{\gamma-1}}{(R_c)^{\gamma-1}} - \dfrac{1}{(R_e)^{\gamma-1}}}{\gamma(\rho - 1)}$$

$$= 1 - \frac{1}{(R_c)^{\gamma-1}} \left[\frac{1}{\gamma} \left(\frac{\rho^\gamma - 1}{\rho - 1} \right) \right] \quad \ldots\ldots(2.12)$$

This expression indicates that the efficiency increases with increasing compression ratio but decreases with increasing the cut-off ratio.

IMPORTANT FORMULAE

Second Law of Thermodynamics and Carnot Cycle

The following formulae are used for solving problems :

1. $\eta = \dfrac{Q_1 - Q_2}{Q_1} = \dfrac{W}{Q_1} = \dfrac{T_1 - T_2}{T_1}$ **(for engine)**

2. $\text{C.O.P.} = \dfrac{Q_2}{W} = \dfrac{Q_2}{Q_1 - Q_2} = \dfrac{T_2}{T_1 - T_2}$ (where $T_1 > T_2$) **(for refrigeration)**

3. $\text{C.O.P.} = \dfrac{Q_1}{W} = \dfrac{Q_1}{Q_1 - Q_2} = \dfrac{T_1}{T_1 - T_2}$ (where $T_1 > T_2$) **(for heat pump)**

4. $\dfrac{Q_1}{T_1} = \dfrac{Q_2}{T_2}$ (for reversible engine or heat pump)

or $\sum_{1}^{n} \left(\dfrac{Q_n}{T_n} \right)_R = 0$

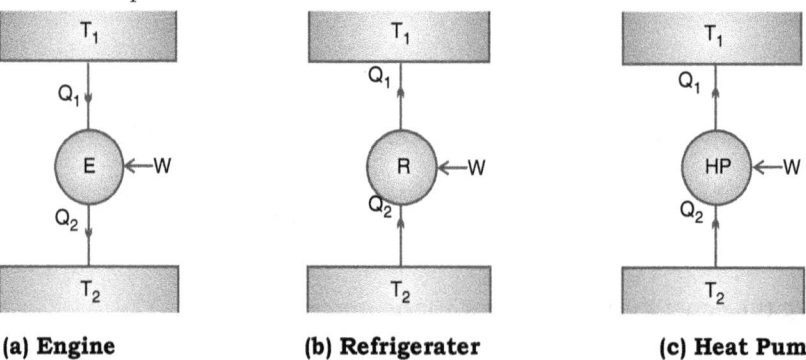

(a) Engine (b) Refrigerater (c) Heat Pump

Fig. 2.11

SOLVED PROBLEMS

Engine, Refrigerator and Heat Pump

Problem 2.1 : A reversible engine with 40% efficiency discharges 1520 kJ of heat per minute at 27°C to a pond. Find the temperature of the source which supplies the heat to the engine and power developed by the engine.

Solution : The arrangement of the system is shown in Fig.

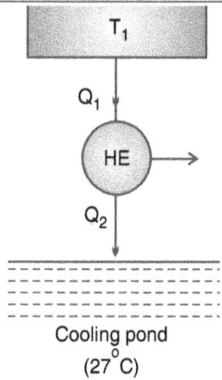

Cooling pond (27°C)

Prob 2.1

The efficiency of the engine is given by,

$$\eta = \frac{T_1 - T_2}{T_1} = \frac{W}{Q_1} = \frac{W}{W + Q_2}$$

$T_1 = ?$, $T_2 = 27 + 273 = 300$ K

$Q_2 =$ **1520 kJ/min (given)**

Substituting the values in the above equation again

$$0.4 = \frac{T_1 - 300}{T_1} = \frac{W}{W + 1520}$$

∴ $0.4 T_1 = T_1 - 300$ ∴ $0.6 T_1 = 300$
∴ $T_1 =$ **500 K**
$W = 0.4 W + 608$ ∴ $0.6 W = 608$
∴ $W =$ **1013.3 kJ/min**
∴ Power $= \dfrac{1013.3}{60}$ kW $=$ **16.9 kW**

Problem 2.2 : A reversible engine receives heat from a mixture of water vapour and liquid water under a pressure of 1.013 bar and rejects 4000 kJ/hr to a mixture of ice and liquid under the pressure of 1.013 bar. Find the power delivered by the engine.

Solution : As per the condition mentioned in the example, the given data is

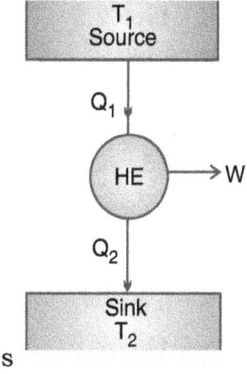

Prob 2.2

$T_1 = 100 + 273 = 373$ and $T_2 = 0 + 273 = 273$ K

The efficiency of a reversible engine is given by,

$$\eta = \frac{T_1 - T_2}{T_1} = \frac{W}{Q_1} = \frac{W}{W + 4000}$$

$$\therefore \quad \frac{373 - 273}{373} = \frac{W}{W + 4000} = \frac{100}{373} = 0.268$$

$$\therefore \quad W = 0.268\,W + 1072$$

$$\therefore \quad 0.732\,W = 1072$$

$$\therefore \quad W = \frac{1072}{0.732} = \mathbf{1465\ kJ/hr}$$

$$\therefore \quad \text{Power} = \frac{1645}{3600} = \mathbf{0.407\ kW}$$

Problem 2.3 : The C.O.P. of a refrigerator operating on reversed Carnot cycle is 5.4 when it maintains − 5°C in the evaporator. Determine the condenser temperature and refrigerating effect if the power required to run the refrigerator is 3.2 kW.

Solution : The arrangement of the system is shown in Fig. 1.27. In this particular system, the source is the evaporator at − 5°C and sink is the condenser at temperature T_1.

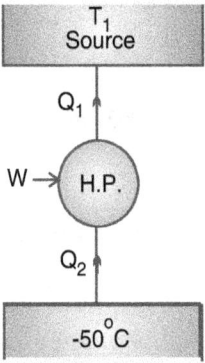

Prob 2.3

The C.O.P. of the refrigerator is given by,

$$\text{C.O.P.} = \frac{Q_2}{W} = \frac{Q_2}{Q_1 - Q_2} = \frac{T_2}{T_1 - T_2}$$

$$T_2 = -5 + 273 = \mathbf{268\ K}\ \text{(given)}$$

$$\therefore \quad 5.4 = \frac{268}{T_1 - 268}$$

$$\therefore \quad T_1 = 268 + \frac{268}{5.4} = 268 + 49.63 = \mathbf{317.63\ K}$$

$$Q_2 = W \times \text{C.O.P.} = 3.2 \times 5.4 = \mathbf{17.3\ kW}$$

Problem 2.4 : An inventor claims to have developed a refrigeration unit which maintains −10°C in the refrigerator which is kept in a room where the surrounding temperature is 25°C and which has C.O.P. of 8.5. How do you evaluate his claim ?

Solution : The maximum C.O.P. of the refrigerator is given by,

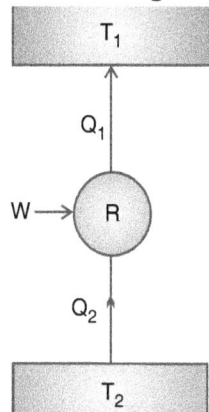

Prob 2.4

$$\text{C.O.P.} = \frac{Q_2}{W} = \frac{Q_2}{Q_1 - Q_2} = \frac{T_2}{T_1 - T_2}$$

$$= \frac{(-10 + 273)}{25 - (-10)} = \frac{263}{35} = 7.5$$

The C.O.P. claimed by the inventor (8.5) is higher than the maximum possible for the given temperature range so his claim is invalid.

Problem 2.5 : A cyclic heat engine operates between a source temperature of 800°C and sink temperature of 30°C. What is the least rate of heat rejection per kW net output of the engine ?

Solution : The efficiency of the engine is given by

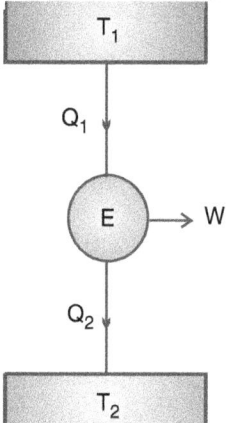

Prob 2.5

$$\eta = \frac{T_1 - T_2}{T_1} = \frac{W}{Q_1} = \frac{Q_1 - Q_2}{Q_1}$$

We have to calculate Q_2 when W = 1 kW. (required)

$$\eta = \frac{800 - 30}{(800 + 273)}$$

$$= 1 - \frac{1}{Q_1}$$

$$= \frac{770}{1073} = 1 - \frac{1}{Q_1}$$

∴ Q_1 = 1.39 kW and η = 0.718 = **71.8%**

$Q_2 = Q_1 - W = 1.39 - 1 = $ **0.39 kW**

Problem 2.6 : A domestic food freezer maintains a temperature of – 15°C. The ambient air temperate is 30°C. If the heat leaks into the freeze 1.75 kJ/s continuously, what is the least power necessary to pump this heat out continuously.

Solution :

$$\text{C.O.P.} = \frac{Q_2}{W} = \frac{Q_2}{Q_1 - Q_2} = \frac{T_2}{T_1 - T_2}$$

Q_2 = 1.75 kW (given)

and we have to find out W.

T_2 = – 15°C and T_1 = 30°C

∴ $$\frac{(-15 + 273)}{[30 - (-15)]} = \frac{1.75}{W}$$

∴ $$W = 1.75 \times \frac{45}{258}$$

$$= \mathbf{0.305 \text{ kW}}$$

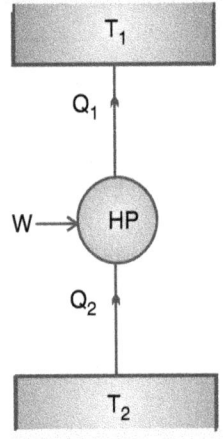

Prob 2.6

Problem 2.7 : The power input required for a grinding mill is 30,000 kNm/min. A heat source at 400°C is available for supplying the energy. The surrounding is at 27°C.

If the actual engine is 30% as efficient as a Carnot engine working between the same temperature limits, find the energy supplied by the source per minute.

Solution : The arrangement is shown in Fig.

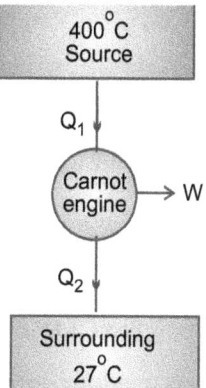

Prob 2.7

The efficiency of the Carnot engine is given by,

$$\eta_C = \frac{W}{Q_1} = \frac{T_1 - T_2}{T_1}$$

$$= \frac{400 - 27}{400 + 273}$$

$$= 0.555$$

Efficiency of the actual engine

$$= 0.555 \times 0.3 = 0.1665$$

$$\therefore \quad \frac{W_{actual}}{Q_1} = 0.1665$$

$$\therefore \quad Q_1 = \frac{W_{actual}}{0.1665} = \frac{30000}{0.1665}$$

$$= 180 \times 10^3 \text{ kNm/min}$$

$$= 180 \times 10^3 \text{ kJ/min} = \mathbf{180 \text{ MJ/min}} = \frac{180 \times 10^3}{60} = \mathbf{3000 kW}$$

Problem 2.8 : A fish freezing plant of *100 tons* capacity is to be maintained at − 50°C when the outside atmospheric temperature is 40°C. The actual C.O.P. of the refrigeration system is 20% of the theoretical Carnot pump working between the same limits of temperature. Calculate the power required to run the plant.

Solution : The arrangement is shown in Fig.

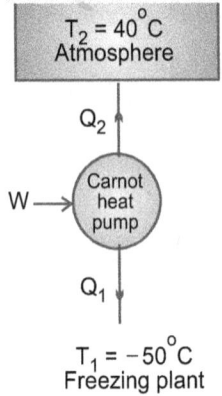

Prob 2.8

C.O.P. of Carnot heat pump (when used for extracting the heat)

$$= \frac{Q_1}{W_1} = \frac{Q_1}{Q_2 - Q_1}$$

$$= \frac{T_1}{T_2 - T_1}$$

$$= \frac{-50 + 273}{40 - (-50)} = \frac{223}{90} = 2.48$$

∴ Actual C.O.P. $= \frac{2.48}{5} = \mathbf{0.466}$

∴ $Q_1 = 100 \times 3.5 = 350$ kJ/s

Actual C.O.P. $= \frac{Q_1}{W} = 0.496$

$W_{actual} = \frac{Q_1}{0.496} = \frac{350}{0.496} = 705$ kJ/s

$= \mathbf{705\ kW}$

Problem 2.9 : A heat pump is used to maintain an auditorium hall at 25°C when the atmospheric temperature is − 5°C. The heat load of the hall is 2400 kJ/min. Calculate the power required to run the actual heat pump if the C.O.P. of the actual heat pump is 25% of the Carnot heat pump working between the same temperature limits.

Solution : The arrangement of the system is shown in Fig.

In this case, the C.O.P. of the Carnot heat pump is given by

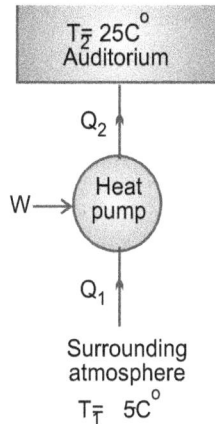

Prob 2.9

$$\text{C.O.P.} = \frac{Q_2}{W} = \frac{Q_2}{Q_2 - Q_1} = \frac{T_2}{T_2 - T_1}$$

$$= \frac{(25 + 273)}{25 - (-5)} = \frac{298}{30} = 9.93$$

∴ Actual C.O.P. = 9.93 × 0.25 = **2.482**

∴ Actual C.O.P. = $\frac{Q_2}{W}$ = 2.482

∴ $W_{actual} = \frac{Q_2}{2.482} = \left(\frac{2400}{60}\right) \times \frac{1}{2.482}$

$\qquad\qquad$ = 16.1 kJ/s = **16.1 kW**

Otto Cycle

Problem 2.10 : An engine 20 cm bore and 30 cm stroke works on Otto-cycle. The clearance volume is 1600 cu cm. The initial pressure and temperature are 1 bar and 60°C. If the maximum pressure is limited to 24 bar, find the following :

(a) The air standard efficiency of the cycle, and

(b) The mean effective pressures for the cycle.

Assume the ideal conditions.

Solution : $\qquad$ vs = $\frac{\pi}{4}$ d2L = $\frac{\pi}{4}$ × 400 × 30 = 9420 cc

$\qquad\qquad$ Re = $\frac{vs + vc}{vc}$ = $\frac{9420 + 1600}{1600}$ = 7.

The air standard efficiency is given by

$$\eta_a = 1 - \frac{1}{(R_c)^{\gamma-1}} = 1 - \frac{1}{7^{0.4}}$$

$$= 0.5408 = \mathbf{54.08\%}$$

For the isentropic process 1 to 2

$$p_2 = p_1 \left(\frac{v_2}{v_1}\right) = 1 \times R_c^{\gamma} = (7)^{1.4}$$

$$= \mathbf{15.245 \text{ bar}}$$

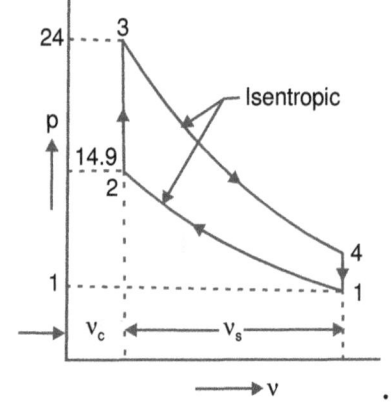

Prob. 2.10

$$\therefore \quad \alpha = \frac{p_3}{p_2} = \frac{24}{15.245} = \mathbf{1.574}$$

The mean effective pressure is given by

$$p_m = p_1 R_c \frac{(\alpha-1)}{(\gamma-1)} \left[\frac{R_c^{\gamma-1}-1}{(R_c-1)}\right] = 1 \times 7 \times \frac{(1.574-1)}{(1.4-1)} \left[\frac{7^{0.4}-1}{7-1}\right] = \mathbf{1.972 \text{ bar.}}$$

Problem 2.11 : An engine works on Otto-cycle. The initial pressure and temperature of the air are 1 bar and 40°C 825 kJ of heat is supplied per kg of air at the end of the compression. Find the temperature and pressures at all salient points if the compression ratio is 6.

Also find the efficiency and mean effective pressure for the cycle.

Assume air is used as working fluid and take all ideal conditions.

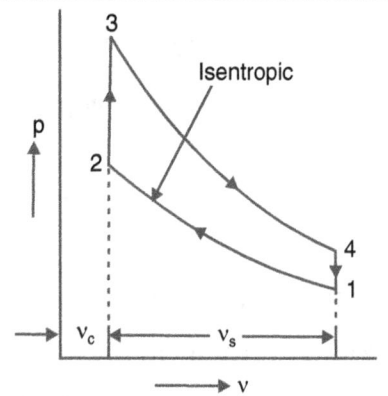

Prob. 2.11

Solution : (a) $p_2 = p_1 \left(\frac{v_1}{v_2}\right)^{\gamma} = p_1 R_c^{\gamma} = 1 \times (6)^{1.4}$

$$= \mathbf{12.286 \text{ bar}}$$

$$T_2 = T_1 \left(\frac{v_3}{v_2}\right)^{\gamma-1} = T_1 R_c^{\gamma-1} = (40+273) \times 6^{0.4} = \mathbf{641 \text{ K}}$$

Heat supplied during the process 2-3 is given by,

$$Q_s = C_v (T_3 - T_2)$$
$$825 = 0.7 (T_3 - 640.92)$$
$$T_3 = 641 + \frac{825}{0.7} = \mathbf{1820 \text{ K}}$$

For the constant volume process 2-3

$$\frac{P_3}{T_3} = \frac{P_2}{T_2}$$

$$P_3 = P_2 \cdot \frac{T_3}{T_2} = 12.3 \times \frac{1820}{641} = \mathbf{34.95 \text{ bar}}$$

(c) For the isentropic process 3-4

$$P_4 = P_3 \left(\frac{v_3}{v_4}\right)^\gamma$$

$$P_4 = P_3 \left(\frac{v_2}{v_1}\right)^\gamma = P_3 \cdot \left(\frac{1}{R_c}\right)^\gamma = 34.95 \left(\frac{1}{6}\right)^{1.4} = \mathbf{2.84 \text{ bar}}$$

$$T_4 = T_3 \left(\frac{v_3}{v_4}\right)^{\gamma-1} = T_3 \cdot \left(\frac{1}{R_c}\right)^{\gamma-1} = \frac{1820}{6^{0.4}} = \mathbf{887.54 \text{ K}}$$

The heat rejected per kg of air is given by

$$Q_r = C_v (T_4 - T_1) = 0.7 (887.54 - 313) = \mathbf{402 \text{ kJ/kg.}}$$

The air-standard efficiency is given by

$$\eta_a = \frac{Q_s - Q_r}{Q_s} = 1 - \frac{402}{825} = 1 - 0.488 = 0.512 \text{ or } \mathbf{51.2\%}$$

It can also be calculated by using direct formula

$$\eta_a = 1 - \frac{1}{R_c^{\gamma-1}} = 1 - \frac{1}{6^{0.4}} = 1 - 0.488 = 0.512 \text{ or } \mathbf{51.2\%}$$

The mean effective pressure is given by

$$P_m = \frac{\text{Work done}}{\text{Stroke volume}} = \left[\frac{p_3 v_3 - p_4 v_4}{\gamma - 1} - \frac{p_2 v_2 - p_1 v_1}{\gamma - 1}\right]\frac{1}{v_s}$$

$$v_2 = v_3 = v_c$$

$$v_1 = v_4 = R_c v_c$$

$$v_s = (R_c - 1) v_c$$

Substituting the values of v_1, v_2, v_3, v_4 and v_s in terms of v_c and R_c and the actual calculated pressures, we can calculate

$$P_m = \frac{1}{v_c (R_c - 1)} \cdot \frac{1}{(\gamma - 1)} (p_2 v_2 - p_4 \times R_c v_c - p_2 v_c + p_1 \times R_c v_c)$$

$$= \frac{1}{(R_c - 1)(\gamma - 1)} (p_3 - p_4 \cdot R_c - p_2 + p_1 R_c)$$

$$= \frac{1}{(6 - 1)(1.4 - 1)} [34.95 - 2.84 \times 6 - 12.286 + 1 \times 6] = \mathbf{5.776 \text{ bar}}$$

It can also be calculated by using direct formula

$$P_m = P_1 \cdot R_c \frac{(\alpha - 1)}{(\gamma - 1)} \left[\frac{R_c^{\gamma-1} - 1}{R_c - 1} \right]$$

$$\alpha = \frac{P_3}{P_2} = \frac{0.95}{12.286} = 2.8388$$

$$\therefore \quad P_m = 1 \times 6 \frac{1.8388}{0.4} \left[\frac{6^{0.4} - 1}{6 - 1} \right] = \frac{6 \times 1.8388}{0.4} \times \frac{1.05}{5} = \textbf{5.776 bar}$$

Problem 2.12 : an engine working on Otto-cycle has a volume of 0.5 m³, pressure 1 bar and temperature 27°C at the beginning of the compression stroke. At the end of the compression stroke, the pressure is 10 bar and 210 kJ of heat is added during constant volume heating process. Calculate the pressures, temperatures and volumes at salient points in the cycle. Also find the percentage clearance, efficiency, net work done per cycle and mean effective pressure. If the number of working cycles is 200 per second, find the power developed by the engine.

Assume the cycle is reversible.

Solution : The given data is

$p_1 = 1$ bar, $p_2 = 10$ bar

$v_1 = 0.5$ m³, $T_1 = 27 + 273 = 300$ K

(a) $$\frac{P_2}{P_1} = \left(\frac{v_1}{v_2}\right)^\gamma = R_c^\gamma$$

$$R_c = \left(\frac{P_2}{P_1}\right)^{1/\gamma} = (10)^{1/1.4} \approx \textbf{5.18}$$

$$T_2 = T_1 \left(\frac{v_1}{v_2}\right)^{\gamma-1} = 300 (5.18)^{0.4}$$

$$= \textbf{579.2°C}$$

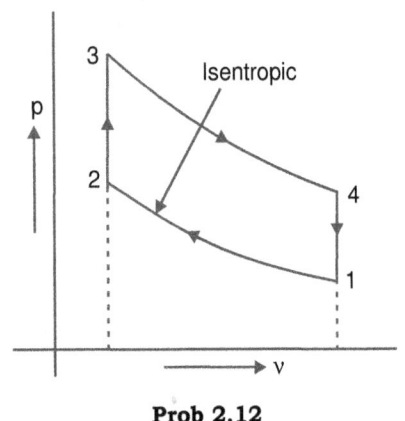

Prob 2.12

Applying the gas law to the points 1 and 2

$$\frac{p_1 v_1}{T_1} = \frac{p_2 v_2}{T_2}$$

$$\therefore \quad v_2 = \frac{T_2}{T_1} \cdot \frac{P_2}{P_1} \cdot v_1 = \frac{579.23}{300} \cdot \frac{1}{10} \times 0.5 = \textbf{0.0965 m}^3$$

(b) The heat supplied during the process 2-3 is given by

$$Q_s = m \cdot C_v (T_3 - T_2)$$

Where, $m = \dfrac{p_1 v_1}{RT_1} = \dfrac{1 \times 10^5 \times 0.5}{287 \times 300} = \mathbf{0.57\ kg}$

$\therefore \quad 210 = 0.57 \times 0.72\ (T_3 - 579.23)$

$\therefore \quad T_3 = 579.2 + \dfrac{210}{0.57 \times 0.72} = \mathbf{1105\ K}$

For the constant volume process 2-3

$$\dfrac{p_3}{T_3} = \dfrac{p_2}{T_2}$$

$\therefore \quad p_3 = \dfrac{T_3}{T_2} \cdot p_2 = \dfrac{1105}{579.2} \times 10 = \mathbf{19\ bar}$

$v_3 = v_2 = \mathbf{0.00965\ m^3}$

(c) For the isentropic process 3-4

$$\dfrac{p_4}{p_3} = \left(\dfrac{v_3}{v_4}\right)^\gamma$$

$\therefore \quad P_4 = P_3\left(\dfrac{1}{R_c}\right)^{\gamma-1} = 19\left(\dfrac{1}{5.18}\right)^{1.4} = \mathbf{19\ bar}$

$$\dfrac{T_4}{T_3} = \left(\dfrac{v_3}{v_4}\right)^{\gamma-1}$$

$\therefore \quad T_4 = T_3\left(\dfrac{1}{R_c}\right)^{0.4} = 11.5\left(\dfrac{1}{5.18}\right)^{0.4} = \mathbf{572.4\ K}$

The percentage clearance is given by

$$= \dfrac{v_c}{v_s} \times 100 = \dfrac{v_2}{v_1 - v_2} \times 100 = \dfrac{0.0965}{0.5 - 0.0965} \times 100 = \mathbf{25\%}$$

It can also be found by

$$= \dfrac{v_c}{v_s} = \dfrac{v_c}{(R_c - 1)v_c} = \dfrac{1}{5.18 - 1} = \mathbf{24.2\%}$$

The heat rejected per cycle is given by

$Q_r = mC_v\ (T_4 - T_1) = 0.58 \times 0.7\ (572.5 - 300)$

$= \mathbf{110.5\ kJ/cycle}$

The air-standard efficiency of the cycle is given by

$\eta_a = \dfrac{Q_s - Q_r}{Q_s} \times 100 = \dfrac{210 - 110.5}{210} \times 100 = \mathbf{47.4\ \%}$

It can also be calculated as

$$\eta_a = 1 - \frac{1}{R_c^{\gamma-1}} = 1 - \frac{1}{(5.18)^{0.4}} = 1 - 0.526 = 0.474 = \textbf{47.2\%}$$

The mean effective pressure is given by

$$P_m = \frac{W}{V_s} = \frac{(210 - 110.5) \times 10^3}{(0.500 - 0.0965) \times 10^4} = \frac{99.5 \times 1000}{0.4035 \times 10^6} = \textbf{2.47 bar}$$

Work done per second

= Work done per cycle × Number of working cycles per second

$$= (210 - 110.5) \times 200 = 99.5 \times \frac{200}{60} = 331.6 \text{ kJ/sec.}$$

Power = **331.6 kW**

Problem 2.13 : An engine works on Otto-cycle. The pressure and temperature of the air at the beginning of the cycle are 1 bar and 40°C. The compression ratio is 6. Assuming the peak pressure is limited to 50 bar, and compression and expansion follow the law $pv^{1.25}$ = constant, find out the following :

1. The thermal efficiency of the cycle.
2. Mean effective pressure of the cycle.
3. If the working cycles per minutes are 300 and cylinder diameter and length of the stroke are 12 cm and 20 cm respectively, find out the power developed by the engine in kW. Working fluid is air.

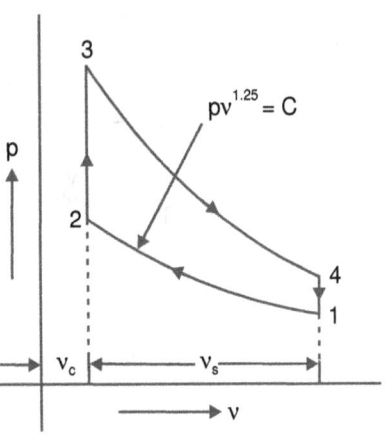

Prob 2.13

Solution : The given data is

p_1 = 1 bar, T_1 = 40 + 273 = 313 K

R_c = 6 and p_3 = 50 bar

$v_1 = v_c + v_s$

$v_s = \frac{\pi}{4} d^2 L = \frac{\pi}{4} \times 144 \times 20 = 2260 \text{ cm}^3$

$v_c = \frac{v_s}{R_c - 1} = \frac{2260}{5} = 452 \text{ cm}^3$

∴ $v_1 = 2260 + 452 = 2712 \text{ cm}^3$

Using the gas law $p_1 v_1 = mRT_1$

∴ $m = \frac{p_1 v_1}{RT_1} \times \frac{1 \times 10^5 \times 2712 \times 10^{-6}}{287 \times 313} = 0.003 \text{ kg/cycle}$

(a) For the polytrophic process 1-2

$$p_2 = p_1\left(\frac{v_1}{v_2}\right)^n = p_1 R_c^n = 1 \times 6^{1.25} = \textbf{9.4 bar}$$

$$T_2 = T_1\left(\frac{v_1}{v_2}\right)^{n-1} = T_1(R_c)^{n-1} = 3131 \times 6^{0.25} = \textbf{490 K}$$

(b) In the constant volume process 2-3

$$\frac{p_3}{T_3} = \frac{p_2}{T_2}$$

$$\therefore \quad T_3 = T_2 \frac{p_3}{p_2} = 490 \times \frac{50}{9.4} = \textbf{2605 K}$$

(c) For the polytropic process 3-4

$$p_4 = \frac{p_3}{R_c^n} = \frac{50}{6^{1.25}} = \textbf{5.32 bar}$$

$$T_4 = \frac{T_3}{R_c^{n-1}} = \frac{2605}{6^{0.25}} = \textbf{1664.45 K}$$

2. Work done per cycle is given by

$$W = \frac{p_3 v_3 - p_4 v_4}{n-1} - \frac{p_2 v_2 - p_1 v_1}{n-1} = p_m v_s \text{ where } p_m \text{ is effective pressure}$$

$$\therefore \quad p_m = \frac{1}{v_s}\left[\frac{p_3 v_3 - p_4 v_4}{n-1} - \frac{p_2 v_2 - p_1 v_1}{n-1}\right]$$

$$v_2 = v_3 = v_c$$
$$v_1 = v_4 = R_c v_c$$
$$v_s = (R_c - 1) v_c$$

$$\therefore \quad p_m = \frac{1}{v_c (R_c - 1)(n-1)} (p_3 v_c - p_4 R_c v_c - p_2 v_c + p_1 R_c v_c)$$

$$= \frac{[(p_3 - p_2) - R_c(p_4 - p_1)]}{(R_c - 1)(n-1)} = \frac{[(50 - 9.4) - 6(5.32 - 1)]}{(6-1)(1.25-1)} = \frac{14.68}{5 \times 0.25}$$

$$= \textbf{11.75 bar}$$

$$v_s = \frac{\pi}{4} d^2 L = \frac{\pi}{4} \times \left(\frac{12}{100}\right)^2 \times \left(\frac{20}{100}\right) = 2.26 \times 10^{-3} \text{ m}^3$$

Work done per cycle

$$= \frac{p_m v_m}{J} = \frac{11.75 \times 10^5 \times 2.26 \times 10^{-3}}{1} = 2655.5 \text{ Nm/cycle}$$

$$= \textbf{2.656 kJ/cycle}$$

Heat supplied per cycle

$$= m C_v (T_3 - T_2) = 0.003 \times 0.72 (2605 - 490) = \textbf{4.43 kJ/cycle.}$$

$$\therefore \quad \eta_a = \frac{W}{Q_s} = \frac{2.656}{4.43} = 0.6 = \mathbf{60\%}$$

Work done per second

$$= 2.656 \times \frac{300}{60} = 13.3 \text{ kJ/sec.}$$

∴ Power of the engine = **13.3 kW**

OR
$$W = \frac{mR}{n-1}[(T_1 - T_n) - (T_2 - T_1')] \text{ J/cycle}$$

Where, m = 0.0003 kg/cycle

P (power) = w × n (number of cycles/sec.)

Where, $n = \frac{300}{60} = 5$ (given)

The students are advised to use this method and check.

Problem 2.14 : Show that the compression ratio for the maximum work to be done per kg of air in an Otto-cycle between upper and lower limits of absolute temperatures T_3 and T_1 is given by

$$R_c = \left(\frac{T_3}{T_2}\right)^{1/2(\gamma-1)}$$

(b) Find the air standard efficiency of the cycle when the cycle develops maximum work with the temperature limit of 300 K and 1200 K and working fluid is air. What will be the percentage changes in the efficiency and work done if helium is used as working fluid instead of air ? The cycle operates between the same temperature limit for maximum work development.

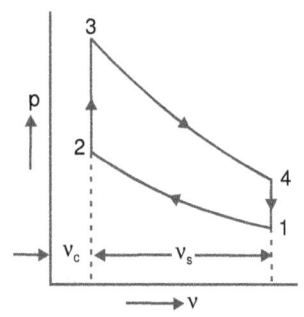

Prob 2.14

Take all ideal conditions.

Solution : The work done per kg of fluid in the cycle is given by

$$W = Q_s - Q_r = C_v(T_3 - T_2) - C_v(T_4 - T_1)$$

But $\quad T_2 = T_1 R_c^{\gamma-1}$ ....(1)

And $\quad T_3 = T_4 R_c^{\gamma-1}$ ....(2)

$$\therefore \quad W = C_v\left[T_3 - T_1 R_c^{\gamma-1} - \frac{T_3}{R_c^{\gamma-1}} + T_1\right] \quad \text{.......(3)}$$

This expression is a function of R_c when T_3 and T_1 are fixed. The value of W will be maximum when

$$\frac{dW}{dR_c} = 0$$

$$\therefore \quad \frac{dW}{dR_c} = T_1(\gamma-1)R_c^{\gamma-1} - T_3(1-\gamma)R_c^{-\gamma} = 0$$

$$T_3 R_c^{-\gamma} = T_1 R_c^{\gamma-2}$$

$$\frac{T_3}{T_1} = R_c^{2(\gamma-1)}$$

$$\therefore \quad R_c = \left(\frac{T_3}{T_1}\right)^{1/2(\gamma-1)}$$

(a) For air $\gamma = 1.4$

$$\therefore \quad R_c = \left(\frac{T_3}{T_1}\right)^{1/2(1.4-1)} = \left(\frac{T_3}{T_1}\right)^{1.25} = \left(\frac{1200}{300}\right)^{1.22} = \mathbf{5.65}$$

The air standard efficiency is given by

$$\eta_a = 1 - \frac{1}{R_c^{\gamma-1}} = 1 - \frac{1}{(5.65)^{0.4}} = 1 - \frac{1}{2} = 0.5 \text{ or } \mathbf{50\%}$$

Work done per kg of air is given by the expression (3),

$$\therefore \quad W = 0.72 \left[1200 - 300 \times 5.65^{0.4} - \frac{1200}{5.65^{0.4}} + 300\right]$$

$$= 0.72 \, (1200 - 600 - 600 + 300) = 0.72 \times 300 = \mathbf{210 \text{ kJ/kg}}$$

(b) If the Helium is used, then the values of

$C_p = 5.25$ kJ/kg-K and $C_v = 3.15$ kJ/kg-K

$$\therefore \quad \gamma = \frac{C_p}{C_v} = \frac{5.25}{3.15} = 1.67$$

The compression ratio for maximum work for the temperature limits T_1 and T_3 is given by

$$R_c = \left(\frac{T_3}{T_1}\right)^{1/2(\gamma-1)} = \left(\frac{1200}{300}\right)^{1/2(1.67-1)} = (0.4)^{0.746} = 2.82$$

The air standard efficiency is given by

$$\eta_a = 1 - \frac{1}{R_c^{\gamma-1}} = 1 - \frac{1}{(2.82)^{0.67}} = 1 - 0.5 = \mathbf{50\%}$$

There is no change in the efficiency.

The work done is given by Equation (3) as

For Helium $\quad W = C_v \left[T_3 - T_1 R_c^{\gamma-1} - \frac{T_3}{R_c^{\gamma-1}} + T_1\right]$

$$= 3.15 \left[1200 - 300 \times (2.82)^{0.67} - \frac{1200}{(2.82)^{0.67}} + 300\right] = 3.15 \times 300$$

$$= \mathbf{945 \text{ kJ/kg}}$$

Percentage increase in the work per kg of fluid

$$= \frac{945 - 210}{210} \times 100 = \mathbf{350\%}$$

Problem 2.15 : An engine working on Otto-cycle in which the salient points are 1, 2, 3 and 4 has upper and lower temperature limits T_3 and T_1. If the maximum work per kg of air is to be done, then show that the intermediate temperature is given by

$$T_2 = T_4 = \sqrt{T_1 T_3}$$

(b) If an engine working on Otto-cycle between temperature limit 1430 K and 300 K, find the maximum theoretical power developed by engine assuming the circulation of air per second 0.4 kg.

Solution : (a) Using the equation (3) of the last problem

$$W = C_v \left[T_3 - T_1 R_c^{\gamma-1} - \frac{T_3}{R_c^{\gamma-1}} + T_1 \right]$$

and differentiating the above equation with respect to R_c and equating to zero.

$$R_c = \left(\frac{T_3}{T_1}\right)^{1/2(\gamma-1)}$$

$$T_2 = T_1 R_c^{\gamma-1} \text{ and } T_4 = \frac{T_3}{R_c^{\gamma-1}}$$

Substituting the value of R_c in the above equations,

$$T_2 = T_1 \left[\left(\frac{T_3}{T_1}\right)^{1/2(\gamma-1)}\right]^{\gamma-1} = T_1 \left(\frac{T_3}{T_1}\right)^{1/2} = \sqrt{T_1 T_3}$$

Similarly, $T_4 = \dfrac{T_3}{\left[\left(\frac{T_3}{T_1}\right)^{1/2(\gamma-1)}\right]^{\gamma-1}} = \dfrac{T_3}{\left(\frac{T_3}{T_1}\right)^{1/2}} = \sqrt{T_3 T_1}$

∴ $T_2 = T_4 = \sqrt{T_1 T_2}$

$W = C_v[(T_3 - T_2) - (T_4 - T_1)]$

$T_2 = T_4 = \sqrt{300 \times 1430} = 655$ K

∴ $W = 0.72[(1430 - 655) - (655 - 300)]$

   = **294 kJ/kg.**

Power developed = 294×0.4 = **117.6 kW**

Diesel Cycle

Problem 2.16 : (a) Determine the air-standard efficiency of the Diesel cycle if the compression ratio is 14 and heat is supplied upto 5% of the stroke. Also find the mean effective pressure.

(b) If the cut-off is increased from 5% to 8% with the original compression ratio, find the percentage change in air standard efficiency. Assume air as working fluid.

(c) If the compression ratio is increased from 14 to 16 with the same cut-off ratio as 5% of stroke, find the change in the air standard efficiency.

Also find the change in the mean effective pressure.

(d) If the compression ratio is increased from 14 to 18 and the cut-off is adjusted to give the same air standard efficiency, find the required change in cut-off.

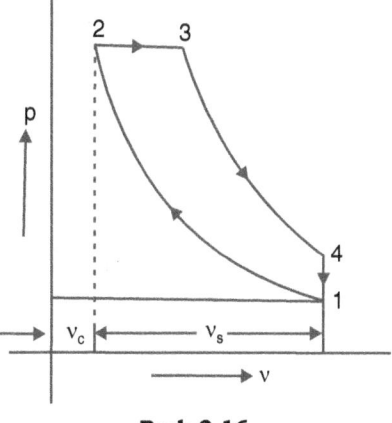

Prob 2.16

Take p_1 (initial pressure) = 1 bar in all the above mentioned cases. Assume all ideal processes.

Solution : (a) $R_c = 14$

$$\rho = 1 + K(R_c - 1) = 1 + \frac{5}{100}(14 - 1) = \mathbf{1.65}$$

$$\eta_a = 1 - \frac{1}{R_c^{\gamma-1}}\left[\frac{\rho^\gamma - 1}{\rho - 1} \cdot \frac{1}{\gamma}\right] = 1 - \frac{1}{14^{0.4}}\left[\frac{(1.65)^{1.4} - 1}{1.65 - 1} \cdot \frac{1}{1.4}\right]$$

$$= 1 - 0.390 = 0.610 = \mathbf{61.0\%}$$

$$p_m = \frac{p_1}{(R_c - 1)(\gamma - 1)} \cdot [R_c^\gamma \cdot \gamma(\rho - 1) - R_c(\rho^\gamma - 1)]$$

$$= \frac{1}{(14-1)(1.4-1)}[14^{1.4} \times 1.4(1.65 - 1) - 14(1.65^{1.4} - 1)]$$

$$= \frac{1}{5.2}[36.4 - 14.2] = \mathbf{4.26 \text{ bar}}$$

(b) If the cut-off is 8% then the value of ρ is given by

$$\rho = 1 + \frac{8}{100}(14 - 1) = \mathbf{2.04}$$

∴ $$\eta_a = 1 - \frac{1}{14^{0.4}}\left[\frac{(2.04)^{1.4} - 1}{2.04 - 1} \times \frac{1}{1.4}\right] = 1 - 0.413 = 0.587 = \mathbf{58.7\%}$$

Decrease in efficiency

$$= 61 - 58.7 = \mathbf{2.3\%}$$

$$p_m = \frac{1}{(14-1)(1.4-1)}[14^{1.4} \times 1.4(2.04 - 1) - 14(2.04)^{1.4} - 1]$$

$$= \frac{1}{5.2}(58.24 - 24.10) = \frac{34.14}{5.2} = \mathbf{6.44 \text{ bar}}$$

Percentage increase in the mean effective pressure = $\frac{6.44 - 4.26}{4.26} \times 100 = \mathbf{53.7\%}$

(c) If the compression ratio is 16 and cut-off ratio is same as previous as 5% of stroke then, $R_c = 16$ and $\rho = 1.65$.

$$\eta_a = 1 - \frac{1}{16^{0.4}}\left[\frac{(1.65)^{1.4}-1}{1.65-1} \times \frac{1}{1.4}\right] = 1 - \frac{1}{3.03} \times \frac{1.12}{1}$$

$$= 1 - 0.37 = 0.63 = \mathbf{63\%}$$

Increase in efficiency = 63 − 61 = **2%**

$$P_m = \frac{1}{(16-1)(1.4-1)}[16^{1.4} \times 1.4(1.65-1) - 16(1.65^{1.4}-1)]$$

$$= \frac{1}{6}(44.10 - 16.20) = \mathbf{4.65 \ bar}$$

Percentage increase in the mean effective pressure $= \frac{4.65 - 4.26}{4.26} \times 100 = \mathbf{9.15\%}$

(d) As the efficiency maintained is 61% with the compression ratio 18, find the value of cut-off ratio.

$$\therefore \quad 0.61 = 1 - \frac{1}{18^{0.4}}\left[\frac{\rho^{1.4}-1}{\rho-1} \times \frac{1}{1.4}\right]$$

$$\therefore \quad \frac{\rho^{1.4}-1}{\rho-1} = 1.73$$

By trial and error method $\rho = 1.95$.

But $\quad \rho = 1 + K(R_c - 1)$

$\therefore \quad 1.95 = 1 + K(18 - 1)$

$\therefore \quad K = \frac{0.95}{17} \times 100 = \mathbf{5.59\%}$

∴ Cut-off occurs at 5.59% of the stroke.

Problem 2.17 : If the mean effective pressure of a Diesel cycle is 7.5 bar and the compression ratio is 12.5, find the percentage cut-off of the cycle if the initial pressure is 1 bar.

Solution : The mean effective pressure is given by an expression.

$$P_m = \frac{P_1}{(R_c - 1)(\gamma - 1)}[R_c^\gamma \cdot \gamma(\rho - 1) - R_c(\rho^\gamma - 1)]$$

Substituting the given values in the above equation, we get,

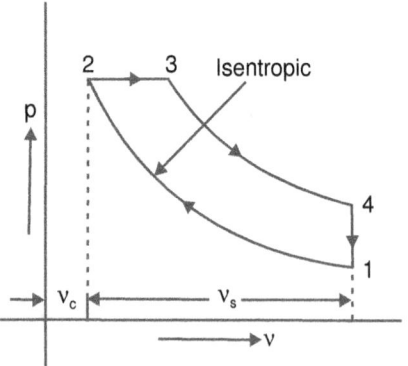

Prob 2.17

$$7.5 = \frac{1}{(1.25-1)(1.4-1)} \times [12.5^{1.4} \times 1.4(\rho-1) - 12.5(\rho^{1.4}-1)]$$

On simplification, it becomes

$1.4\rho - 0.36\,\rho^{1.4} - 2.05 = 0$.

Solving by trial and error method,

$\therefore \quad \rho = 2.25$

$$\rho = 1 + K(R_c - 1)$$

$$\therefore \quad K = \frac{(2.25 - 1)}{(12.5 - 1)} \times 100 = \mathbf{10.88\%}.$$

cut-off occurs at 10.88% of the stroke.

Problem 2.18 : An oil engine with 20 cm cylinder diameter and 30 cm stroke works on theoretical Diesel cycle. The initial pressure and temperature of the air used are 1 bar and 30°C. The cut-off is 10% of the stroke. Find the following :

1. Pressure and temperatures at all salient points.
2. Theoretical air standard efficiency.
3. Mean effective pressure.
4. The power developed by the engine if the working cycles per minute are 400.

Assume the compression ratio is 16 and working fluid is air.

Take all ideal conditions.

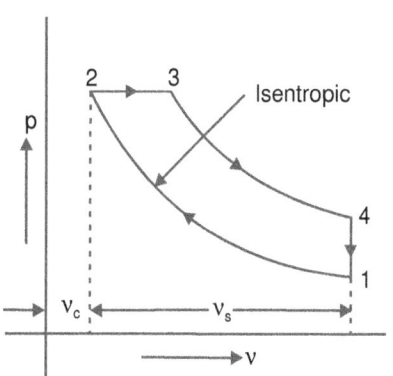

Prob 2.18

Solution : The given data is

$p_1 = 1$ bar, $T_1 = 30 + 273 = 303$ K and $R_c = 16$

$$v_s = \frac{\pi}{4} d^2 L = \frac{\pi}{4} \times 400 \times 30 \times 10^{-6} = 9.42 \times 10^{-3} \text{ m}^3$$

$$v_1 = v_s + v_c = v_s + \frac{v_s}{R_c - 1} = \frac{R_c}{R_c - 1} \times v_s = \frac{16}{15} \times 9.42 \times 10^{-3} = 10 \times 10^{-3} \text{ m}^3$$

The mass of this air in the cylinder can be calculated by using the gas equation

$$p_1 v_1 = mRT_1$$

$$\therefore \quad m = \frac{p_1 v_1}{RT_1} = \frac{1 \times 10^5 \times 10 \times 10^{-3}}{287 \times 303} = \mathbf{0.0115 \text{ kg/cycle}}$$

1. For the isentropic process 1 to 2.

(a) $\quad p_2 = p_1 R_c^{\gamma} = 1 \times 16^{1.4} = 48.5$ bar

$\quad T_2 = T_1 R_c^{\gamma-1} = 303 \times 16^{0.4} = 920$ K

$$V_2 = V_c = \frac{V_s}{R_c - 1} = \frac{9.42 \times 10^{-3}}{15} = \mathbf{0.628 \times 10^{-3} \, m^3}$$

(b) $\quad p_2 = p_3 = \mathbf{48.5 \, bar} \quad v_3 = \rho v_2$

where, ρ is given by $\rho = 1 + K(R_c - 1) = 1 + \frac{10}{100}(16 - 1) = \mathbf{2.5}$

$\therefore \quad v_3 = 2.5 \times 0.628 \times 10^{-3} = \mathbf{1.57 \times 10^{-3} \, m^{-3}}$

For the constant pressure process 2-3

$$\frac{V_3}{T_3} = \frac{V_2}{T_2}$$

$\therefore \quad T_3 = T_2 \frac{V_3}{V_2} = T_2 \rho = 920 \times 2.5 = \mathbf{2300 \, K}$

(c) $\quad R_e = \frac{R_c}{\rho} = \frac{16}{2.5} = 6.4$

For the isentropic process 3-4

$$p_4 = \frac{p_3}{R_e^\gamma} = \frac{48.5}{6.4^{1.4}} = \frac{48.5}{13.5} = \mathbf{3.6 \, bar}$$

$$T_4 = \frac{T_1}{R_e^{\gamma-1}} = \frac{2300}{6.4^{0.4}} = \frac{2300}{2.1} = \mathbf{1095 \, K}$$

$v_4 = v_1 = \mathbf{10 \times 10^{-3} \, m^{-3}}$

3. The air standard efficiency is given by

$$\eta_a = 1 - \frac{Q_r}{Q_s} = 1 - \frac{C_v (T_2 - T_1)}{C_p (T_3 - T_2)} = 1 - \frac{1095 - 303}{1.4 \, (2300 - 920)}$$

$$= 1 - 0.41 = 0.59 = \mathbf{59\%}.$$

The air standard efficiency can also be calculated by using the formula

$$\eta_a = 1 - \frac{1}{R_c^{\gamma-1}} \left[\frac{\rho^\gamma - 1}{\rho - 1} \times \frac{1}{\gamma}\right] = 1 - \frac{1}{16^{0.4}} \left[\frac{2.5^{1.4} - 1}{25 - 1} \times \frac{1}{1.4}\right] = 0.59 = \mathbf{59\%}$$

4. The mean effective pressure of the cycle is given by

$$p_m = \frac{1}{v_s} \left[p_2(v_3 - v_2) + \frac{p_3 v_3 - p_4 v_4}{\gamma - 1} - \frac{p_2 v_2 - p_1 v_1}{\gamma - 1}\right]$$

$v_1 = v_4 = R_c v_c, \, v_2 = v_c$

$v_3 = \rho v_c, \, v_s = (R_c - 1) v_c.$

Substituting these values in the above equation

$$P_m = \frac{1}{(R_c - 1)v_c}\left[P_2(\rho v_c - v_c) + \frac{P_3 \rho v_c - P_4 R_c v_c}{\gamma - 1} - \frac{P_2 v_2 - P_1 R_c v_c}{\gamma - 1}\right]$$

$$= \frac{1}{R_c - 1}\left[P_2(\rho - 1) + \frac{P_3 \rho - P_4 R_c}{\gamma - 1} - \frac{P_2 - P_1 R_c}{\gamma - 1}\right]$$

$$= \frac{1}{15}\left[48.5 \times (2.5 - 1) + \frac{48.5 \times 2.5 - 3.6 \times 16}{1.4 - 1} - \frac{48.5 - 1 \times 16}{1.4 - 1}\right]$$

$$= \frac{1}{15}(72.75 + 159.125 - 81.25) = \textbf{10 bar}$$

It can also be calculated by using the formula,

$$P_m = \frac{P_1}{(R_c - 1)(\gamma - 1)} = [R_e^\gamma \times \gamma(\rho - 1) - R_c(\rho^\gamma - 1)]$$

$$= \frac{1}{15 \times 0.4} = [16^{1.4} \times 1.4 (2.5 - 1) - 16(2.5^{1.4} - 1)]$$

$$= \frac{1}{6}(102 - 41.8) = \textbf{10 bar}$$

The work done per cycle can be calculated as

$$W = P_m v_s = \frac{10 \times 10^5 \times 9.42 \times 10^{-3}}{1000} = 9.42 \text{ kJ/cycle}$$

∴ Power = $\frac{\text{Work done}}{\text{Cycle}} \times \frac{\text{No. of cycles}}{\text{Seconds}}$ = $9.42 \times \frac{400}{60}$ = **62.8 kW**

Problem 2.19 : An oil engine works on Diesel cycle. The compression ratio is 20 and heat addition at constant pressure takes place upto 10% of the stroke. The initial pressure and temperature of air are 1 bar and 67°C.

Assume the compression follows the law $pv^{1.32} = C$ and the expansion follows the law $pv^{1.30} = C$.

Find the following :

(a) The temperatures and pressures at all salient points.

(b) The mean effective pressure of the cycle.

(c) The efficiency and power developed by the engine if the working cycles per minute are 300.

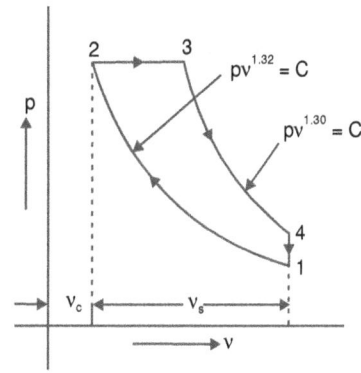

Prob 2.19

Assume bore and stroke of the engine are 16 cm and 20 cm.

Solution : The given data is

(a) $p_1 = 1$ bar, $T_1 = 67 + 273 = 340$ K

$R_c = 20$, $n_1 = 1.32$ and $n_2 = 1.3$

(2) For the polytropic process 1-2

$$p_2 = p_1 R_c^{n_1} = 1 \times 20^{1.32} = 52 \text{ bar}$$

$$T_2 = T_1 R_c^{n_1-1} = 340 \times 20^{0.32} = 884 \text{ K}$$

and $\rho = 1 + K(R_c - 1) = 1 + \dfrac{10}{100} \times 19 = \mathbf{2.9}$

(3) For the constant pressure process 2-3

$$T_3 = T_2 \times \dfrac{v_3}{v_2} = T_2 \rho = 8.84 \times 2.9 = \mathbf{2560 \text{ K}}$$

$$p_3 = p_2 = \mathbf{52 \text{ bar}}$$

$$R_e = \dfrac{R_c}{\rho} = \dfrac{20}{2.9} = \mathbf{6.9}$$

(4) For the polytropic process 3-4

$$p_4 = \dfrac{p_3}{R_e^{n_2}} = \dfrac{52}{(6.9)^{1.3}} = \mathbf{4.23 \text{ bar}}$$

$$T_4 = \dfrac{T_3}{R_e^{n_2-1}} = \dfrac{2560}{6.9^{0.3}} = \dfrac{2560}{1.785} = \mathbf{1435 \text{ K}}$$

(b) The mean effective pressure of the cycle can be calculated as follows :

$$p_m = \dfrac{\text{Work done per cycle}}{\text{Stroke voluem}}$$

∴ $$p_m = \dfrac{1}{v_s}\left[p_2(v_3 - v_2) + \dfrac{p_3 v_3 - p_4 v_4}{n_2 - 1} - \dfrac{p_2 v_2 - p_1 v_1}{n_2 - 1}\right]$$

$v_1 = v_4 = R_c \times v_c$, $v_2 = v_c$, $v_3 = \rho v_c$ and $v_s = (R_c - 1)v_c$

Substituting these values in the above equation

$$p_m = \dfrac{1}{(R_c - 1)v_c}\left[p_2(\rho v_c - v_c) + \dfrac{p_3 \rho v_c - p_4 R_c \cdot v_c}{n_2 - 1} - \dfrac{p_2 v_2 - p_1 R_c v_c}{n_1 - 1}\right]$$

$$= \dfrac{1}{(R_c - 1)}\left[p_2(\rho - 1) + \dfrac{p_3 \rho - p_4 R_c}{n_2 - 1} - \dfrac{p_2 - p_1 R_c}{n_1 - 1}\right]$$

$p_1 = 1$ bar, $p_2 = 52$ bar, $p_3 = 52$ bar, $p_4 = 4.23$ bar

$R_c = 20$, $\rho = 2.9$, $n_2 = 1.3$, $n_1 = 1.32$.

Substituting these values in the equation

$$p_m = \frac{1}{19}\left[52(2.9-1) + \frac{52 \times 2.9 - 4.23 \times 20}{(1.3-1)} - \frac{52 - 1 \times 20}{1.32 - 1}\right]$$

$$= \frac{1}{19}(98.8 + 22.07 - 100) = \mathbf{11.55\ bar}$$

(c) The work done per kg of air is given by

$$W = \left[p_2(v_3 - v_2) + \frac{p_3 v_3 - p_4 v_4}{n_2 - 1} - \frac{p_2 v_2 - p_1 v_1}{n_1 - 1}\right]\ \text{Joules}$$

Considering the mass of air one kg

$$W = \left[R(T_3 - T_2) + \frac{R}{n_2 - 1}(T_3 - T_4) - \frac{R}{n_1 - 1}(T_2 - T_1)\right]$$

$$= 0.287\left[(2560 - 884) + \left(\frac{2560 - 1435}{1.3 - 1}\right) - \left(\frac{884 - 340}{1.32 - 1}\right)\right]$$

$$= 0.287\,[1676 + 3750 - 1700] - 1069\ \text{kJ/kg.}$$

∴ Q_s (heat supplied/kg of air) $= C_p(T_3 - T_2)$

$$= 1.0\,(2560 - 884) = 1676\ \text{kJ/kg.}$$

$$\eta = \frac{W}{Q_s} = \frac{1069}{1676} = 0.638 = \mathbf{63.8\%}$$

$$v_1 = v_c + v_s = \frac{v_s}{R_c - 1} + v_s = v_s\left(\frac{1}{R_c - 1} + 1\right) = v_s \cdot \left(\frac{R_c}{R_c - 1}\right)$$

$$v_s = \frac{\pi}{4}d^2 L = \frac{\pi}{4} \times \left(\frac{16}{100}\right)^2 \times \frac{20}{100} = 4021 \times 10^{-6}\ m^3 = 4 \times 10^{-3}\ m^3$$

∴ $$v_1 = 4 \times 10^{-3} \times \frac{20}{19} = 4.21 \times 10^{-3}\ m^3$$

The man of v_1 is given by

$$m = \frac{p_1 v_1}{RT_1} = \frac{1 \times 10^{+5} \times 4.21 \times 10^{-3}}{287 \times 340} = 0.0043\ \text{kg.}$$

∴ $P = $ (Power developed/cycle) $\times$ (No. of cycles/sec.)

$$= (1069 \times 0.0043) \times \frac{300}{60} \approx \mathbf{23\ kw}$$

EXERCISES

1. Draw a neat diagram of an I.C. engine and explain the functions of different parts.
2. How the internal combustion engines are classified ?
3. What do you understand by four-stroke cycle and two-stroke cycle engine ?
4. Explain the working of 4-stroke diesel engine giving neat sketches. How it differs from 4-stroke petrol engine ?
5. Explain the working of 2-stroke petrol engine with neat sketches. In what respect it differs from 2-stroke diesel engine ?
6. What are the merits and demerits of four-stroke engines over two-stroke engines ?
7. Discuss the merits and demerits of diesel engine with petrol engine.
8. Why two-stroke engines are preferred for two wheelers ?
9. Why two-stroke cycle engine is more suitable for diesel engine compared with petrol engine ?
10. Give the reasons for the following :
    (i) I.C. engines need cranking.
    (ii) I.C. engines need water cooling.
    (iii) Some method of ignition is required in petrol engine but diesel engines do not need any system.
    (iv) The cam shaft speed is half of the crank-shaft speed of 4-stroke cycle engine.
11. Prove that the ideal thermal efficiency of an engine working on Otto cycle is given by $\eta_{th} = 1 - \dfrac{1}{(R_c)^{\gamma-1}}$ where, R_c is compression ratio.
12. Prove that the ideal thermal efficiency of an engine working on diesel cycle is given by $\eta_{th} = 1 - \dfrac{1}{(R_c)^{\gamma-1}} \left[\dfrac{(\rho^\gamma - 1)}{\gamma(\rho - 1)} \right]$
13. In what respect diesel cycle differs from Otto cycle? Which cycle gives higher efficiency for the same compression ratio ?

Cycles

Second Law of Thermodynamics

14. Discuss whether the following processes are reversible or irreversible. Give reasons for the conclusion.

(a) Water is evaporated at constant temperature by (i) adding heat and (ii) by adding work.

(b) Air is expanded slowly against a frictionless piston in an insulated cylinder.

(c) Two gases mix in an insulated vessel (i) at same temperature (ii) at different temperatures.

(d) Water under a piston of constant weight is stirred unit and 20% of it evaporates.

(e) Gas expands through a small orifice from a high pressure chamber to low pressure chamber.

(f) A stream of water at 20°C is mixed with a stream of water at 80°C.

What is the check to decide whether a given process is reversible or irreversible ?

15. Give the following statements of the Second Law of Thermodynamics : (a) Kelvin Plank statement and (b) Clausius statement. Is the second law independent of the first law ? If so, prove it.

16. Define heat engine, refrigerator and heat pump. Explain why the performance of heat engine is measured in terms of efficiency but that of refrigerators and heat pumps in terms of C.O.P. Why does the expression for C.O.P. differ for refrigerator and heat pump ?

17. A reversible heat engine, a reversible heat pump and a reversible refrigerator are operating between a high temperature reservoir at T_1 and a low temperature reservoir at T_2, prove that

$$\eta_{engine} = \frac{1}{(C.O.P)_{heat\ pump}}$$

and $C.O.P._{heat\ pump} = 1 + C.O.P._{refrigerator}$.

18. The air in air-conditioned room is maintained at 24°C when the outside temperature was – 10°C. During one hour, 20 MJ of heat is lost from the room through the walls and roof. Determine the net change of entropy of the universe.

19. A vessel contains 10 kg water at 30°C. A mass of ice of 1 kg at –4°C is dropped into the water. Assuming the system is an isolated one, determine the temperature and net change in entropy when the system comes to equilibrium.

Take C_p (ice) = 2.1 kJ/kg-K;

h_{fl} (latent heat of ice) = 334.5 kJ/kg-K; and

  C_p (water) = 4.18 kJ/kg-K.

20. An inventor claims to have developed an engine working between 400 K and 200 K taking 100 kJ of energy and rejecting 40 kJ of energy and delivering 15 kWh of work.

Verify whether his claim is correct or not.

21. An inventor claims to have developed an engine that takes 100 MJ of heat at 400 K and rejects 40 MJ at 150 K and delivers 15 kWh of work. Discuss the possibility of this engine on the market (1 kWh = 3600 J/s).

22. An inventor claims that by passing 3 kg of air at 300 K and 10 bar, through an instrument, it is possible to get 1 kg of air at 100°C and 2 kg of air at − 40°C at pressure of 1 bar. Verify his claim using the second law of thermodynamics.

23. An inventor claims that the heat engine developed by him has the following specifications :

    Power developed 76 kW, Fuel burned = 4 kg/hr, C.V. of fuel = 50 KJ/kg, and Working temperature limit = 700 K and 300 K.

    Check whether his claim is correct or not.

24. A household refrigerator absorbs heat at 5°C and rejects heat at 40°C. Its compressor is driven by 2 kW motor and 25 MJ heat are absorbed per hour at the low temperature. Find the amount of heat rejected per hour.

25. A Carnot engine receives 1000 kJ of heat at 300°C and rejects heat at temperature of 30°C. (a) Determine the heat rejected and work output of the engine and (b) show that the entropy increase is zero.

26. Find the temperature that will be maintained in a refrigerator when its power consumption is 100 watts and heat leaking into the refrigerator is 2200 kJ/hr. The surrounding temperature is 40°C. Assume that the refrigerator works on a reversible cycle.

27. A house in winter is heated by a reversible heat pump. The heat transfer from the house is 80 MJ/hr. The house is to be maintained at 25°C while outside air is at 5°C. Determine the power required to drive the pump.

28. An ice making plant produces ice at atmospheric pressure and at 0°C from water at 0°C. The mean temperature of cooling water circulated through the condenser of the refrigerating machine is 18°C. Evaluate minimum electric input in kWh required to produce one tonne of ice (enthalpy of fusion of ice = 354.5 kJ/kg).

29. An office block is heated by means of a heat pump. The temperature maintained in the block is 20°C when the surrounding temperature is − 4°C. The heat transfer rate of the pump is 108 MJ/hr and the power required to run the pump is 10 kW. (a) Evaluate the heat transfer rate to the building and C.O.P. of the pump. (b) Also evaluate the maximum possible C.O.P. and minimum power requirement to run the heat pump to satisfy the heating requirements.

30. A warming machine operating on the Cranot reversed cycle abstracts heat from a cold reservoir at 280 K and rejects heat to hot reservoir at 45°C. Find (a) the heat rejected for each kWh of work, and (b) C.O.P.

31. A Carnot cycle refrigerator operates in a room in which the temperature is 25°C. It is required to transfer 100 kW form the cold space being held at – 30°. What is the power of the motor required to run the refrigerator ?

32. It is proposed to heat a house using a heat pump. The heat transfer from the house is 15 kW. The house is to be maintained at 22°C while the outside air is at a temperature of – 10°C. What is the minimum power required to drive the heat pump ?

33. A heat pump is used to heat a house in the winter and then reversed to cool the house in the summer. The interior temperature is to be maintained at 20°C. Heat transfer through the walls and roof is estimated to be 2400 kJ/hr per degree temperature difference between the inside and outside. (a) If the outside temperature in the winter is 0°C, what is the minimum power required to drive the heat pump ? (b) If the power input is same as that in part (a), what is the maximum outside temperature for which the inside can be maintained at 20°C ?

34. An engine working on Otto cycle has a compression ratio 5. If its compression ratio is increased from 5 to 6, determine the percentage increase in the air standard efficiency.

35. A petrol engine 10 cm in diameter and 15 cm stroke works on Otto-cycle. The clearance volume is 250 cm3. Determine the air standard efficiency of the cycle.

36. The pressure and temperature of the air at the beginning of compression stroke in an engine working on Otto cycle are 1 bar and 100°C. The temperature at the end of compression is 473°C and the maximum pressure of the cycle is limited to 23 bar. Determine the air standard efficiency of the cycle and work done per kg of air.

37. The pressure at the end of compression is 15 times its initial pressure. The initial temperature of air is 40°C and maximum temperature of the cycle is limited to 1677°C. Determine the air standard efficiency of the cycle if the heat added is at constant volume. Also calculate the work done per kg of air.

38. The pressure and temperature of air in an engine cylinder working on Otto cycle at the beginning of compression are I bar and 50°C. The compression ratio is 5. The heat supplied per kg of air is 500 kJ/kg. Determine : (a) air standard efficiency of the cycle, (b) maximum temperature, and (c) work done per kg of air.

39. The compression ratio of a Diesel engine is 14 and cut-off takes place at 6% of the stroke. Determine the air standard efficiency of the cycle.

40. Determine the percentage loss in the ideal efficiency of a Diesel engine with compression ratio 15 when the cut-off is increased from 5% to 10% of the stroke.

41. The diameter and stroke of an engine cylinder working on Diesel cycle are 170 mm and 250 mm respectively. The clearance is 450 cm3 and cut-off is at 6% of stroke. Determine the air standard efficiency of the cycle.

42. The pressure and temperature of air at the beginning of compression of Diesel cycle are 1.1 bar and 15°C. The pressure of the air at the end of compression is 35 bar. The expansion ratio is 5. Determine the air standard efficiency of the cycle and the maximum temperature in the cycle.

43. The temperatures at the beginning and end of compression in Diesel cycle are 32°C and 615° respectively. The maximum temperature of the cycle is limited tc 1780°C. Determine the air standard efficiency of the cycle and cut-off as percentage of stroke.

44. An engine works on diesel cycle with compression ratio of 18 and cut-off is al 10% of the stroke. The pressure and temperature at the beginning of the compression are 1 bar and 27°C. Determine the air standard efficiency and mean effective pressure of the cycle.

3

INTRODUCTION TO REFRIGERATION AND AIR CONDITIONING

3.1 Introduction to Refrigeration
3.2 Unit of Refrigeration and Performance Factor
3.3 Vapour Compression Refrigeration Systems
3.4 Vapour Absorption Refrigeration System
3.5 Solar Refrigeration System
3.6 Domestic Refrigerator
3.7 Required Properties of Ideal Refrigerant
3.8 Some Important Refrigerants
3.9 Phychrometry and Air Conditioning
3.10 Concept of Comfort
3.11 Air Conditioning Systems
3.12 Window Air-Conditioner
   Exercises

3.1 INTRODUCTION TO REFRIGERATION

The art of producing and maintaining the temperature in an enclosed space below surrounding temperature is known as refrigeration. In order to maintain the low temperature in the refrigerated space, it is necessary to remove heat continuously equal to the amount of heat leaking into the system and reject the same to the surrounding atmosphere at higher temperature.

A machine which produces cold is known as refrigerator and the process is known as refrigeration. Refrigeration has wide applications in chemical industries, food industries, air-conditioning plants and many other industrial processes.

3.2 UNIT OF REFRIGERATION AND PERFOMANCE FACTOR

The capacity of engine is given in kW, similarly the capacity of refrigeration system is given in tonnes of refrigeration. A tonne of refrigeration is the amount of heat to be removed in order to form one tonne of ice at 0°C in 24 hours when the temperature of water supplied is 0°C. It is commonly taken as 3.5 kJ/sec. or 3.5 kW.

The performance of a refrigeration machine is measured by a factor known as coefficient of performance (C.O.P.). It is defined as the ratio of heat extracted from the refrigerator to the work supplied and it is given by

$$\text{C.O.P.} = \frac{Q}{W}$$

The Q is the quantity of heat removed by the refrigeration system and W is the work supplied to the system during the same time.

Refrigerator : A refrigerator is used to remove the heat continuously from the space and maintain the temperature below surrounding temperature and reject the heat extracted to the surrounding atmosphere.

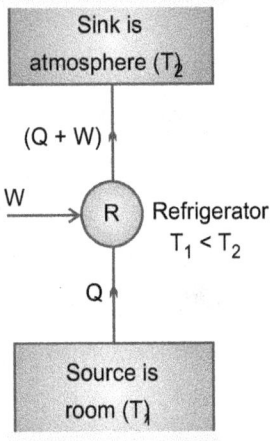

Fig. 3.1 : Carnot Refrigerator

The C.O.P. of refrigeration system is given by

$$\text{C.O.P.} = \frac{Q}{W} \text{ (refrigeration system)}$$

If the refrigerator works on Carnot cycle as shown in Fig. 3.2 on p-v and T-s diagrams, the C.O.P. of the cycle is given by

$$\text{C.O.P.} = \frac{\text{Heat absorbed}}{\text{Work done}}$$

$$= \frac{\text{Heat absorbed}}{\text{Heat rejected} - \text{Heat absorbed}} = \frac{T_1 (s_2 - s_1)}{T_2 (s_2 - s_1) - T_1 (s_2 - s_1)}$$

$$= \frac{T_1}{T_2 - T_1}$$

where, $T_2 > T_1$.

where, T_1 is the temperature of refrigeration system and T_2 is the temperature of the surrounding.

The working cycle of Carnot Refrigerator is shown on p-v and T-s diagram as shown in Fig. 3.2

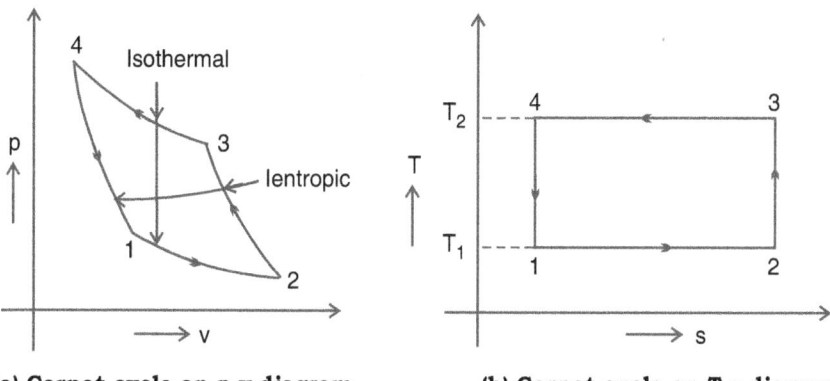

(a) Carnot-cycle on p-v diagram   (b) Carnot cycle on T-s diagram

Fig. 3.2

3.3 VAPOUR COMPRESSION REFRIGERATION SYSTEM

In vapour compression refrigeration system, the refrigerant used alternately, undergoes a change of phase from vapour to liquid and liquid to vapour during the cycle. The latent heat of vaporisation is used for absorbing the heat at low temperature from the refrigerated space and the same is rejected during the condensation at high pressure and high temperature also.

The arrangement of the components of this refrigeration system is shown in Fig. 3.3. The liquid refrigerant coming out from a condenser at high pressure is passed through a throttle valve and the pressure of the refrigerant is reduced. The temperature

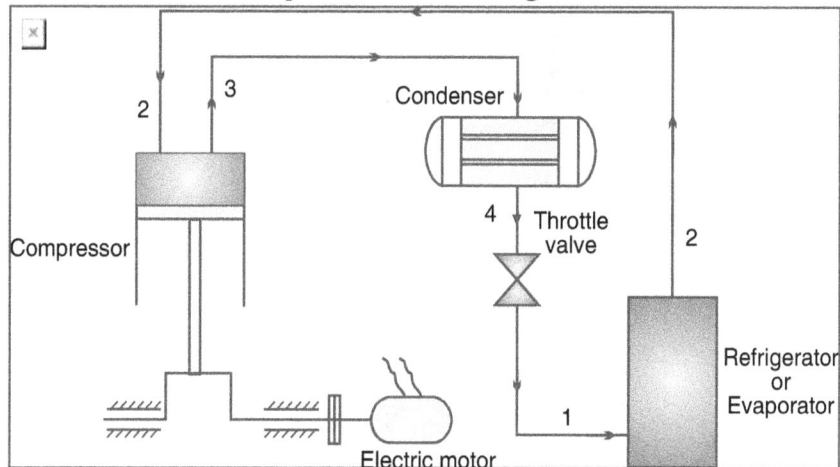

Fig. 3.3

of the refrigerant falls as its pressure is reduced. A mixture of vapour and liquid coming out of the throttle at low temperature enters the evaporator and absorbs the heat from the evaporator in the form of latent heat and is converted into vapour. Then, it is further passed to compressor where its pressure is increased by the compression and consequently temperature also. The high pressure, high temperature vapour coming out of compressor enters the condenser where the latent of refrigerant is removed by using water or air and converted into liquid. The high pressure liquid refrigerant is again passed through the throttle valve and cycle is repeated.

The process 1-2 is the absorption of heat in the evaporator.

The process 2-3 is the isentropic compression in compressor.

The process 3-4 is the desuperheating and liquifying the refrigerant in the condenser. The process 4-1 is the throttling process.

The major advantages of this system are smaller size of the machine and high C.O.P. (4 to 5) as the heat transfer in the evaporator and condenser takes place in the form of latent heat instead of sensible heat.

3.4 VAPOUR ABSOSSRPTION REFRIGERATION SYSTEM

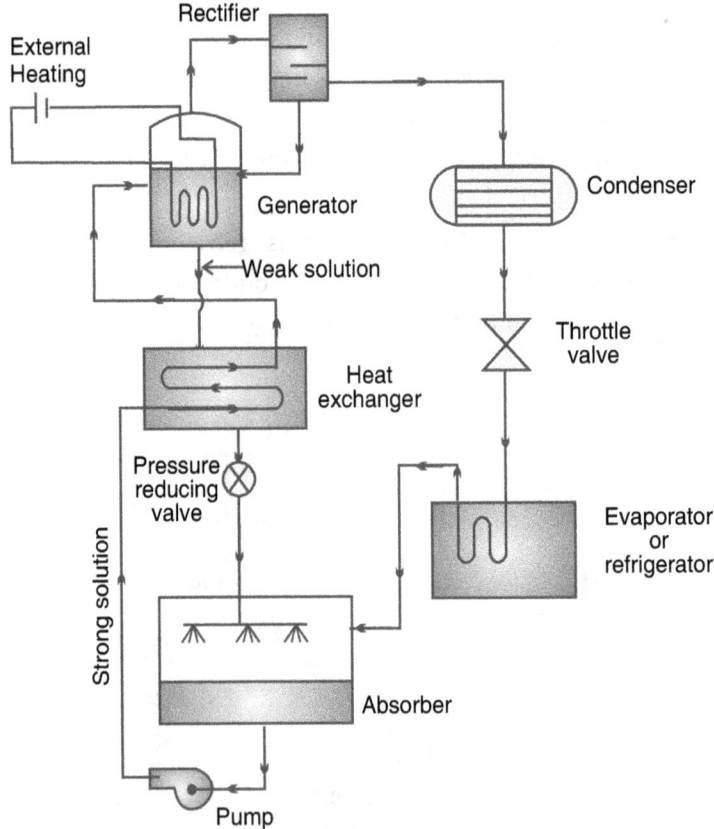

Fig. 3.4

The arrangement of the components of the system is shown in Fig. 3.4. In this system, ammonia vapour is produced in the generator at high pressure (6 bar) by heating strong solution of ammonia in water with the help of external heat source. The water particles and water vapour carried by ammonia vapour are removed in the rectifier and dehydrated ammonia vapour enters into the condenser. The high pressure NH_3 vapour is condensed in the condenser using water as cooling medium. The high pressure NH_3 liquid coming out of condenser is throttled passing through a throttle valve. The low temperature liquid-vapour refrigerant mixture enters into the refrigerator and absorbs heat in the form of latent heat and comes out in the form of vapour. The vapour coming out of the evaporator enters into the absorber where it is absorbed by weak ammonia solution sprayed as shown in the figure. As weak ammonia solution (known as aqua ammonia) absorbs gas ammonia coming from the evaporator becomes strong aqua solution. The strong aqua solution is pumped back to the generator with the help of pump through a heat exchanger. The weak hot ammonia solution from the generator is passed through a heat exchanger where it gives its sensible heat to the incoming strong ammonia solution. This transfer of heat increases the overall performance of the system. The weak ammonia solution is passed through a pressure reduction valve before spraying into the absorber. The absorbing capacity of weak ammonia solution in the absorber is further increased by cooling the absorber surface with the help of cooling water (not shown in figure).

The advantages of this system over vapour compression system are :

1. It is quiet in operation as compressor is removed from the system.
2. The maintenance is low.
3. Any low grade heat source can be used for its operation.
4. It can be built well above 1000 tonnes capacity.
5. It can be operated at variable evaporating temperature without affecting its capacity.

3.5 SOLAR REFRIGERATION SYSTEM

This system is used only for **Vapour-absorption Refrigeration System.** The principle of its operation is same as discussed earlier, except the source of heat used is solar energy.

In this system, the water is heated in solar Flat-plate collector upto 80 to 90°C and the heat collected by the water is used in the generator to generate the refrigerant vapour at the desired pressure (mostly 2 to 5 bar).

The common configuration of the system used is shown in Fig. (3.5). In this system, ammonia vapour is generated from rich aqua-ammonia supplying the heat from solar heated water. The water coming out from the generator is recirculated through solar heater with the help of pump.

The high pressure NH_3 vapour coming out of generator is passed through rectifier as shown in Fig. (3.5) where water particles carried by NH₃ vapour are removed. Then the high pressure, dry vapour of ammona is condensed in the condenser. Then high pressure liquid - NH₃ is passed through the throttle valve and its pressure (temperature also) is reduced. This low temperature mixture of NH₃ (with dryness fraction of 0.8 to 0.9) is passed through the refrigerator for absorbing the heat and to maintain required low temperature. The ammonia vapour carring out of refrigerator enters into the absorbing chamber, where weak aqua-ammona from the generator is passed through the pressure reducing value and sprayed in the absorbing chamber as shown in Fig. (3.5). The weak aqua-ammonia absorbs the ammonia vapour coming in from the refrigerator and becomes strong aqua-ammonia. This aqua ammonia is supplied back to the generator with the help of pump as shown in the Fig. (3.5) and cycle is completed.

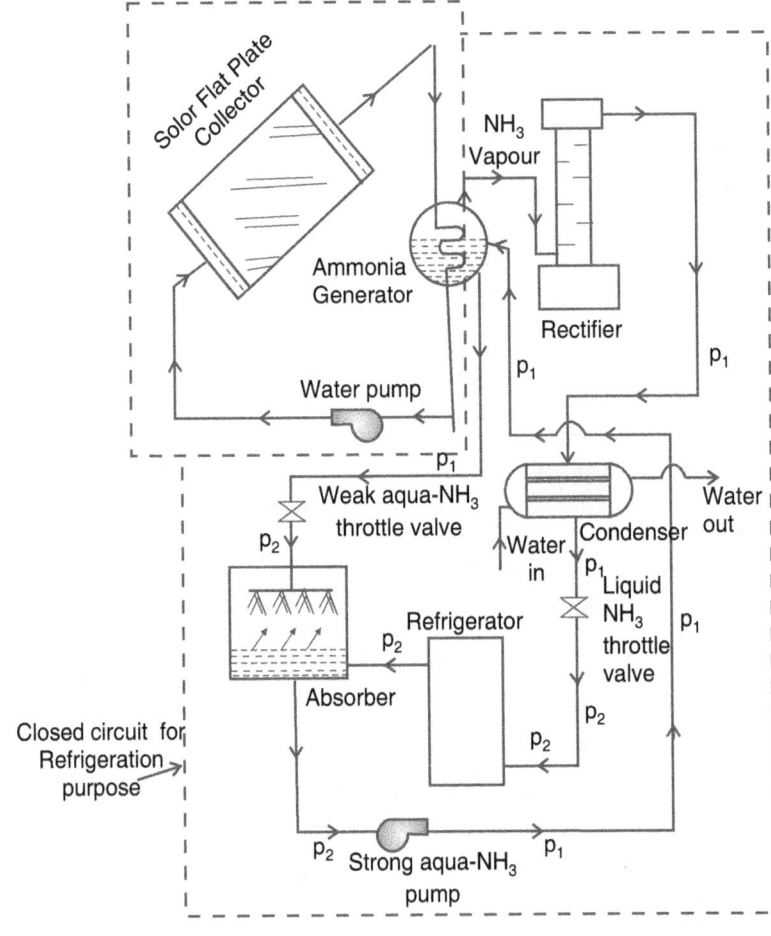

Fig. 3.5 : Solar Flat Plate Collector

3.6 DOMESTIC REFRIGERATOR

The domestic refrigerator works on a compression refrigeration cycle and also uses compressor, condenser, capillary and evaporator which are the basic components of the system. But the arrangement of these components is different from the refrigeration system used for other purposes. The compressor is directly coupled to an electric motor and both are sealed in a steel box therefore this is known as sealed unit. This arrangement helps to reduce the noise of the motor, prevents the leak of the refrigerant and motor is cooled by the refrigerant vapour as it is exposed to the same. Such systems are very popular as they are very rigid and compact. The condenser is generally made of a grid of copper tubes provided with fins, mounted behind the unit and cooled by natural air convection. Capillary is used as a throttling device for reducing the pressure and temperature of the refrigerant. The refrigerator is the box which forms the evaporator part of the system and it is heavily insulated around with thermocole to reduce the heat flow from the surrounding to the evaporator. This evaporator is generally divided in three compartments. The top compartment works as a freezer where the temperature of the refrigerant is minimum as the refrigerant first enters in this compartment. Other middle and bottom, compartments are known as cold chambers. The other two compartments, middle and bottom, are cooled by natural convection as the cooled air in the freezer descends and then goes up after absorbing the heat from the middle and bottom compartments.

The top compartment of the refrigerator is used for making ice, kulfi or ice-cream. The middle and bottom compartments are used for preserving milk, curd, vegetables and fruit. The door of the refrigerator is also provided with space which is used for putting the water bottles, cold drinks, sauce and jam bottles. The top of the door is used for putting the

The control used is on-off control and it is operated automatically by a thermostat valve.

The refrigerant F-12 is only used in domestic refrigerator as it is most safe refrigerant. It does not spoil the foods even if it comes in contact due to lead.

The power consumption of 165 litres capacity refrigerator is about 60 to 80 kWh per month.

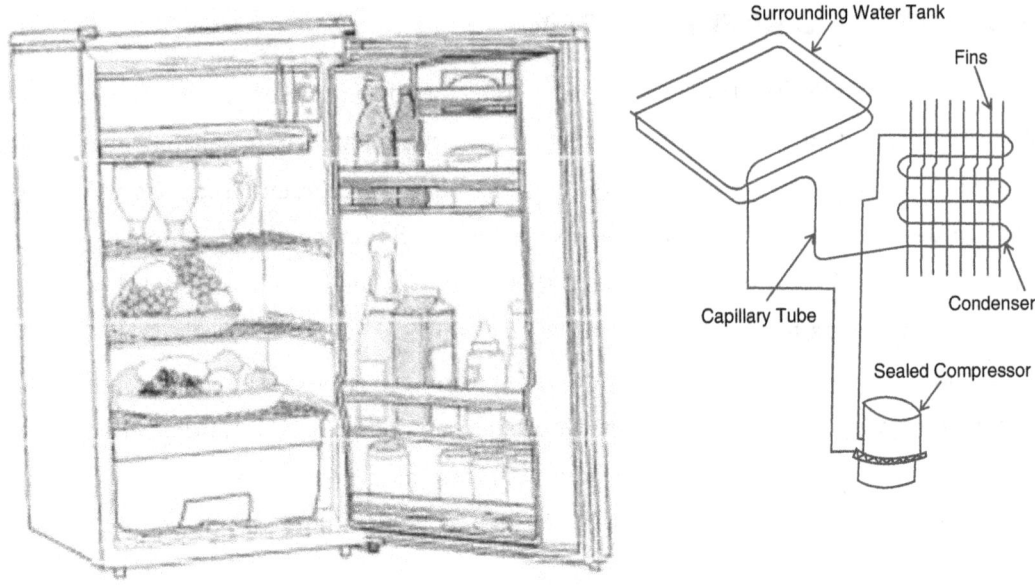

Fig. 3.6

3.7 REQUIRED PROPERTIES OF AN IDEAL REFRIGERANT

1. Low boiling point at atmospheric pressure is essential to maintain low temperature in the evaporator without the problem of leakage.
2. The vapour pressure corresponding to 40°C should not be high as water or air at 25-30°C is used for condensing the refrigerant.
3. High latent heat of the refrigerant reduces the quantity of refrigerant circulated in the system.
4. It should be non-flammable and non-toxic.
5. It must have good miscibility with lubricating oil as oil is returned back to compressor by refrigerant and avoids its accumulation in the condenser or evaporator.
6. It should have high critical pressure and temperature and also should have low freezing point.
7. It should be easily available at low cost.
8. It should give high C.O.P.

3.8 SOME IMPORTANT ENGINEERING REFRIGERANTS

1. Ammonia : It is the oldest and most widely used refrigerant in ice plants and cold storages. Its boiling point at atmospheric pressure is −33°C. It is considered most suitable as it has large latent heat (1320 kJ/kg,) moderate working pressure and high critical temperature. It is less expensive compared with any other refrigerant.

It is toxic and attacks on many foods, therefore, it is rarely used in domestic refrigerator. It is widely used in absorption system as it is highly soluble in water and easily expelled out when heated.

2. Freon-12 : It is most widely used refrigerant for many applications. It is non-toxic and non-flammable and therefore more safe. It is fully miscible with oil therefore it simplifies the problem of lubrication. It is excellant electric insulator therefore it is universally used in sealed type domestic refrigerator. Its boiling point at atmospheric pressure is –30°C. It is much costlier than ammonia, therefore perfect design and fabrication should be adopted to prevent its leak from the system.

3. Freon-22 : It is another widely used refrigerant and is superior to F-12 in many respects. It is used for low temperature industrial and commercial systems as its boiling temperature at atmospheric pressure is –40°C. All other safe properties are similar to F-12. It has also equally good oil miscibility. The only disadvantage is, it has very low latent heat (88 kJ/kg). The principal advantage of F-22 over F-12 is the smaller compressor displacement (40% less than F-12). The major disadvantage compared with F-12 is high discharge temperature which essentially requires water cooling of the compressor head and cylinder.

Comparison of different refrigerants is shown in the following table.

Refrigerant	Boiling temperature at atmospheric pressure °C	Pressure at 30°C and –15°C (bar)	Specific volume at –15°C (m³/kg)	Latent heat at –15°C (kJ/kg)	Compressor displacement per ton of refrigeration	Power per ton of refrigeration (–15 to 30°C) in kW	C.O.P. as percentage of Carnot cycle as standard condition
NH_3	–33.3	11.9 and 2.4	0.51	1320	5.83	1.6	82.9
F-12	–29.8	7.58 and 1.86	0.093	160	9.85	1.65	80
F-22	–41.3	12.26 and 3.03	0.0778	218	5.85	1.7	82

3.9 PSYCHROMETRY AND AIR-CONDITIONING

The simultaneous control of temperature, humidity, purity and air motion within an enclosed space is known as air-conditioning. Air-conditioning is used in residences, theatres, offices, hospitals, railway coaches and aeroplanes. The use of air-conditioning for industrial purposes is also increasing in this country with rapid industrial development. The purpose of this chapter is to introduce the thermodynamic principles of air-conditioning and its applications to the students.

3.9.1 Concept of Air-conditioning

Man feels comfortable at a particular temperature, humidity and air motion. Therefore, severe winter and summer are equally uncomfortable for human beings. The simultaneous control of temperature, humidity, purity and air motion within enclosed space is known as air-conditioning. The controlled atmosphere which provides comfort is known as comfort air-conditioning. The air-conditioning provides comfortable and healthy conditions for the occuptants in residences, theatres, office buildings, hospitals and railway coaches. Air-conditioning increases the working efficiency of the employees in factories and offices. The conditioned air has comfort effect on health and psychological effect on the human minds. Air-conditioning used for improving the quality of the manufactured materials is known as industrial air-conditioning. The temperature and humidity conditions for industrial air-conditioning are always different from comfort air-conditioning.

3.9.2 Psychrometry and Psychrometric Terms

Air always contains water vapour and its content plays very important role in the design of air-conditioning system as it directly affects the comfort. The study of the properties of moist air is known as **psychrometry** and the terms used in psychrometry are known as **psychrometric properties.**

1. **Dry air :** Air except water vapour is known as dry air.
2. **Moist air :** It is a mixture of dry air and water vapour. The maximum quantity of water vapour that can be present in the air depends upon the temperature of the air. The maximum quantity of water vapour presents in air at particular air temperature is known as saturation capacity of air. When the air is saturated with water vapour, the partial pressure of water vapour is equal to saturation pressure of water vapour corresponding to air temperature. If the air is not saturated, the water vapour exists in superheated condition.
3. **Moisture :** The water vapour present in the air is known as moisture.
4. **Dry Bulb Temperature (DBT) :** The temperature of air measured by ordinary thermometer is known as dry bulb temperature of air.
5. **Wet Bulb Temperature (WBT) :** The temperature of air measured by a thermometer when its bulb covered with wet colth is known as wet bulb temperature. The difference between dry bulb and wet bulb is known as wet bulb depression. When DBT and WBT are simultaneously measured by a combined thermometer, it is known as psychrometer.
6. **Dew Point Temperature (DPT) :** It is the temperature at which moisture present in the air begins to condense when the air is cooled. The DBT, WBT and DPT will be same for saturated air.

7. **Specific Humidity :** It is the mass of water vapour present with one kg of dry air. It is generally given in grams per kg of air.

8. **Relative Humidity :** It is equal to the ratio of actual mass of water vapour in a given volume to the mass of water vapour if the same volume of air is saturated at the same temperature. It is given by (p_v/p_{vs}) where p_v is the actual partial pressure of water vapour in air and p_{vs} is the partial pressure of water vapour in the air when air is fully saturated.

9. **Sensible Heat of Air :** The quantity of heat which can be measured by measuring the dry bulb temperature of air is known as sensible heat.

10. **Total Heat of Air :** It is the sum of sensible heat of dry air and sensible and latent heat of water vapour associated with dry air.

3.10 Concept of Comfort

The body of a man like engine emits heat to the surrounding atmosphere. This heat is nearly 400 kJ/hr by a man at rest. This amount increases with the activity of a man. This heat should be carried out by the surrounding air, otherwise it will be accumulated in the body and man feels uneasy.

The heat from the body is emitted in the form of sensible heat and latent heat. For carrying out the heat by the air from the body, the temperature of the air must be below the body temperature (36.4°C). The heat carried away from the body in the form of latent heat is due to the sweating from the body. The sweating maintains the softness of the body. Therefore, it is necessary that 30% of the total heat from the body should be carried out in the form of latent heat and remaining 70% in the form of sensible heat. If this balance is not maintained, the man feels uncomfortable even if air is capable of carrying the total heat from the body.

To maintain this balance of heat carried away by the air, certain DBT and R.H. of the air are absolutely essential. In addition to DBT and R.H., the air movement over the body is also equally important. If the air speed over the body is above a particular value, the man feels draft and if it is below, the required heat carrying rate from the body cannot be maintained.

3.11 AIR-CONDITIONING SYSTEM

The arrangements of equipments used for different air-conditioning plants are discussed below :

1. Summer air-conditioning system for hot and wet weather : When the outside air temperature (32-35°C) and humidity (75-80%) are high, this type of air-conditioning system is generally used. This system can be used for the cities like Mumbai, Chennai and Kolkatta which are along the sea-shore. The comfort condition commonly specified in the air-conditioning space is 26°C DBT and 55% R.H.

The arrangement of the required components is shown in Fig. 3.7.

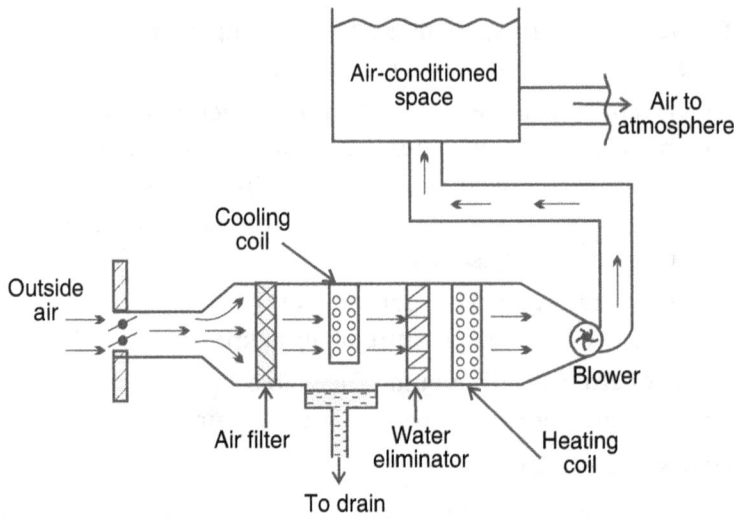

Fig. 3.7 : **Summer air-conditioning system for hot and wet weather**

The air is first filtered and then cooled below dew point temperature. Then, condensed water is removed and further heated to required temperature as it is cooled below D.B.T for removing extra humidity. Lastly, it is supplied to the required space with the help of blower.

2. Summer air-conditioning system for hot and dry weather : This type of air-conditioning system is used for the places where the temperature is high (40-45°C) and relative humidity is low (15-25%). This system can be used for cities like Delhi, Nagpur and Gaya. The comfort condition commonly specified for air-conditioned space is 25°C DBT and 55% R.H.

The arrangement of the equipments is shown in Fig. 3.8.

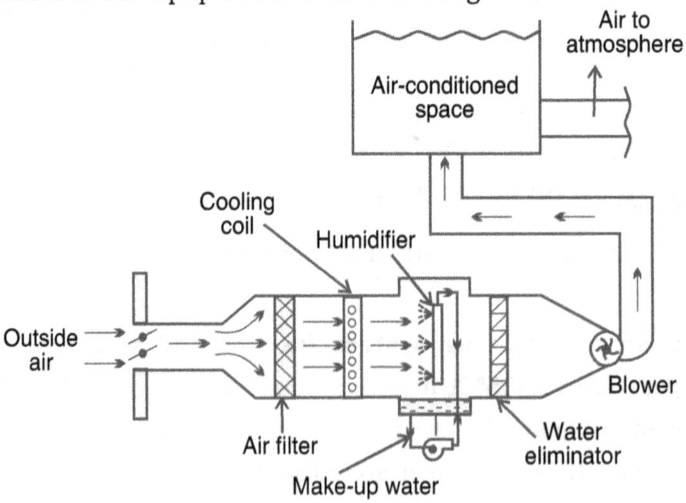

Fig. 3.8 : **Summer air-conditioning system for hot and dry weather**

First air is filtered and then cooled to required temperature with the help of cooling coil and then passed through water spray to increase the humidity to the required value.

Then it is passed through eliminator where unevaporated water particles are removed. Lastly, it is supplied to the conditioned space with the help of blower.

3. Winter air-conditioning system : This type of air-conditioning system is used for the places where the temperature is considerably low (5-10°C). The system can be used for cities like Delhi, Chandigarh and Patna during winter. The comfort condition commonly used in the air-conditioned space is 26°C D.B.T. and 55% R.H.

The arrangement of the equipments is shown in Fig. 3.9.

The air is passed through the filter and heating coil to heat and then through humidifier to increase the humidity. The unevaporated water is removed with the help of eliminator. Again it is passed to the second heater and then supplied to the air-conditioned space with the help of blower. Two-stage heating provides better control compared with single heating.

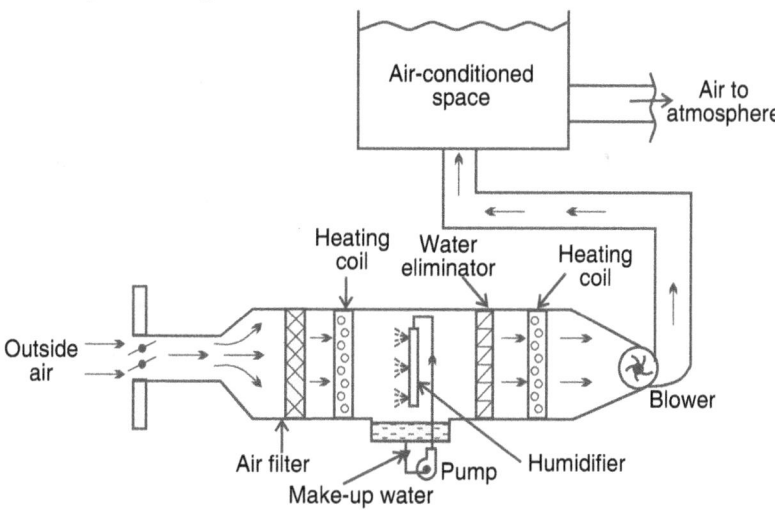

Fig. 3.9 : Winter air-conditioning system

3.12 WINDOW AIR-CONDITIONER

It is the simplest example of refrigeration cycle used in a packed air-conditioner. In this unit, filtering, coolig and air-distribution system are combined in a compact package. Compact air-conditiioners in completely self contained packaged units not only lowers the equipment cost but also made installation, servicing and operation simple and inexpensive. These units work very satisfactorily as long as the air-conditioner is properly selected, installed and serviced.

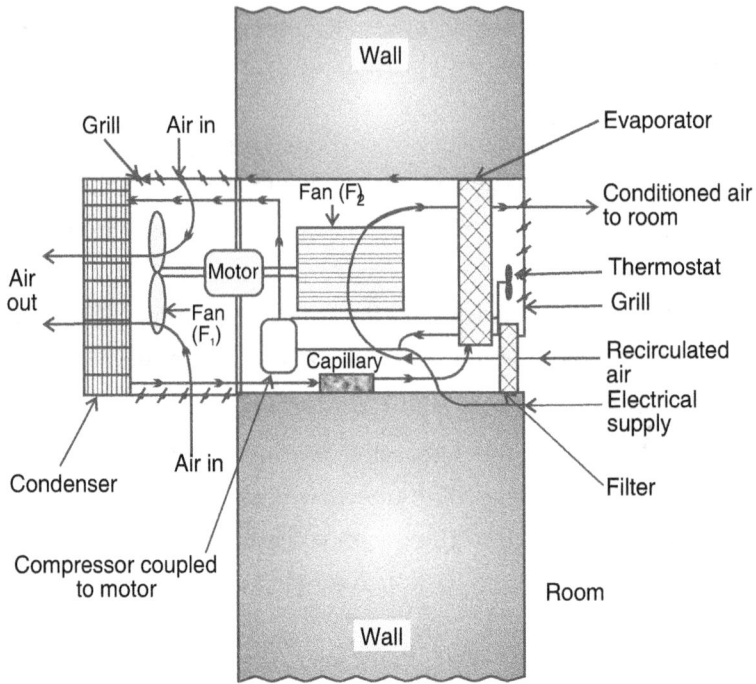

Fig. 3.10 : Window air-conditioner

A window air-conditioner consists of a case which is divided in two parts such as outdoor part and indoor part by a partition as shown in Fig. 3.10. The outdoor part consists of hermetically sealed motor. compressor, condenser, motor driven fan and a tray as shown in the figure. The outdoor portion is also divided into two parts by a partition. The hermetically sealed compressor and motor and the tray are housed in the bottom part and condenser and fan with small motor to run the fan are housed to the top part.

The indoor part is divided into bottom and top parts. The evaporator, the fan with small motor to run the fan are housed at the top portion. The control panel is fitted at one side of the conditioner. A tray is also provided below evaporator to collect the water removed from the air by dehumidifying. Both trays below are connected by a pipe line and fed to outside for draining (not shown in figure). The air filter and power connections are housed in the bottom part as shown in figure.

The air conditioner is fitted in an opening of the wall such that the outdoor portion remains outside the wall seal. The indoor portion is fitted with bottom and top shutters which can be set at different incinations.

When the conditioner is working, the low pressure vapour refrigerant is drawn from the evaporator to the compressor and it is compressed to high pressure and temperature. This high pressure, high temperature vapour is condensed passing through the condenser. The condensed liquid at high pressure is passed through the capillary and then flows through the evaporator. As the refrigerant comes out of capillary, its pressure and temperature fall and it starts boiling and absorbing the latent heat in the evaporator compartment from the air and vaporised. This low pressure vapour is again drawn by the comperssor and the cycle is repeated.

For condensing the high pressure refrigerant vapour, the air is drawn by the fan F_1 from the bottom of the outside compartment and passed over the condenser and discharged to the atmosphere from the top of the outside compartment.

The air from the room to be cooled is drawn with the help of the fan F_2 through air filter from the bottom of the inside compartment and passed over the evaporator. It loses its heat and moisture giving out its heat to the refrigerant passing through the evaporator. The cooled and dehumidified air is thrown into the room through the dampers from the top of the inside compartment as shown in figure. The moisture removed from the air by the evaporator drips into the pan located at the bottom of the evaporator (not shown in the figure) and fed to atmosphere through the pipe.

The water collected in the pan located outside the compartment evaporates to some extent and helps in cooling the compressor and condenser.

3.12.1 Split Air-Conditioner

In the conventional window air-conditioner, all the four components (cooleror evaporater compressor, condenser and. throttle) are grouped together to make the system most compact. This creates sufficient noise because of the compressor and creates discomfort.

To avoid the noise discomfort, two components (compressor and condenser) are located away from the room, mostly on the roof of the room and the cooler and air-circulating-fan (as one unit) is located (hanged) in the required room. This reduces the noise level to 10% of the window air-conditioner as major noise is created by the compressor.

The basic components of the system are shown in Fig. 3.11 which are same as window air-conditioner. The basic functions of all the components are also same.

This type of air-conditioner is commonly used now-a-days for officer's room, class-rooms, conference hall and banks. They are available from 2 to 5 tons capacity.

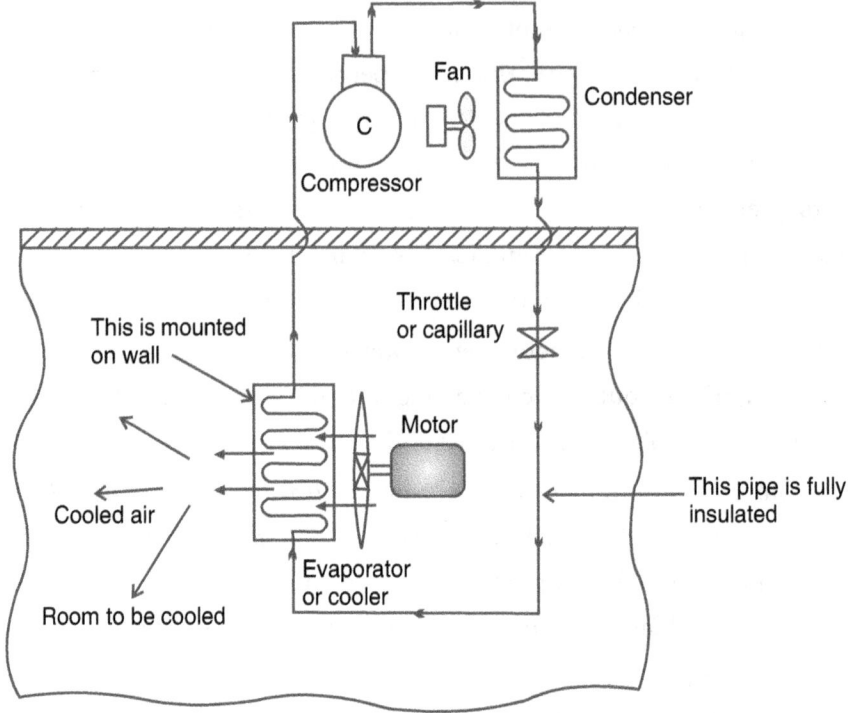

Fig. 3.11 : Split Air-conditioner

EXERCISES

3.1 Define Refrigeration and define the ton of refrigeration.

3.2 What do your understand by performance factor ? Find out the performance factor of carnot cycle when used for Refrigeration plant.

3.3 Draw a neat line diagram of vapour compression refrigeration system and explain its working.

3.4 Draw a neat line diagram of vapour absorption refrigeration system and explain its working.

3.5 Draw a neat diagram of solar assisted refrigeration system and explain its working.

3.6 Discuss relative merits and demerits of vapour compressior system with vapour absorption system.

3.7 List out the required properties of an ideal refrigerant.

3.8 What do understand by air conditioning?

3.9 Draw the line diagrams of air conditioning system used for summer Air conditioning and winter Air-conditioning and explain the working.

3.10 Draw line diagrams of Domestic refrigerator and window air conditioner and explain their working.

Section II

4

ENERGY SOURCES AND POWER PLANTS

Part A

4.1 Introduction (Renewable and Non Renewable energy sources)
4.2 Thermal Power Plant
4.3 Hydroelectric Power Plant
4.4 Nuclear Power Plant

Part B

4.5 Non-conventional (Renawable) Energy Sources
4.6 Solar Power Plant
4.7 Biogas System
4.8 Bio-Diesel
4.9 Photo Voltic Soler Cell
Exercises

Part A

4.1 INTRODUCTION

Electric energy occupies the top grade in the energy hierarchy. It finds innumerable uses in home, industry, agriculture and even in transport. The electric energy became more attractive than any other sources of energy due to the facts that electricity can be transported easily with negligible loss; it can be transported within no time i.e. instantaneously. It is almost pollution free at the consumer level and its use can be controlled very easily. Electric energy can be easily converted into other forms of energy e.g. It can be converted into mechanical energy using motor, fan etc. It can be converted into heat using electric heater, electric iron etc.

Therefore there is a huge demand of electric energy. A power station (also referred to as a generating station, power plant, or powerhouse) is an industrial facility for the generation of electric power. The major sources which can be used to generate electricity are fossil fuels and water. The power plants are classified according to the methodology adopted in the plant to generate electricity.

1. Steam Power Plant (Thermal Power Plant)
2. Hydroelectric Power Plant
3. Nuclear Power Plant
4. Diesel Power Plant
5. Gas Turbine Power Plant
6. Power plants those use renewable energy sources like Solar Power Plant, Wind Mills, Tidal plant, Geothermal Plant etc.

We will discuss Steam Power Plant, Hydroelectric Power Plant and Nuclear Power plants in detail.

4.2 THERMAL POWER PLANT

A major portion of the demand for electrical power is met by thermal power plants. These plants can be operated safely, efficiently and economically. The steam power plant can be considered to have two major divisions, namely boiler plant and turbine plant. The boiler plant converts the chemical energy of the fuel into heat energy and the turbine plant converts the heat energy of the steam into electricity.

In thermal power plants, fossil fuel such as coal, crude oil/furnace oil and natural gas are used. The selection of the fuel is decided by availability and economic considerations. In our country, coal is used in many thermal power plants.

Thermal Power Plants in Maharashtra:

1. Koradi Thermal Power Station, Nagpur
2. Nashik Thermal Power Station
3. Bhusawal Thermal Station
4. Paras Thermal Power Station, Akola
5. Parli Thermal Power Station
6. Chandrapur Thermal Power Station
7. Trombay Thermal Power Station
8. Dahanu Thermal Power Station

9. Wardha Warora Power Station
10. Khaparkheda Thermal Power Station

4.2.1 Site Selection for Thermal Power Plant

The following factors are to be considered while selecting a location for thermal plant.

(a) Availability of coal : The major source of fuel used for thermal power plant is coal. The huge quantity of coal is required for large power plants. A power plant of 400MW capacity requires 5000 to 6000 tons of coal per day. Therefore it is necessary to erect power plant near coal mines, so that the coal transportation charges to be minimised.

(b) Availability of Water : Large quantity of water is required for running condenser, for disposal of ash and as feed water to the boiler and drinking water to the working staff. It is therefore necessary to locate the power plant near the water source which will be able to supply the required quantity of water throughout the year.

(c) Ash Disposal Facilities : The ash disposal problem is more serious because the coal used for power generation contains large percentage of ash (20 to 40%). The quantity of ash to be handled is as large as 1500 to 2000 tons per day. The ash handling problem is more serious than coal handling because it comes out in hot condition and it is highly corrosive. Its effect on atmosphere is more serious as the human health is considered. Therefore there must be sufficient space to dispose off large quantity of ash. The ash can be disposed off to river, sea or lakes economically but presently the ash from the power plants is used for many industrial processes, therefore the question of its disposal to sea or river does not arise.

(d) Space Requirement : The average land requirement is 3 to 5 acres per MW capacity which includes the space required for coal storage, ash disposal, staff colony, space required for whole machinery. The cost of land adds in the final cost of the plant therefore it should be available at cheap rates which may be available at outskirts of the city.

(e) Transportation Facilities : This is another important consideration in locating the thermal power station. It is always necessary to have a railway line available near the power station for bringing the coal. It is always preferable to select the site of thermal power plants near coal mines to reduce transportation cost.

(f) Electric Power Transmission : A power plant should provide a reliable supply of electricity at minimum cost to the customer. Heavy transmission lines are to be erected from power station to load station. Therefore if the distance of load centre from power station is less then the installation cost of transmission lines can be reduced. Along with the reduction in distance the power losses associated with transmission are also get reduced. But it is always thought that the site of thermal plant near the coal mines is more economical than selecting the site near load centre.

(g) Availability of Labour : Cheap labour should be available at the proposed site as enough labour is required during construction of the plant. If the plant is at moderate distance from the towns then the labour availability for running the plant can be easily satisfied and the labour transportation cost is also reduced.

4.2.2 General Layout of Thermal Power Plant

The general layout of coal fired thermal power plant consists of mainly four circuits as shown in fig. Namely,

1. Coal and Ash Circuit
2. Air and Gas Circuit
3. Feed Water and Steam Flow Circuit
4. Cooling Water circuit

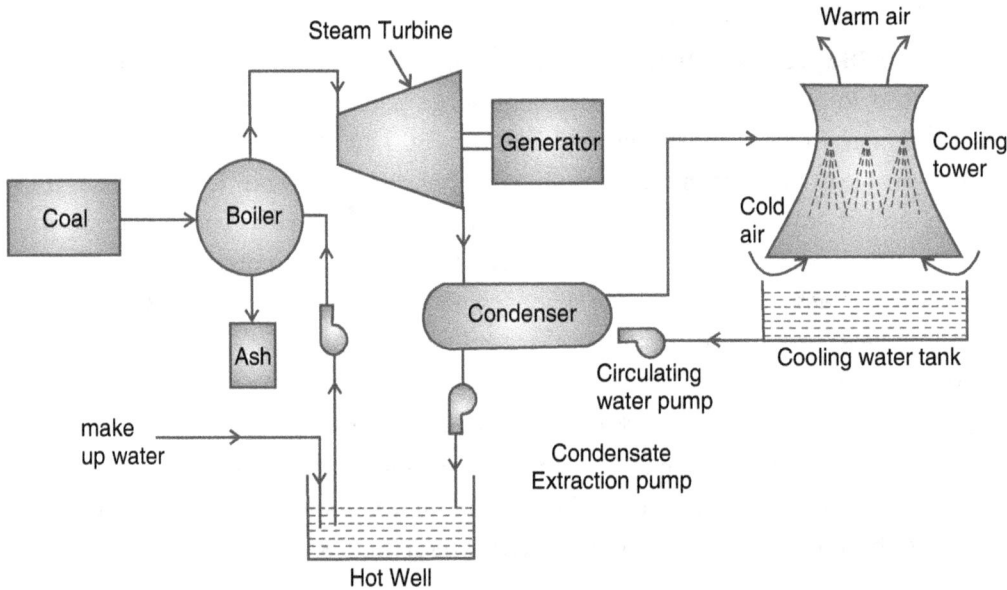

Fig. 4.1 : General Layout of Steam Power Plant

In this plant, steam is generated in the boiler which then is expanded in the turbine and again condensed in the condenser and fed into the boiler again with the help of pump.

1. Coal and Ash Circuit : Coal is supplied inside the boiler with the help of coal handling device. Usually coal is fed in the powdered form (pulverised coal) to the boiler so that there should be effective combustion. Coal is burnt inside the boiler. In the boiler, the chemical energy inside the coal is converted into heat energy, which is used for heating the water. After burning the coal, ash is formed, which can disposed separately by ash handling equipment.

2. Air and Gas Circuit : Air is supplied to the combustion chamber of the boiler through the (forced draft) fan. The dust from the air is removed before supplying to the combustion chamber.

The flue gases carrying sufficient quantity of heat and ash are passed through the air heater (called as air preheater) where the heat of the gases is given to the air and then the gases are passed through the dust collectors where most of the dust is removed before exhausting the gases to the atmosphere through chimney.

Economiser : Flue gases coming out of the boiler carry lot of heat. Function of economiser is to take some of the heat from the heat carried away in the flue gases through chimney and utilize for heating the feed water to the boiler. It is placed in the passage of flue gases in between the exit from the boiler and the entry to the chimney (not shown in fig.4.1).

The use of economiser results in saving in coal consumption, increase in rate of steam production and high boiler efficiency but it needs extra investment and increase in maintenance costs.

Air Preheater : The remaining heat of flue gases is utilised by air preheater. It is a device used in steam boilers to transfer heat from the flue gases to the combustion air before the air enters the furnace. Also known as air heater.

It is not shown in the figure. It is kept at a place near by where the air enters in to the boiler.The purpose of the air preheater is to recover the heat from the flue gas from the boiler to improve boiler efficiency by burning warm air which increases combustion efficiency, and reducing useful heat lost from the flue.

As much heat is utilised from the flue gases in the economiser and air preheater, before releasing through the chimney, the temperature of gases going out of chimney become very less, which are less harmful.

1. Feed Water and Steam Flow Circuit : The steam generated in the boiler is fed to the steam turbine. The steam coming out of the turbine is condensed in the condenser and then fed to the boiler again with the help of feed pump. The make up water is added in the hot well to recover the losses due to leakage.

2. Cooling Water Circuit : The quantity of cooling water required to condensate the steam is considerably large and it is taken either from lake or river. The cooling water is passed through the condenser which absorbs heat from the steam passing through the condenser. The water coming out of the condenser is cooled in cooling tower.

4.2.3 Working of the Thermal Power Plant

Steam is generated in the boiler using the heat of the fuel burned in the combustion chamber. The steam generated is passed through steam turbine where part of its thermal energy is converted into mechanical energy which is further used for producing electric power. The steam coming out of the steam turbine is condensed in the condenser and the condensate is supplied back to the boiler with the help of feed pump and the cycle is repeated.

4.2.4 Advantages of Coal Based Thermal Power Plant

- They can respond to rapidly changing loads without difficulty
- A portion of the steam generated can be used as a process steam in different industries
- Steam engines and turbines can work under 25 % of overload continuously
- Fuel used is cheaper
- Cheaper in production cost in comparison with that of diesel power stations.

4.2.5 Disadvantages of Coal Based Thermal Power Plant

- Maintenance and operating costs are high
- Long time required for erection and putting into action
- A large quantity of water is required
- Great difficulty experienced in coal handling
- Presence of troubles due to smoke and heat in the plant
- Unavailability of good quality coal
- Maximum of heat energy lost
- Problem of ash removing

4.3 HYDROELECTRIC POWER PLANT

In hydroelectric power plants, the potential energy of water due to its high location is converted into electrical energy. The total power generation capacity of the hydroelectric power plants depends on the head of water (height of water from ground level) and volume of water flowing towards the water turbine. It is the most widely used form of renewable energy.

The hydroelectric power plant, also called as hydel or hydropower plant, is used for generation of electricity from water on large scale basis. The dam is built across the large river that has sufficient quantity of water throughout the river. In certain cases where the river is very large, more than one dam can built across the river at different locations.

4.3.1 Working Principle of Hydroelectric Power Plant

The water flowing in the river possesses two type of energy: the kinetic energy due to flow of water and potential energy due to the height of water. In hydroelectric power plants or dams potential energy of water is utilized to generate electricity. The energy stored in the system at the height from datum is called as potential energy. Rain falling upon the earth's surface has a potential energy relative to oceans due to its flow. Potential energy of rain falling on earth's surface with respect to sea level is converted into mechanical energy by using suitable hydraulic turbines. The power developed by a hydraulic turbine 'P' is given as,

$$P = \rho Q g h \text{ watts}$$

Where,
- Q = flow rate, m^3/sec
- H = head, (m), Level difference between reservoir and tail race
- ρ = density of water, (kg/m^3)
- g = gravitational acceleration (m/sec^2)

Therefore, to generate hydraulic power economically, ample quantity of water (Q) at sufficient height [head (h)] must be available.

To obtain the high head of water the reservoir of water should be as high as possible and power generation unit should be as low as possible. The maximum height of reservoir of water is fixed by natural factors like the height of river bed, the amount of water and other environmental factors. The location of the power generation unit can be adjusted as per the total amount of power that is to be generated. Usually the power generation unit is constructed at levels lower than ground level so as to get the maximum head of water.

4.3.2 Selection of Site for Hydro Power Plant

The following factors are considered for the selection of site.

1. Large quantity of water at reasonable head should be available.
2. The site should provide strong and high mountains on the two sides of the river reservoir with minimum gap for economical dam construction.
3. The rain fall should be sufficient to maintain desired water level in the reservoir throughout the year.
4. The catchment area for the reservoir to collect rain water should be large.
5. There site should have the firm rock for foundation.

4.3.3 Hydroelectric Power Plants in Maharashtra:

1. Koyna Power Plant
2. Bhatghar Pumped Storage Scheme
3. Mulshi Dam
4. Jayakwadi Dam (Pump storage Type)
5. Pench Power Plant (Near Nagpur)

4.3.4 Classification of Hydro-Electric Power Plants

(a) According to the availability of head

1. Low head plants - head below 30 m
2. Medium head plants - head between 30 m to 180 m
3. High head plants - head 180 m and above.

(b) According to the nature of load:

1. Base load plants: These plants operate at maximum output. They shut down or reduce power only to perform maintenance or repair. These plants produce electricity at the lowest cost of any type of power plant, and so are most economically used at maximum capacity

2. Peak load plants: Peaking power plants, also known as peaker plants, are power plants that generally run only when there is a high demand, known as peak demand, for electricity. A peaker plant may operate many hours a day, or it may operate only a few hours per year, depending on the condition of the region's need.

(c) According to the quantity of water available :

1. Run of river plant: Run-of-river hydro power does not have a large reservoir, if any. If there is a dam across a river, it will create power from the power that collects behind the dam. In other forms, the run-of-river plant is one large part of the river flow, while another part flows on unobstructed. Some even smaller run-of-river systems simply use a turbine placed in the middle of the flow of the river, or something similar to a water wheel. These systems are generally much smaller, perhaps only a few kilowatts in size

2. Pump storage plant: Pumped-hydro storage requires two reservoirs at different elevations. When power demand is high, water is run out of the higher reservoir to generate electricity. When demand is low, water is pumped upwards from the lower reservoir to the higher one, effectively storing it for later use.

3. Storage reservoir plant: Storage reservoir type hydel power plant is explained as follows:

Storage Reservoir Plant: (Refer fig.4.2)

The storage type hydro-electric power plant is as shown in Fig. 4.2. Such plant has a large storage capacity of water, therefore water collected in rainy season is utilized during dry period of the year. The collection of water is done on yearly basis, therefore, the capacity of the reservoir required is extremely large compared with the other types of hydro-electric power plant.

The elements of the hydel power plant are explained as follows:

1. Reservoir: Dams are built over rivers to stop the water flow and form a reservoir. The reservoir stores the water flowing down the river. This water is diverted to turbines in power stations. The dams collect water during the rainy season and store it, thus making the provision to use it throughout the year. Dams are also used for controlling floods and irrigation. The dams should be water-tight and should be able to withstand the pressure exerted by the water on it. The height of water in the dam is called *head race.*

2. Track Rash: Its function is to prevent the entry of debris into the penstock which may damage the wicket gates of turbine runner or chock up the nozzle of the impulse turbine.

3. Penstock: It is a pipe from reservoir to the surge tank. The penstock has to bear heavy pressure from inside during decreased load conditions of generator and on outside surface during increased load conditions of generator. Therefore, it is constructed in heavy reinforced cement concrete or M.S. plates.

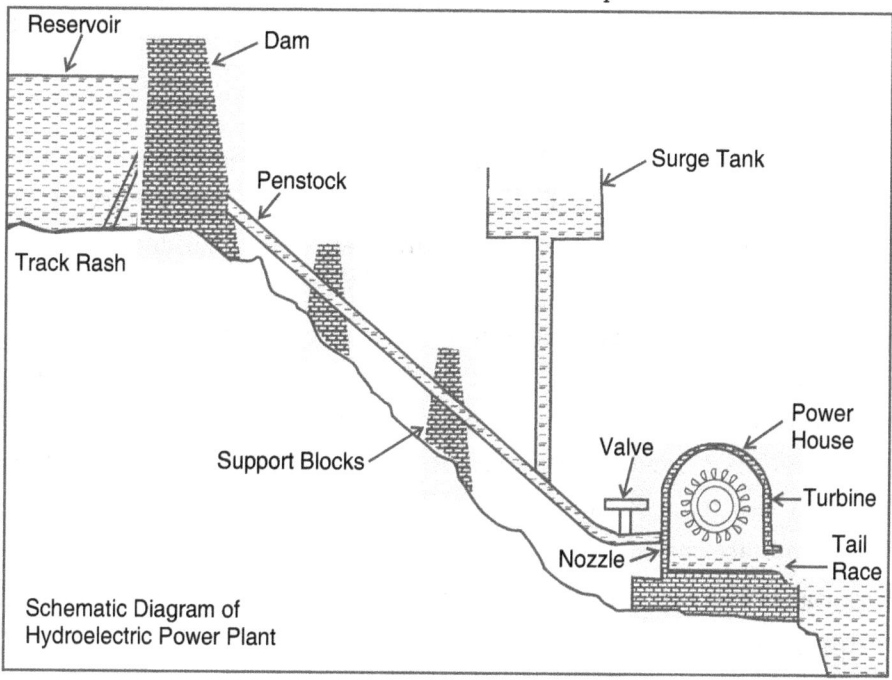

Fig. 4.2

4. Surge Tank: There is sudden increase of pressure in the penstock due to sudden decrease in the rate of flow of water to the turbine when the gate (valve) admitting water to the turbine is suddenly closed. This sudden rise of pressure in the penstock above normal pressure due to reduced load on the generator is known as "water hammer". To avoid water hammering and vacuum forming tendencies, surge tank is introduced near the power house.

5. **Power House:** Power house contains a turbine coupled to a generator. The water brought to the power station rotates the vanes of the turbine producing torque and rotation of turbine shaft. This rotational torque is transferred to the generator and is converted into electricity.

A superstructure is built to protect the turbine and generator unit from atmospheric effects. If conventional geographic area is not available, then power stations are preferred to build underground which also increases the head.

6. **Turbine:** The main purpose of turbine is to convert the K.E. of water into mechanical energy to generate electric power. The turbines are classified into two categories.

Impulse Turbine

It uses the kinetic energy of water to move the runner and discharges to atmospheric pressure. The water stream hits each bucket on the runner. Water flows out the tail race after hitting the runner. This type of turbine is suitable for high head power plants.

Reaction Turbine

This turbine develops power from the combined action of pressure energy and kinetic energy of water. Runner is placed directly in the water stream flowing over the blades rather than striking each blade individually .Such turbine is used for sites with lower head.

7. **Draft tube:** It is used in reaction turbines. It is a device, which is having gradual increasing area. It is placed in between the turbine and tailrace. The function of draft tube is to increase the pressure energy of the water flowing towards tailrace. This is used because pressure energy of the water after striking the turbine blades is much less than the atmospheric pressure because of this water can not be discharged to tail race easily.

4.3.5 Advantages of Hydro-Electric Power Plant

1. Operating cost is extremely low.
2. Nuisance of smoke, exhaust gases, etc.
3. Labour required to operate the plant is less.
4. As these are located away from the developed areas, so the cost of land is not a problem.

5. Easy start and stop facilities.
6. These are able to respond to rapidly changing loads without loss of efficiency.
7. No fuel is required. Therefore, there is no cost of fuel as well as the costs in connection with handling, storage and disposal of ash and flue gases.

4.3.6 Disadvantages of Hydro-Electric Power Plant

1. Initial cost of the plant including the cost of the dam is too high.
2. Power generation from such plant is dependent on the quantity of water which in turn depends on the natural phenomenon of rain. Thus, the availability of power is not very reliable.
3. These are usually away from the consumers. Therefore, transmission of power from power station to the load centers involves use of long transmission lines and consequent investment and loss of power in transmission are unfavourable.

4.4 NUCLEAR POWER PLANT

The energy needs of the country can not be met from a single source. Hydroelectric stations produce cheap power but it depends upon rainfall. The thermal plants need lot of coal. The coal reserves of the world are fast depleting. The nuclear plant is the only source which can satisfy the future energy demands of the world.

Nuclear Power Stations use a fuel called uranium, a relatively common material. Energy is released from uranium when an atom is split by a neutron. The uranium atom is split into two and during the process; a large amount of heat energy is released. This nuclear reaction is called the fission process. The heat energy in the fission process is used for raising steam to run turbines.

4.4.1 Nuclear Fission

In the fission process, the nuclei of heavy atom of Uranium or Plutonium are bombarded by the neutrons. The nuclei then become highly excited due to absorption of these slow neutrons. The original nuclei are split up into two different masses. These masses are also highly excited; they try to become stable by emitting neutrons. Thus heat energy is produced on vast scale along with kinetic energy. This spontaneous disintegration is known as a radioactive decay. This decay gives out electromagnetic radiation such as α, β, γ rays. The unstable heavy nuclei are converted into stable light nuclei during the process. The products obtained at the end of the process are known as the fission products.

Nuclear Chain Reaction

The natural Uranium isotope is very easily and readily fissionable. It is bombarded by a neutron. The nucleus is split up and release enormous energy that binds the nucleus together.

If a U^{235} atom is bombarded with a neutron, it splits into two lighter nuclei, Barium^{141} and Krypton ^{92} along with 3 neutrons. The three neutrons again hit the other U nuclei. This process goes on multiplying. It is known as chain reaction. It is a continuous splitting process of neutrons. This chain reaction is performed and controlled in a special closed device known as reactor.

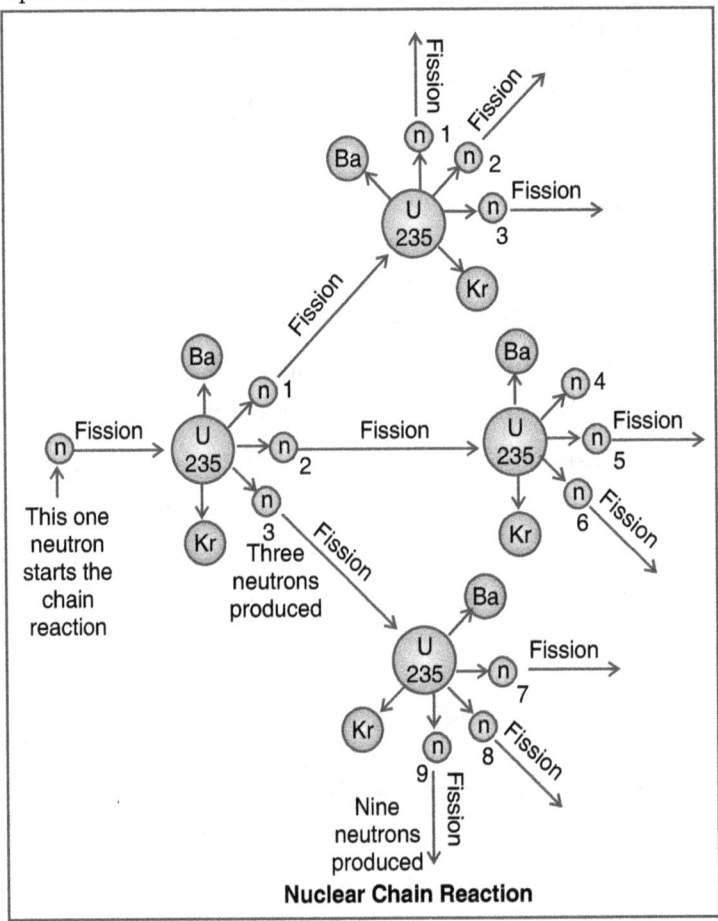

Nuclear Chain Reaction

Fig. 4.3

4.4.2 Location of Nuclear Power Plant

The following factors are considered are taken into considerations while selecting a site for the nuclear power plant.

1. Availability of water: This plant requires water as a secondary working fluid and for cooling. So the plant should have its location near the river or lake.
2. Distance from populated area: It should be located reasonably away from the thickly populated area for safety considerations against radioactivity.
3. Nearness to load centre: The site should be near to load centre as far as possible to reduce the cost of transmission of large amount of electric power.
4. Disposal of Nuclear waste: The nuclear waste obtained by burning nuclear fuel is radioactive. It should be buried deeply in the ground or disposed in the sea far away from sea shore. The location of the plant should allow these things easily.
5. Transport facility: The location of the plant should be accessible for transportation of heavy equipment during erection of site.

4.4.3 Nuclear Power Plants in India
1. Kaiga Atomic Station, Karnataka.
2. Tarapur Atomic Station Maharashtra.
3. Madras Atomic Station Kalpakkam, Tamilnadu.
4. Rajasthan Atomic Station Rawatbhata, Rajasthan.
5. Narora Atomic Station, Narora, Uttar Pradesh.
6. Kakrapar Atomic Power Station Kakrapar, Gujarat.

4.4.4 Main Parts of Nuclear Plant

A nuclear power plant consists of a nuclear reactor (for heat generation), heat exchanger (for converting water into steam by using the heat generated in reactor), steam turbine, generator, condenser etc. It is similar to a steam power plant except that the nuclear reactor and heat exchanger replace the boiler. Thus some of the auxiliaries are similar to those in the steam plant. But the reactor and the cooling circuit have to be heavily shielded to eliminate radiation hazards. Fig. 4.4 shows the main parts of a nuclear power plant.

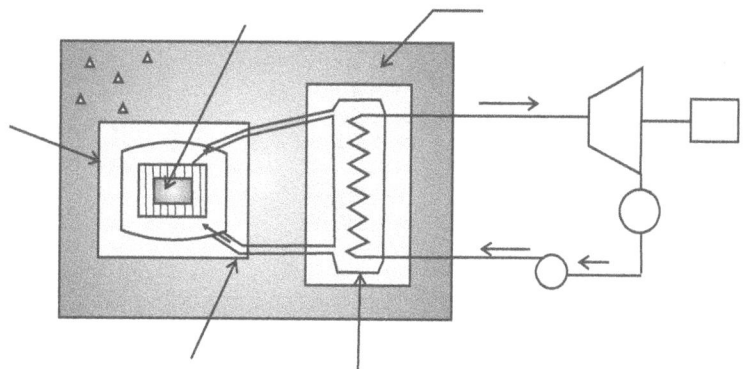

```
ERROR: undefined
OFFENDING COMMAND: 650.0720.

STACK:

193.464
646.76
190.152
329.216
```

5
MECHANICAL POWER TRANSMISSION AND ENERGY CONVERSION DEVICES

Part A

5.1 Introduction
5.2 Classification of Drives
5.3 Couplings
5.4 Bearings
5.5 Belt and Belt Drives
5.6 Chain Drive
5.7 Gear Drive

Part B

5.8 Air Compressors
5.9 Water Pumps
5.10 Hydraulic Turbines (Water Turbine)
    Solved Problems
    Exercises

Part A

5.1 INTRODUCTION

In most of the cases, the power generated cannot be used at the point of generation and it is to be taken at the point of use. The device used for the purpose is known as Mechanical Drive. The drive takes the power from the source of power to the point of use. For example, the power of the electrical motor is taken to the cutting point in case of lathe, milling machine, shaper machine in machine tool industry. The power of engine is taken to the propeller shaft in automobiles.

In majority cases, the motor or engine can be directly coupled to the machine to be operated and therefore, a mechanical device is to be introduced in between the two.

Many times, it becomes necessary to regulate the speed of the shaft on which the job is mounted as per requirement (low speed for hard material and high speed for soft material). This is essential in case of Lathe and Milling machine.

In addition to this, it becomes necessary to disconnect the power from driving shaft to driven shaft in case of automobiles as well as it also becomes necessary to brake (to reduce the speed) the moving vehicle under emergency condition. Engaging and disengaging the driving and driven shaft is done by clutch. The braking of the moving vehicle is done by braking system.

All such components which are used for transmitting power, regulating speed, disengaging the power from one to another and braking the power are discussed in this chapter.

The requirements of a good mechanical drive are listed below.

1. The drive should be efficient and reliable.
2. Its capital and maintenance cost should be low.
3. It must be able to change the speed in steps as per the requirement without stopping the motor.
4. It must be able to transfer power from one plane to another required plane.
5. The drive should be compact and (weight/power) ratio should be as minimum as possible.

5.2 CLASSIFICATION OF DRIVES

The drives are classified as Individual drive and Group drive.

1. Individual Drive :

In this system of drive, every machine tool has its own electric motor and the power from motor is brought to the machine spindle or to the tool through belts or gears. In addition to this, the prime mover can also be coupled directly to the required equipment like pump. Motor-pump sets of different capacity are available in the market. The power arrangements mentioned above are shown in Fig. 5.1.

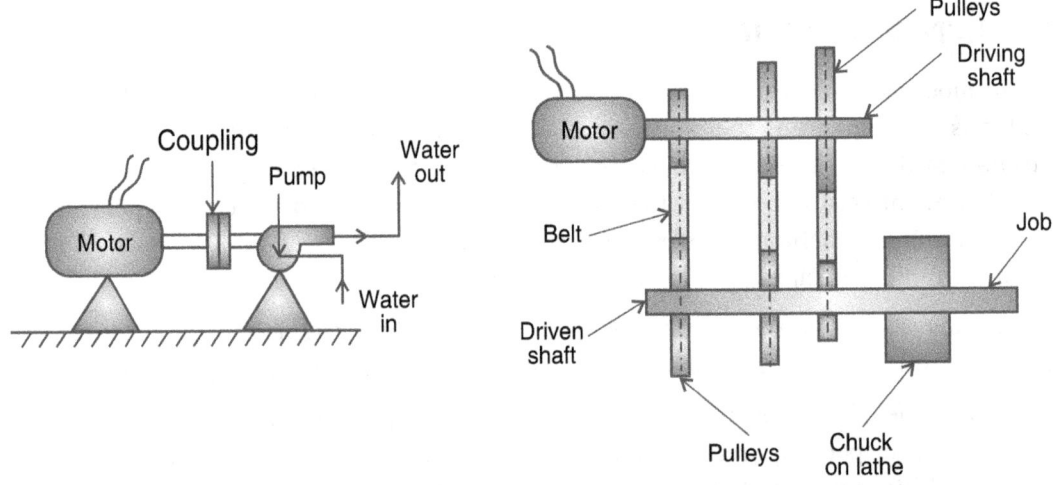

(a) Directly coupled   (b) Variable speed with belt and pulley

Fig. 5.1 : Individual drive

Advantages and Disadvantages of Individual Drive
Advantages :
1. The shop appearance is very good.
2. In a work shop, if one motor fails then only one machine stops and other machines remain working.
3. The chances of accidents are less as there are no overhead shafts and belts.
4. Machine repair is easy and less costly.
5. Machine can be removed and replaced by new machine till the failed machine is repaired.
6. The power losses are minimum.
7. It is possible to provide a range of speed to the job as used with Lathe.

Disadvantages :
1. Initial cost is high.
2. More space is required compared with group drive system.

2. Group Drive :

When a single prime mover (motor or engine) is used to drive more than one machines then the system is known as group drive. Such type of system is commonly used in villages for grinding corn, extracting oil from ground-nut and spinning seeds from cotton.

Such a system is shown in Fig. 5.2. The prime mover first transfers the power to the another shaft as shown in Fig. 5.2 and then the power is distributed to the number of machines. In this system, the driven shaft drives the different machine shafts at different speeds as per requirements through the pulleys and belts. The driven shaft transmits the power to each machine shaft when it is connected with fast pulley and machine remains idle when loose pulley is engaged as shown in Fig. 5.2.

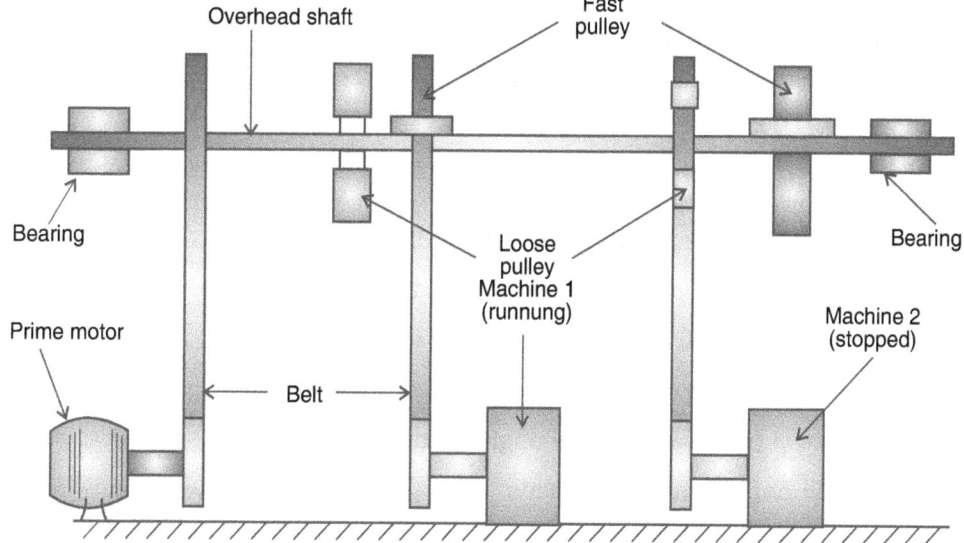

Fig. 5.2 : Group drive

Advantages and Disadvantages of Group Drives :

Advantages :

1. It saves capital cost as one high capacity motor can be used instead of several motors in case of individual drive.

2. It is always preferred when number of machines for different purposes are to be operated simultaneously.

3. The maintenance cost is low compared to individual drive.

4. Group drive is suitable when power variation in case of individual machine is extremely variable.

Disadvantages :

1. A big prime mover (motor or engine) has to run even a few machines are working in the whole machine shop.

2. The whole machine shop stops when the motor fails.

3. The possibility of accident is more because of overhead shafts and long belts.

4. Wide variation of speed, if required, is not possible.

5. The environment in the work shop becomes very noisy.

6. The overall efficiency of the system is low as the losses exit at many places like pulleys and belts.

7. The overhead crane cannot be used because of number of shafts and belts existing in the shop.

5.3 COUPLINGS

A coupling is a device used to connect two co-axial shafts permanently so that necessary torque and power can be transmitted. The connection of motor shaft (driving) with water pump shaft (driven) is best example where coupling can be used.

A clutch is also a device used in automobiles to connect two co-axial shafts for power transmission. However, the clutch permits rapid connection and disconnection of driving and driven shafts at the will of the driver.

The requirements of a good coupling are listed below :

1. It must transmit full power of the driving shaft.

2. It should be easy to connect and disconnect the coupling.

3. It must keep the shaft in 100% alignment.

4. It should not transmit shock loads.

The couplings are classified as rigid couplings and flexible couplings.

(A) Rigid Couplings : The rigid couplings are used to connect two co-axial shafts rigidly. Some of the rigid couplings are discussed below.

1. Sleeve or Muff Coupling : The arrangement of this coupling is shown in Fig. 5.3.

It consists of a cast iron hollow cylinder known as sleeve or muff. The sleeve is fitted over the ends of the shaft with the help of gib-head sunk key in the keyways of the shafts and sleeve. The power is transmitted from driving shaft through the key, through the sleeve then again through key to the driven shaft.

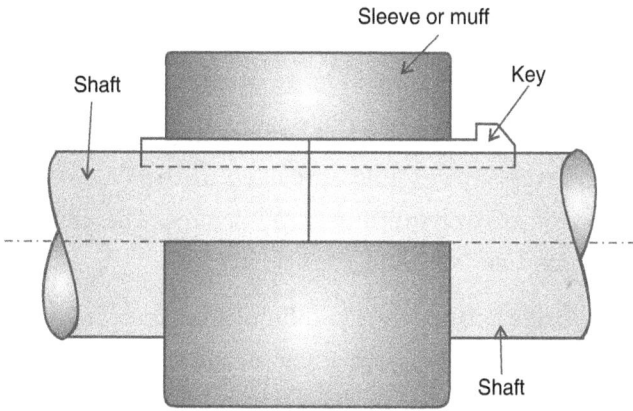

Fig. 5.3 : Muff Coupling

2. Clamp or Compression Coupling : The configuration of this coupling is shown Fig. 5.4. In this case, the sleeve is split into two halves which are assembled over two co-axial shafts to be connected. One part of the sleeve is fixed from the top and other half from the bottom and these are clamped together by means of nuts and bolts as shown in Fig. 5.4. This is generally used for transmitting large torques.

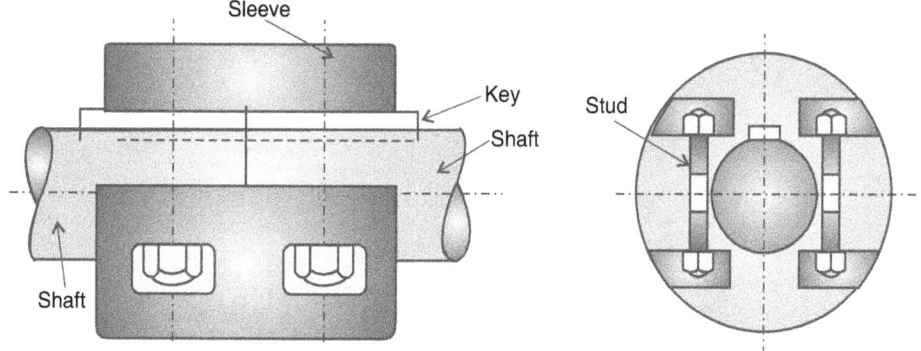

Fig. 5.4 : Clamp or compression coupling

3. Flange Coupling : The configuration of this coupling is shown in Fig. 5.5. It

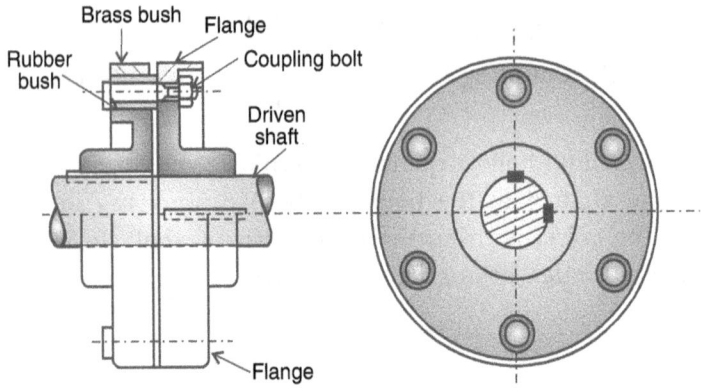

Fig. 5.5 : Flange coupling

consists of two flanges each being keyed to the driving and driven shafts. Both flanges are joined by bolts and nuts in the holes provided in the flanges as shown in Fig. 5.5. This coupling is also used for transmitting large torques. The advantage of this coupling is equal distribution of load on bolts.

(B) Flexible Couplings : It is always difficult to connect two co-axial shafts with 100% alignment because of installation error or unequal wear in the bearing. Such misalignment causes stress reversal in the shafts and excessive wear of the bearings. The flexible coupling is used to avoid these adverse effects because of lateral or angular misalignment.

A few important flexible couplings are discussed here.

1. Bushed Pin Type Flexible Coupling : The configuration of this coupling is shown in Fig. 5.6. It is basically a modification of rigid type flanged coupling.

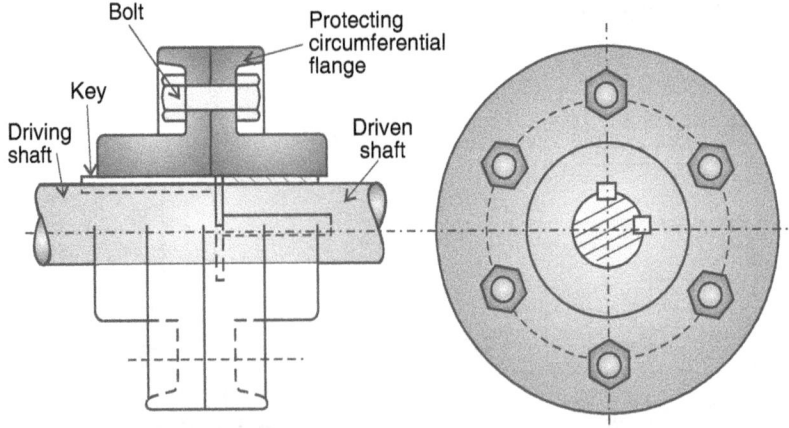

Fig. 5.6 : Bushed pin type flexible coupling

The coupling bolts made of special shape (known as pins) are rigidly fixed by nuts to one of the flanges. The enlarged portion of the pin is fitted with brass-bush and covered with a ring of rubber. The power from the driving shaft to the driven shaft is transmitted through the rubber bushes which take care of misalignment. This is very commonly used for coupling the motor shaft and centrifugal pump shaft.

2. Oldham's Coupling : This is generally used to connect two parallel shafts and are at a very short distance apart. The configuration of the coupling is shown in Fig. 5.7. The flanges A and B are rigidly fixed on the driving and driven shafts respectively. In between the flanges A and B, the coupling has an intermediate piece C which has two projections X and Y and these projections slide in the grooves provided in the flanges of the shaft. These projections are formed at right angle to each other but in opposite sides of the piece C.

If the driving shaft starts rotating, then flange A also rotates at the same speed as the flange A is rigidly fixed on the shaft. Then flange A transmits the same motion to the intermediate piece C and from C to flange B and finally to the driven shaft. The projections provided on piece C slide into the grooves on the flanges where the motion is transmitted through the coupling.

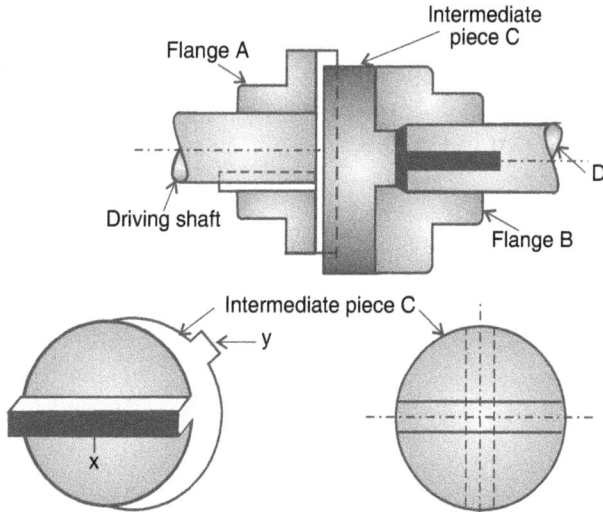

Fig. 5.7 : Oldham's coupling

3. Universal Coupling or Hooke's Joint : This coupling is used to transmit the power from one shaft to another which are non-parallel intersecting shafts. This is universally used to transmit the power from the gear box of the automobile engine to the rear axle. The configuration of this coupling is shown in Fig. 5.8. The driving and driven shafts are inclined at an angle α in their fixed bearings. Each shaft has a fork at its

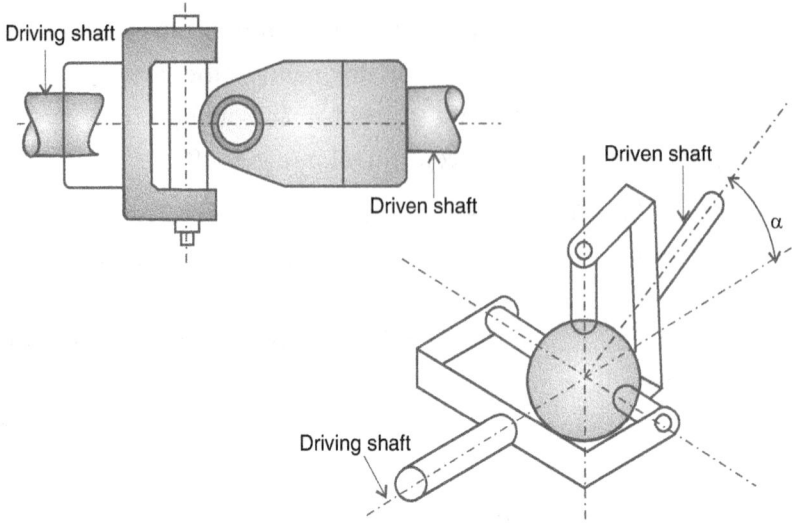

Fig. 5.8 : Universal coupling

ends. The four ends of the forks are connected by an intermediate block connecting pins in the form of a cross. The cross pins rest on the needle bearings in the fork ends. The four arms of the cross are at right angles to each other. The intermediate block may be in the form of cube or sphere.

In this coupling, one rotation of driving shaft provides one rotation to the driven shaft but with varying angular speed. In order to transmit constant angular velocity from driving shaft to driven shaft, two universal couplings (one to gear box and other to rear axle) are used as shown in Fig. 5.9.

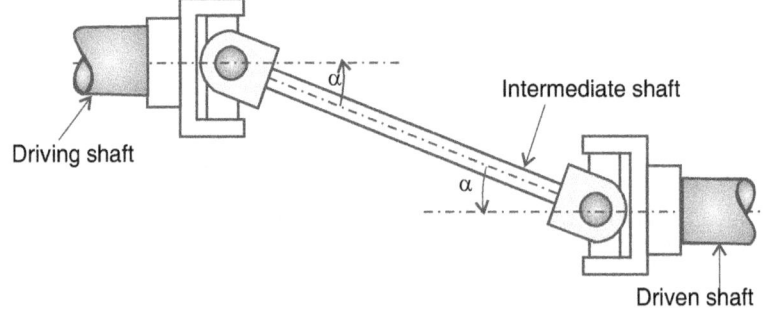

Fig. 5.9 : Double universal coupling

5.4 BEARINGS

It is a machine element used for supporting rotating shaft and to carry the loads applied to them. It permits relative motion between bearing surface and shaft surface and facilitates smooth running. Because of relative motion between two surfaces, sets up frictional force and certain amount of power is lost to overcome this frictional force. The frictional force generates heat and it becomes necessary to remove this heat. Therefore, lubrication is provided between these two surfaces having relative motion and reduces the wear, power loss and heat generation.

The Fig. 5.10 shows a simple type of bearing. The bearings are generally classified as slide contact bearings and rolling contact (antifriction) bearings.

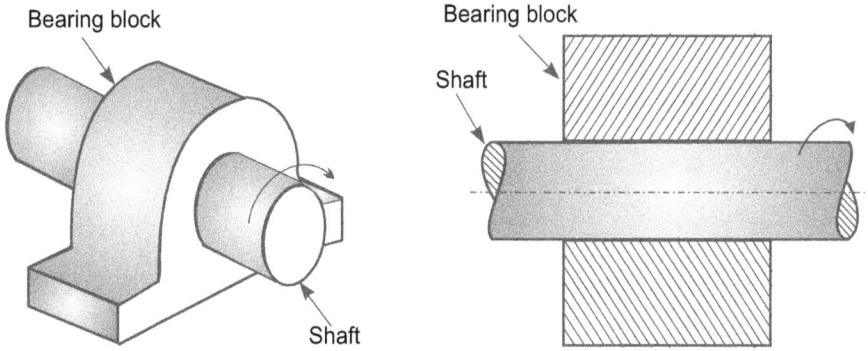

Fig. 5.10

[A] Sliding Contact Bearings

In this bearing, the nature of motion between the shaft and bearing is purely sliding. Therefore, the friction is high and requires more lubrication.

These bearings are further classified as given below :

Journal Bearing : The configuration is shown in Fig. 5.11 (a). In this bearing, the sliding action is along the circumference of the circle.

Thrust Bearing : The configuration of this bearing is shown in Fig. 5.11 (b) and Fig. 5.11 (c). These bearings are used to support axial loads of rotating members. These are used for ship propeller shaft and steam turbine shaft.

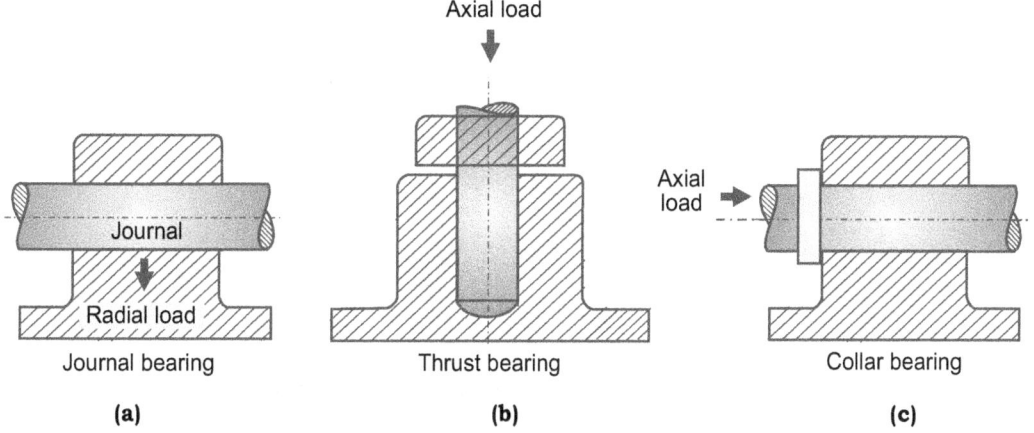

Fig. 5.11 : Sliding contact bearings

1. Bush Bearing : The bush bearing is used for supporting radial loads. This is the simplest type of journal bearing as shown in Fig. 5.12. This is used for supporting the long shafts.

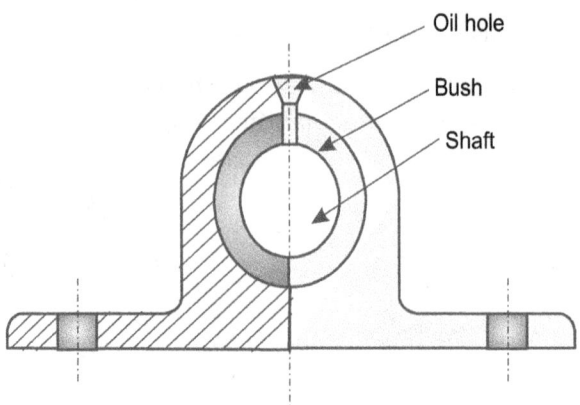

Fig. 5.12 : Bush bearing

2. Split Journal Bearing : The configuration of this bearing is shown in Fig. 5.13. This is used for high speed rotating shaft and carrying heavy radial loads. It consists of cast iron base. The bearing is split into two parts in which top part is called cap. The bush is also split into two halves called brasses. The cap and base along their brasses are fastened together by means of nut and bolts shown in Fig. 5.13. An oil groove is provided for the purpose of lubricating the bearing. The flanges are provided to prevent axial movement of brasses and its rotation is prevented by providing projections called **snugs** which fits into the corresponding hole in the housing.

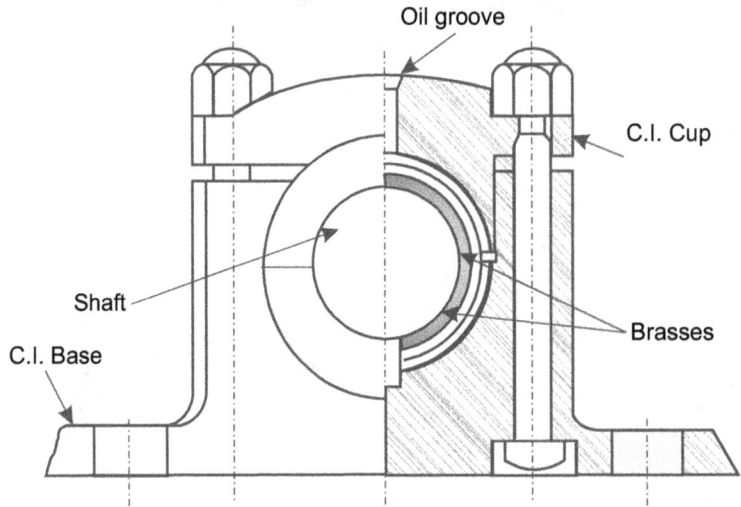

Fig. 5.13 : Split journal bearing or plumber block

3. Foot Step Bearing : This bearing is used to support axial load and it is provided at the end of the shaft. The configuration is shown in Fig. 5.14. The end part of the shaft rests on a flat surface of the bearing and rotates on a gun-metal bush which is press-fitted in the pedestal. Such bearings are difficult to lubricate since the lubricating oil is thrown outwards from the centre of the shaft due to centrifugal force.

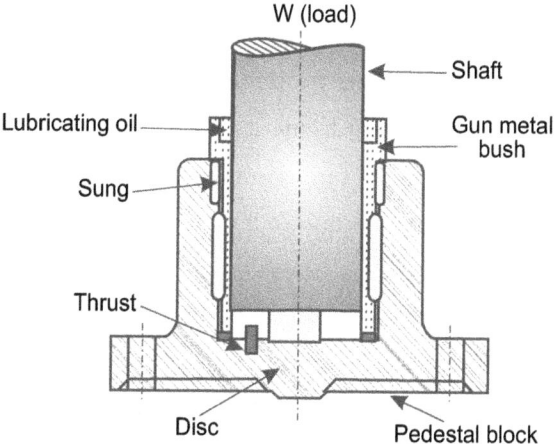

Fig. 5.14 : Foot step bearing

This is generally used for low speed shaft and carrying light loads.

4. Collar Thrust Bearing : The configuration is shown in Fig. 5.15 (a). These are generally used to reduce the bearing pressures by providing collar as it increases the surface area of contact. These are used for horizontal shaft carrying heavy axial loads. If the load to be carried is considerably large, then multi-collar thrust bearing is used as shown in Fig. 5.15 (b).

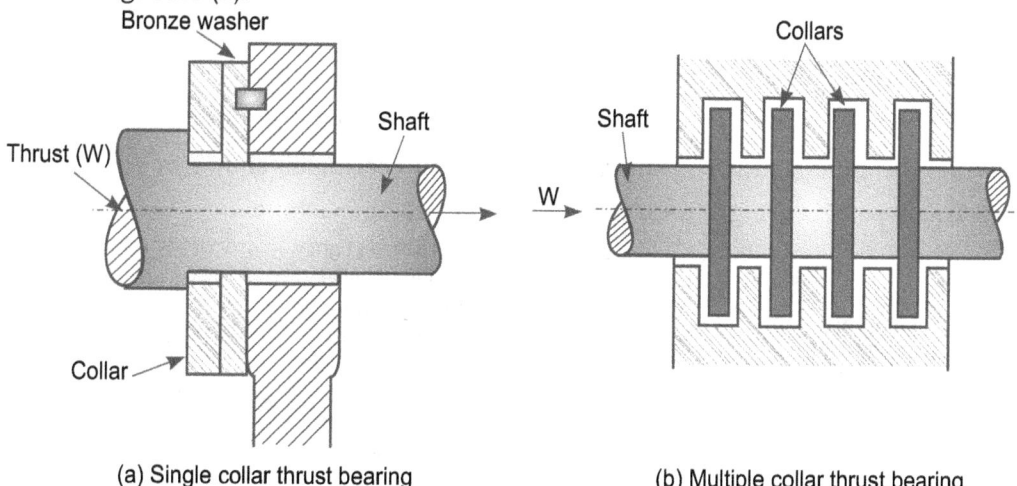

(a) Single collar thrust bearing   (b) Multiple collar thrust bearing

Fig. 5.15

Advantages and Disadvantages of Sliding Bearing over Roller Bearing :

Advantages :

1. Requires less space.
2. They are quieter in operation.
3. The cost is low.
4. It provides greater rigidity.

Disadvantages :

1. Higher power loss due to higher frictional losses.
2. More stringent lubrication requirements.
3. More susceptible to damage if foreign materials are carried in lubrication.
4. Less life because of fatigue action.

The common materials used for these types of bearings are babitt materials, cadmium alloys, bronze sintered materials and plastic.

[B] Roller Contact or Antifriction Bearings

In these type of bearings, the sliding motion between the contact surface is replaced by rolling motion between the mating members with the help of spherical balls or cylindrical rollers. Such arrangement reduces the frictional power loss considerably and increases the life of the bearings.

These bearings are further classified as ball bearings and roller bearings.

1. Radial Ball Bearing : A simplest type of ball bearing is shown in Fig. 5.16 (a). In this bearing, hardened steel balls are positioned between the two suitable grooves as shown in figure. The balls are retained in position in a cage as shown in figure. The balls can freely rotate in the races only when rolling friction exits.

This bearing helps in carrying large amount of load compared with slide bearings. For increasing load carrying capacity further, two rows of balls are used.

When the axial load is considerable, thrust ball bearing as shown in Fig. 5.16 (b) is used. This type of bearing is used with lathe and milling machine.

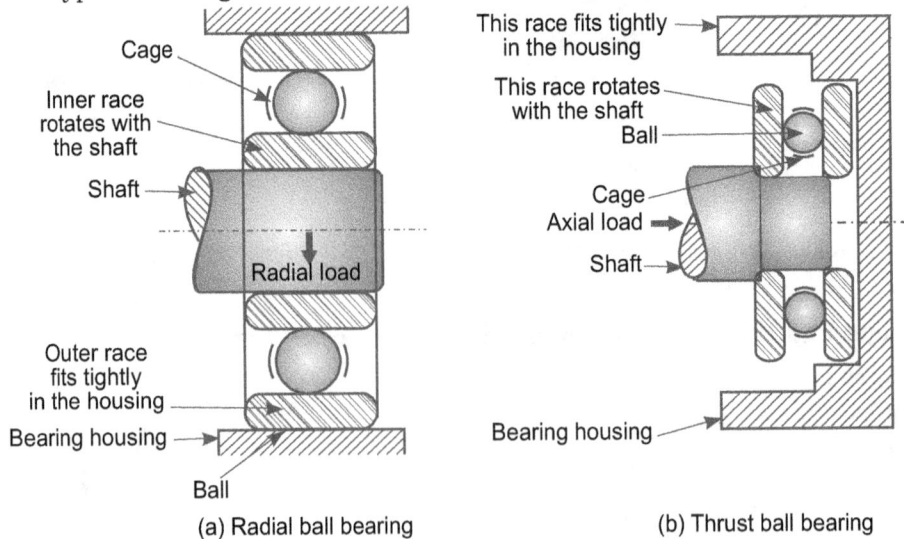

(a) Radial ball bearing   (b) Thrust ball bearing

Fig. 5.16

2. Roller Bearing : The configuration of this bearing is just similar to ball bearing except the balls are replaced by roller as shown in Fig. 5.17 (a). These bearings are better suited for heavy loads than the ball bearings as the contact is along a line instead of at a point in case of ball bearing. The number of rollers to be fitted depends upon the total load coming on the bearing.

When the load acting is of radial load and thrust load. then the tapered roller bearing is used as shown in Fig. 5.17 (b). It finds its application in machine tools and automobile industries.

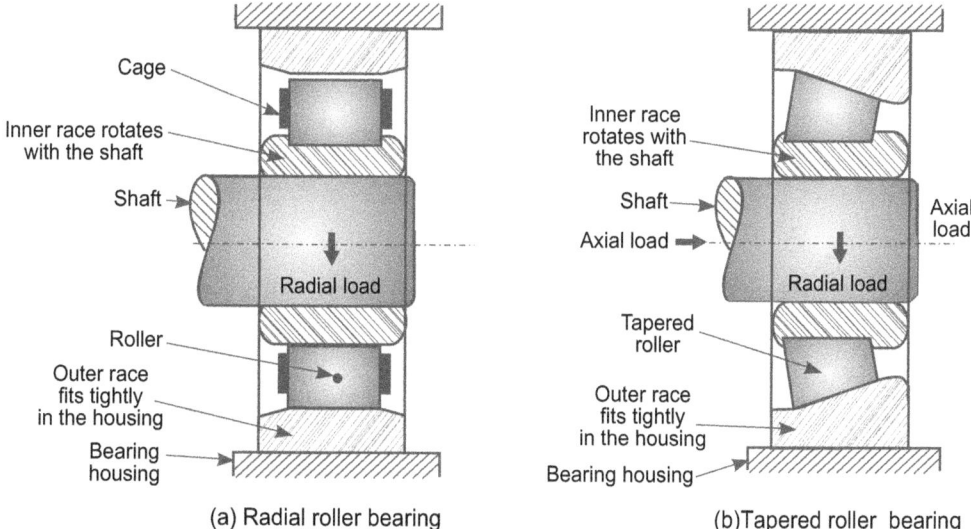

(a) Radial roller bearing   (b) Tapered roller bearing

Fig. 5.17

Advantages and Disadvantages of Rolling Bearings over Sliding Bearings

Advantages :

(a) Low friction loss even at high speed.

(b) It can withstand shock load.

(c) Maintenance cost is less as no lubrication is required.

(d) It is easy to mount and erect.

(e) Shaft alignment is perfect.

Disadvantages :

(a) Creates noise at high speed.

(b) Capital cost is high.

(c) Bearing housing design is complicated.

Bearing Materials :

The bearing materiales must possess high compression strength, high corrosion resistance, good thermal conductivity and resistance to wear. The materials used are classified as metallic and non-metallic. The metallic group includes brass, bronzes, zinc and babits material (alloy of aluminium with lead and tin). The non-metallic group includes plastic and graphites.

A few common materials used are listed below.

Material	Materials (% by weights)			Applications
Aluminium	Al 80 – 92	Sn 20 - 8		Diesel engines and air-craft engines.
Lead bronze	Cu 70	Pb 25	Sn 5	Small pumps and home appliances.
Phosphor bronze	Cu 80	Pb 10	Sn 10	Lathes, milling machines and high capacity pumps.
Babbit (tin base)	Sn 84	Cu 8	Sb 8	Electric motors.
Babbit (lead base)	Pb 75	Sn 10	Sb 15	Crank shaft bearings and electric motors.

5.5 BELT AND BELT DRIVES

The belt drives are generally used to transmit power from one shaft to another between the parallel shaft as shown in Fig. 5.18.

The belt drive consists of three elements - driving pulley mounted on driving shaft, driven pulley on driven shaft and a belt. The power is transmitted from driving pulley to driven pulley because of friction between the belt and pulley surface.

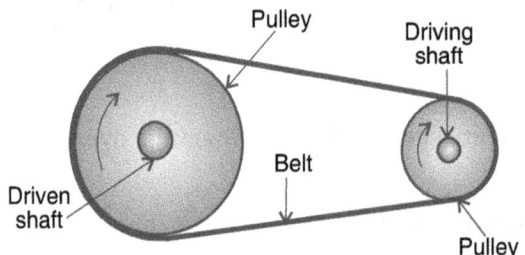

Fig. 5.18

The power transmitted from the driving to driven shaft depends upon the material of the belt, friction factor between the belt and pulley surfaces, the velocity of the belt, the arc of contact between the belt and smaller pulley and tension in the belt.

Classification of the Belt :

The belts are classified on the basis of material used for the belt as leather belt, rubber belt, fabric belt and Balata belt.

1. Leather Belts : These belts are used in both dry and wet weather conditions.

2. Rubber Belts : Rubber belts are preferred in chemical industries. They are used in saw mills and paper mills where they are exposed to moisture. They are not preferred where they are exposed to heat and oil because they are quickly destroyed. The advantage is, it can be easily made endless.

3. Fabric Belts : These belts are made from canvas or cotton and impregnated with linseed oil to make it water-proof. These can also be used in dry and wet atmosphere. They are preferred in farm-industry as they are cheaper.

4. Balata Belts : These belts are made from layers of fabric impregnated with balata gum. They are water-proof, acid-proof and are not affected by oils and alkalies. The only drawback of this belt is, it cannot withstand more than 40°C, therefore not preferred in dry-hot conditions.

The belts are further classified as per the cross-selection of the belt as flat belt, V-belt and rope belt as shown in Fig. 5.19.

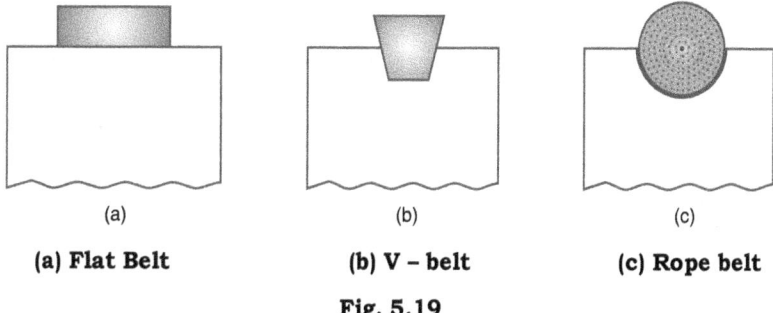

(a) Flat Belt   (b) V – belt   (c) Rope belt

Fig. 5.19

1. Flat Belt : It is used for transmitting small power from one pulley to another and their distance is not more than 8 m.

2. Vee Belt : This is generally used for transmitting large power. They are suitable for short distances only. The groove angle lies between 30° to 40°.

3. Ropes : They are made of cotton or steel and circular in cross-section. The advantage of rope drive is that the number of separate drives may be taken from one driving pulley. Steel ropes are preferred when large power is to be transmitted over long distance (100 - 150 m) as in mining, cranes, conveyors and suspension bridges.

Advantages and Disadvantages of Flat Belt :

Advantages :

    1. Its design is simple and it is relatively cheap.

    2. It can be easily repaired if broken.

    3. It can absorb shock and vibration as it is flexible.

    4. It can be used for considerably long distances (20 - 30 m).

    5. It can be used in abrasive atmosphere as in machine shop.

Disadvantages :

    1. It has always a slip.

    2. It cannot give constant velocity because of variable slip.

    3. It has short life and is not preferred for high speed ratio.

    4. It cannot transfer high power.

Advantages and disadvantages of V-belts :
Advantages :
1. It is compact drive as distance through which the power transmitted is less (5 m).
2. As the slip does not exist between the pulley groove and belt, it can provide constant velocity ratio.
3. The drive is smooth as it is endless and there is no joint trouble.
4. The operation is not noisy as flat belt as grip is better.
5. This belt can absorb shock easily particularly at starting.
6. It provides high velocity ratio (10) and also long life.

Disadvantages :
1. It cannot be used for transmitting power through large distances.
2. Repairing is difficult once breaks and generally it is to be replaced.
3. The construction of pulley and belt is complicated and costly also.
4. The life of this belt is very much influenced by changes in temperature, improper belt tension and mismatching of belt lengths.

Comparison between Flat and V-belts :

	Flat Belt	V-belt
1.	Used for distance upto 10 m.	Used for very small distance.
2.	Efficiency of transmission is low.	Efficiency of transmission is high.
3.	The construction is simple.	The construction is difficult and costly.
4.	These are cheaper in initial and repair costs.	They are costly as well as repair is not possible.
5.	Suitable for moderate power transmission.	Suitable for high power transmission.
6.	It cannot give constant velocity ratio because of slip.	It proves constant velocity as slip does not exist.

The belts are also classified according to its arrangement and they are discussed below.

1. Open Belt Drive : This is used when shafts are parallel. Rotation of both the shafts has same direction. This arrangement is shown in Fig. 5.20 (a).

2. Cross Belt Drive : This is used when the shafts are parallel and they rotate in opposite direction as shown in Fig. 5.20 (b).

Velocity Ratio of Belt Drives :

Let,
d_1 = diameter of the driver
d_2 = diameter of the follower
N_1 = speed of driver in r.p.m.
N_2 = speed of the follower in r.p.m.
ω_1 = Angular speed of the driver in rad/ sec.
ω_2 = Angular speed of the follower in rad/sec.

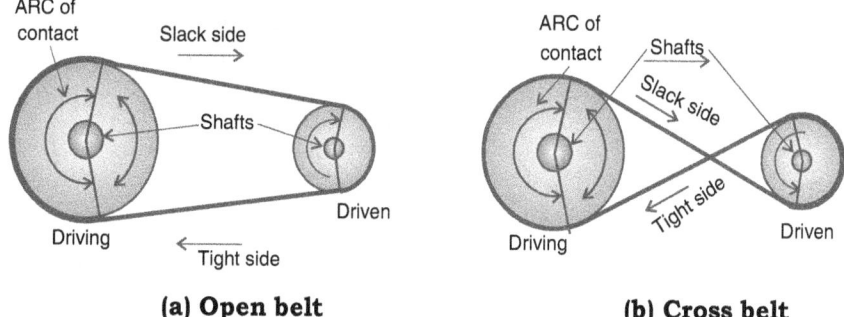

(a) Open belt   (b) Cross belt

Fig. 5.20 : Types of belt drives

Assuming that there is no slip between the belt and the pulley, the linear speed of the belt over the two pulleys must be the same.

$$\therefore \quad \pi d_1 N_1 = \pi d_2 N_2$$

or $\quad d_1 N_1 = d_2 N_2$

$$\therefore \quad \frac{N_2}{N_1} = \frac{d_1}{d_2} \qquad \ldots(5.1)$$

or $\quad \dfrac{\text{Speed of the follower}}{\text{Speed of the Driver}} = \dfrac{\text{Diameter of the driver}}{\text{Diameter of the follower}}$

Thus, in a belt drive, the speeds are inversely proportional to the diameters of the pulleys.

The ratio $\dfrac{N_2}{N_1}$ is called the velocity ratio of the drive.

Velocity ratio in terms of angular speed :

Angular speed of the driver, $\omega_1 = \dfrac{2\pi N_1}{60}$ rad/sec.

Angular speed of the driven, $\omega_2 = \dfrac{2\pi N_2}{60}$ rad./sec. or follower

Dividing, we get, $\quad \dfrac{N_2}{N_1} = \dfrac{\omega_2}{\omega_1} \qquad \ldots(5.2)$

Hence, from equations (5.1) and (5.2)

$$\frac{N_2}{N_1} = \frac{d_1}{d_2} = \frac{\omega_2}{\omega_1}$$

Effect of thickness of belt on the velocity ratio :

Let, $\quad t = $ Thickness of the belt

Then, $\quad \pi(d_1 + t)N_1 = \pi(d_2 + t)N_2$

Or $\quad \dfrac{N_2}{N_1} = \dfrac{d_1 + t}{d_2 + t}$

As the belt runs over the pulley, its outermost fibres are under tension and the innermost fibres are under compression. The section which is at the centre of the belt is neither under tension or compression and is called the neutral section.

Effect of slip on the velocity ratio : When the belt becomes loose, it does not have perfect contact over the pulley while transmitting the motion and the slip takes place between the belt and pulley. It causes a loss of motion and power.

Let S = Total percentage slip between the belt and driven pulley. Then the velocity ratio becomes

$$\frac{N_2}{N_1} = \frac{d_1}{d_2}\left(1 - \frac{S}{100}\right)$$

Combined effect of slip and thickness of belt on the velocity ratio : If the slip and thickness of the belt are taken into account, then the velocity ratio is given by

$$\frac{N_2}{N_1} = \frac{d_1 + t}{d_2 + t}\left(1 - \frac{S}{100}\right)$$

Compound drive : When the motion is transmitted from a pulley A to a pulley F through a number of intermediate pulley B, C, D, E) of which B and C, are fixed to one shaft and D and E fixed to an other then velocity ratio is

$$\frac{N_6}{N_1} = \frac{d_1}{d_2} \cdot \frac{d_3}{d_4} \cdot \frac{d_5}{d_6}$$

Here $d_1, d_2, d_3, \ldots d_6$ are the diameters of pulleys A, B, C, D, E, and F respectively and $N_1, N_2, N_3, \ldots N_6$ their speeds.

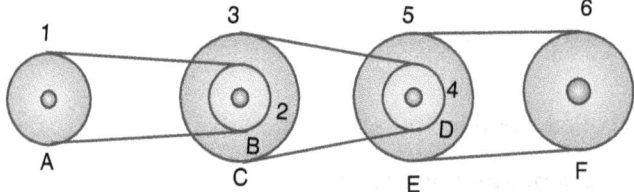

Fig. 5.21

Thus, in a compound drive,

$$\text{Velocity ratio} = \frac{\text{Product of diameter of the drivers}}{\text{Product of diameters of the followers}}$$

If the thickness of the belt is taken into account, then

$$\frac{N_6}{N_1} = \frac{(d_1 + t)}{(d_2 + t)} \cdot \frac{(d_3 + t)}{(d_4 + t)} \cdot \frac{(d_5 + t)}{(d_6 + t)}$$

The slip is also taken into account, then

$$\frac{N_6}{N_1} = \frac{(d_1 + t)}{(d_2 + t)} \cdot \frac{(d_3 + t)}{(d_4 + t)} \cdot \frac{(d_5 + t)}{(d_6 + t)} - \left(1 - \frac{S}{100}\right)$$

Where S being the percentage total slip at all the drives which is given by

$$\left(1 - \frac{S}{100}\right) = \left(1 - \frac{S_1}{100}\right)\left(1 - \frac{S_2}{100}\right)\left(1 - \frac{S_3}{100}\right)$$

and $\frac{S_1}{100}$ is the % slip between A and B, $\frac{S_2}{100}$ is the % slip between C and D,

And $\frac{S_3}{100}$ is the % slip between E and F.

Length of the Belts :

(1) Length of Open Belt : Let the two pulleys A and B are connected by an open drive as shown in Fig. 5.22.

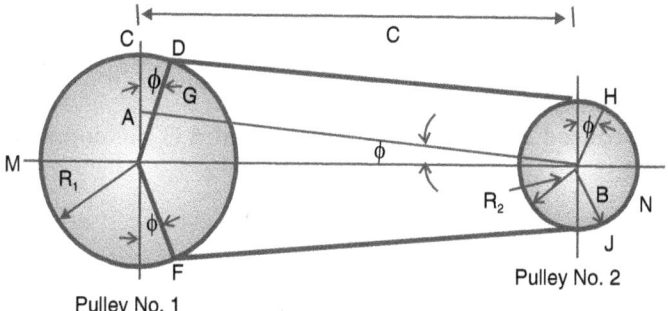

Fig. 5.22 : Length of open belt

Let R_1 = Radius of pulley A

R_2 = Radius of pulley B

C = centre distance between A and B

D and H are the points of contact of the belt on the upper side of the two pulleys. Angle CAD is represented by ϕ.

Then BG = HD = C· cos ϕ.

Length of belt $L = 2$ [arc MD + DH + arc HN]

$$= 2\left[\left(\frac{\pi}{2} + \phi\right) R_1 + BG + \left(\frac{\pi}{2} - \phi\right) R_2\right]$$

$$= 2\left[\frac{\pi}{2}(R_1 + R_2) + \phi(R_1 - R_2) + C \cdot \cos\phi\right]$$

$$= \pi(R_1 + R_2) + 2\phi(R_1 - R_2) + 2C \cdot \cos\phi \quad \ldots (5.3)$$

Where, $\phi = \sin^{-1} = \dfrac{R_1 - R_2}{2C^2}$

Equation (5.3) gives the exact length of the belt. If the two pulleys are nearly of the same diameters then ϕ will be very small.

∴ For small angle ϕ, $\sin\phi = \dfrac{R_1 - R_2}{C}$

And $\cos\phi = (1 + \sin^2\phi)^{1/2}$

$$\cong \left(1 + \frac{1}{2}\sin^2\phi\right) \quad \ldots \text{by Binomial theorem.}$$

$$= 1 + \frac{(R_1 - R_2)^2}{2C^2}$$

Putting this value of cos ϕ in equation (5.3)

$$L = \pi(R_1 + R_2) + \frac{2(R_1 - R_2)}{C}(R_1 - R_2) + 2C\left[1 + \frac{(R_1 - R_2)}{2C^2}\right]$$

$$= \pi(R_1 + R_2) + \frac{2(R_1 - R_2)^2}{C} - \frac{(R_1 - R_2)^2}{C} + 2C$$

$$= \pi(R_1 + R_2) + \frac{(R_1 - R_2)^2}{C} + 2C$$

(2) Length of Crossed Belt : Let the pulleys A and B are connected by crossed belt as shown in Fig. 5.23.

From B, draw a line BG parallel to JD to meet AD produced at G so that,

$$BG = JD = C \cdot \cos \phi$$

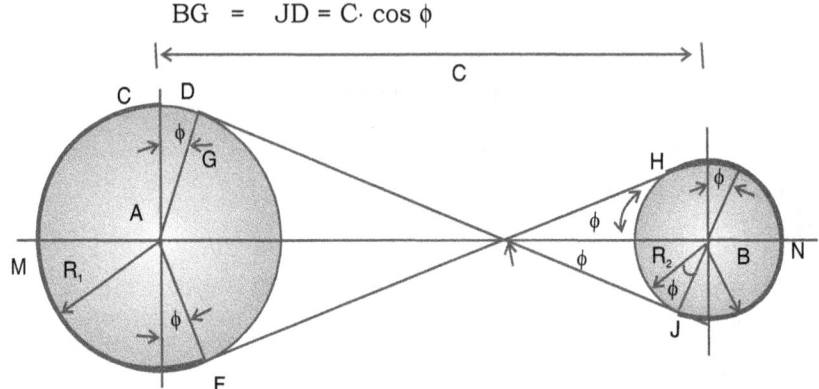

Fig. 5.23 : Length of crossed belt

∴ Length of the crossed belt,

$$\begin{aligned}
L &= 2\,[\text{arc MD} + DJ + \text{arc JN}] \\
&= 2\left[\left(\frac{\pi}{2} + \phi\right) R_1 + BG + \left(\frac{\pi}{2} + \phi\right) \cdot R_2\right] \\
&= 2\left[\left(\frac{\pi}{2} + \phi\right)(R_1 + R_2) + C \cdot \cos \phi\right] \\
&= (\pi + 2\phi)(R_1 + R_2) + 2C \cdot \cos \phi
\end{aligned}$$

where $\phi = \sin^{-1} \dfrac{R_1 + R_2}{C} = \dfrac{R_1 + R_2}{C}$ if ϕ is very small.

∴ Approximate length of the crossed belt is given by,

$$L = \left[\pi + 2\left(\frac{R_1 + R_2}{C}\right)\right](R_1 + R_2) + 2C\left[1 + \frac{(R_1 + R_2)^2}{2C^2}\right]$$

$$= \pi(R_1 + R_2) + \frac{(R_1 + R_2)^2}{C} + 2C$$

Ratio of Driving Tensions in a Belt : The ratio of driving tensions in a belt just on the point of slipping is given by,

$$\frac{T_1}{T_2} = e^{\mu\theta}$$

Where, T_1 and T_2 are the tensions in the belt on the tight and slack side respectively.

θ = Angle of contact of belt and pulley (in radians)

μ = Coefficient of friction for the belt on the pulley

e = base of the Napierian log = 2.718

Angle of Contact : In the case of open belt :

$$\text{Angle of contact, } \theta = \pi - 2 \sin^{-1}\left(\frac{R_1 - R_2}{C}\right) \text{ radians,}$$

In the case of crossed belt :

$$\text{Angle of contact, } \theta = \pi + 2 \sin^{-1}\left(\frac{R_1 + R_2}{C}\right) \text{ radians.}$$

Power Transmitted by a Belt : Due to the difference in tensions, the belt exerts a force $F = (T_1 - T_2)$ on the pulley in Newton. If V is the linear speed of the pulley in metres/sec., then,

$$\text{Work done per sec.} \quad W = F \times V = (T_1 - T_2) \cdot V$$
$$V = \pi D_1 N_1 = \pi D_2 N_2$$
$$\therefore \quad \text{Power transmitted} = \frac{(T_1 - T_2) V}{1000} \text{ kW}$$

Centrifugal Tension in the Belt (T_c) : When the belt starts moving then the centrifugal force acts on the belt and tends to lift the belt from the pulley. Therefore, the tension on the tight side as well as slag side will increase. In this case,

$$T_{t1} = T_1 + T_c$$
$$T_{t2} = T_2 + T_c$$

Where, $\quad T_c = mV^2$

Where m is the mass of belt in kg/m length of the belt and V is linear velocity of the belt in m/s.

Note : When V < (10 m/s) then Te can be neglected.

Initial Tension in the Belt (T_i) : The ends of the belt passing over two pulleys must be joined. In order to maintain a firm grip between the pulley and belt, the two ends of the belt are pulled. Such an initial pull maintained in the belt at the time of joining the ends is known as **Initial Tension (T_i)**.

$$\therefore \quad T_i = \frac{T_1 + T_2}{2} \text{ (Neglecting } T_C\text{)}$$
$$= \frac{T_1 + T_2 + 2T_c}{2} \text{ (Considering } T_C\text{)}$$

(3) Slip of Belt : It is the difference between the velocity of belt and the peripheral velocity of pulley. The slip occurs due to insufficient frictional grip between the belt and surface of pulley. Generally, Slip is expressed in percentage.

Let $\quad S_1$ = Percentage slip between driver and belt

$\quad S_2$ = Percentage slip between belt and follower

First, slip 'S_1' occurs in the driving pulley and belt. Here velocity of belt reduces due to 's_1'.

This belt then drives the follower. The velocity of follower reduces due to slip between belt and follower 'S_2'.

∴ Velocity of the belt passing over the driver pulley,

$$v = \frac{\pi d_1 N_1}{60} - \left(\frac{\pi d_1 N_1}{60} \times \frac{S_1}{100}\right)$$

$$v = \frac{\pi d_1 N_1}{60}\left(1 - \frac{S_1}{100}\right) \quad \ldots (1)$$

Velocity of follower pulley,

$$\frac{\pi d_2 N_2}{60} = v - \frac{vS_2}{100} = \left(1 - \frac{S_2}{100}\right) \quad \ldots (2)$$

From equation (1)

$$\frac{\pi d_2 N_2}{60} = \frac{\pi d_1 N_1}{60}\left(1 - \frac{S_1}{100}\right)\left(1 - \frac{S_2}{100}\right)$$

$$\frac{N_2}{N_1} = \frac{d_1}{d_2}\left[\left(1 - \frac{S_1}{100}\right)\left(1 - \frac{S_2}{100}\right)\right]$$

$$= \frac{d_1}{d_2}\left[1 - \frac{S_1}{100} - \frac{S_2}{100}\right] \text{ Neglecting } \frac{S_1 \times S_2}{100 \times 100}$$

$$\frac{N_2}{N_1} = \frac{d_1}{d_2}\left[1 - \frac{(S_1 + S_2)}{100}\right]$$

$$\boxed{\therefore \frac{N_2}{N_1} = \frac{d_1}{d_2}\left(1 - \frac{S}{100}\right)} \text{ where } S = S_1 + S_2 = \text{total Slip \%}$$

If thickness of the belt is considered,

$$\boxed{\frac{N_2}{N_1} = \frac{d_1 + t}{d_2 + t}\left(1 - \frac{S}{100}\right)}$$

(4) Creep of Belt : When the belt passes from the slack side to the tight side, certain part of the belt expands (elongates) and it contract when the belt passes from the tight to the slack side. Because of changes of length, there is a relative motion between the belt and pulley. This relative motion is termed as creep. The net effect of creep is to reduce the speed of driven pulley or follower. This reduction in speed of follower is very small.

Velocity ration, considering the creep of belt is given by

$$\boxed{\frac{N_2}{N_1} = \frac{d_1}{d_2}\frac{(E + \sqrt{\alpha_2})}{(E + \sqrt{\alpha_1})}}$$

Where
- α_1 = Stress in tight side of belt
- α_2 = Stress in slack side of belt
- E = Young's Modulus of belt material

5.6 CHAIN DRIVE

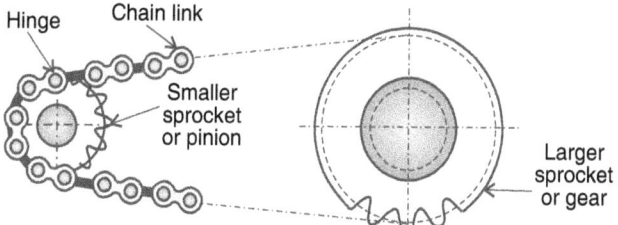

Fig. 5.24 : Chain Drive

The chains are made of number of rigid links which are hinged together by pin joints round the driving and driven wheels as shown in Fig. 5.24. The toothed wheels are known as sprocket. The chains are commonly used for transmitting motion and power from one shaft to another when centre distance between the driving and driven shaft is small and 100 % positive power transmission is essential. The chains are used in bicycles, motorcycles, conveyors, rolling mills and road rollers.

Advantages and Disadvantages of Chain Drives

Advantages :

1. There is zero slip and therefore constant velocity ratio is obtained.
2. This is used for short and long distances also.
3. Its transmission efficiency is high (98- 99%).
4. It transmits large power compared with belts.
5. It operates under any environmental conditions as it is made of metal.

Disadvantages :

1. The production cost is high as well as repair cost also.
2. It requires very accurate mounting.
3. It creates more noise than belt drives.

5.7 GEAR DRIVES

A gear is defined as a machine element used to transmit motion and power between the two rotating shafts by means of progressively meshing teeth.

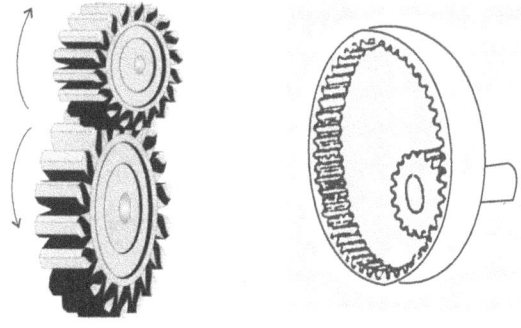

(a) External gearing   (b) Internal gearing

Fig. 5.25

There are different types of gears used to suit various applications. The gear drives transmit power between two shafts when their axes are parallel, intersecting or neither parallel nor intersecting. The different types of gears used in practice are discussed here.

1. Spur Gears : These gears are used to transmit the power and motion when the shafts are parallel to each other. The speed ratio lies upto 1 : 8. The gearing can be external or internal meshing as shown in Fig. 5.25. These are very commonly used in machine tools and automobile gear boxes.

As the spur gears are very commonly used in practice, it is expected that the students should know the terminology used with this gear. The gear with different terminologies of different geometry is shown in Fig. 5.25.

The terms are defined as follows :

(i) Pitch Circle and Pitch Circle Diameter : It is an imaginary circle which can be produced by rolling action. Pitch diameter is the diameter of the pitch circle. The gear size is specified by pitch circle diameter.

Circular pitch is distance of a point on a tooth to the corresponding point on the next adjustment tooth along the pitch circle.

(A) ∴ Circular Pitch, $P_c = \dfrac{\pi D_1}{T_1} = \dfrac{\pi D_2}{T_2}$ ...(5.1)

Or $\dfrac{D_1}{D_2} = \dfrac{T_1}{T_2}$

Where, D_1 and D_2 are two different pitch diameters and T_1 and T_2 are number of teeth on those diameters.

(B) Diametal pitch is defined as the ratio of number of teeth to pitch circle diameter.

$$P_d = \dfrac{T}{D}$$ ...(5.2)

∴ From equations (5.1) and (5.2) we get

$$P_c \cdot P_d = \pi$$ ...(5.3)

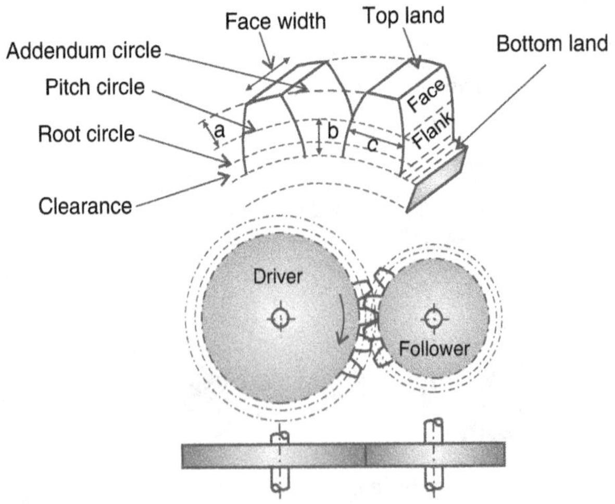

Fig. 5.26 : Spur Gears

(ii) Module : It is the ratio of pitch circle diameter in mm to the number of teeth.

$$\therefore \text{Module, } m = \frac{D}{T} \qquad \ldots(5.4)$$

From equations (5.4) and (5.5), $m = \frac{P_c}{\pi}$

$$P_c = \pi m \qquad \ldots(5.5)$$

(iii) Addendum and Addendum Circle : Addendum is the radial distance of the tooth from pitch circle to the top of the tooth and addendum circle is the circle passing through the top of the teeth and concentric to the pitch circle.

(iv) Dedendum and Dedendum Circle : Dedendum is the radial distance of the tooth from the pitch circle to the bottom of the tooth and dedendum circle is the circle passing through the bottom of the teeth and concentric to the pitch circle.

(v) Width of Tooth Space : It is the length of an arc between two adjacent teeth at pitch circle.

(vi) Tooth Thickness : It is the width of tooth measured along the pitch circle. The difference between tooth space and tooth thickness is known as Backlash.

(vii) Face of Tooth : It is the surface of tooth above pitch surface and face width is the width of tooth face measured parallel to gear axis.

(viii) Flank of Tooth : It is the surface of tooth below pitch surface.

(ix) Profile : It is the curve formed by the face and flank of the tooth. It can be involute or cycloid.

(x) Path of Contact : It is the path traced by the contact point of two teeth from the beginning to the end of engagement.

2. Helical Gears : In this gear also, the shafts are parallel to each other as shown in- Fig. 5.27, except the teeth are cut in the form of helix. The matting gears have the same helix angle, but one gear has right handed helix, while the other gear has left handed helix. A speed ratio can be obtained upto 1 : 12. The advantage of this gearing is that their engagement is shock-free and operation is silent. These are generally used in power transmission system of automobiles.

This gear transfers large load at higher speed and very smoothly compared with spur gear. The disadvantages are high manufacturing cost, difficult to manufacture and imposes radial as well as axial thrust on the shaft.

3. Spiral Gears : This is generally used when the shafts are not parallel and non-intersecting also as shown in Fig. 5.27. In this type of gearing system, a left hand helical. gear can mesh with right hand helical gear or with left hand helical gear and the helix angles of both the gears may be of different values.

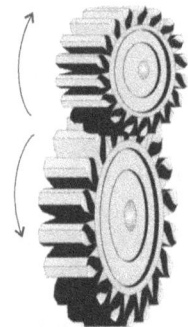

Fig. 5.27

These are used to transmit small power from one shaft to another shaft. They are used to drive camshafts and oil pumps used with I.C. engines.

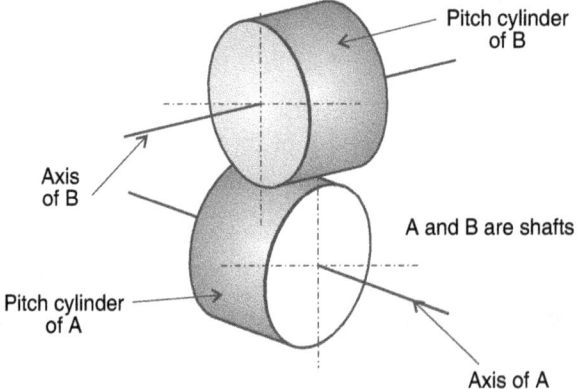

Fig. 5.28 : Spiral gears

4. Bevel Gears : The bevel gears are used when the shafts are intersecting with each.

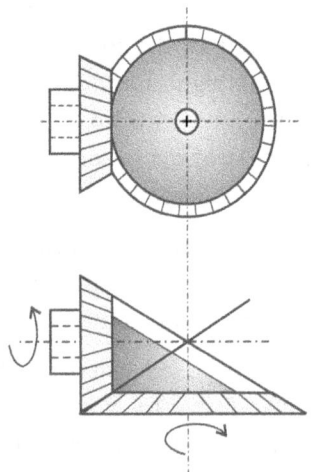

Fig. 5.29 : Bevel gears are used to transmit rotary motion between intersecting shafts

other and coplanar. These gears have the shape of truncated cone as shown in Fig. 5.29. The bevel gears are used when the shaft axes are at right angles to each other. The bevel gear can be cut straight for low speed purposes and spiral teeth for high speed applications. It can transmit power from one shaft to another when the intersecting angle is 90° or less or more than 90° also. They are difficult to manufacture and cost is more.

5. Rack and Pinion : This is a special case of a spur gears where the rack is a straight sided gear and pinion is a spur gear as shown in Fig. 5.30. The system transmits the rotary motion of pinion into translatory motion of rack or vice versa. This arrangement is used with diesel engine to change the helical space to be filled by the oil according to the load on the engine as well as in lathe where rack transmits the motion to the saddle.

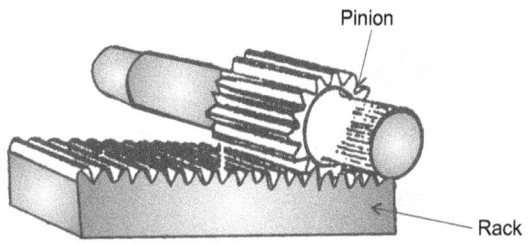

Fig. 5.30 : Rack and Pinion

6. Worm Gear : In this arrangement, the axes of two gears do not intersect and their axes are at right angles and non-coplanar as shown in Fig. 5.31. The smaller gear (driving gear) is called worm and larger gear (driven gear) is known as worm wheel.

These gears are used for transmitting power when the reduction in speed ratio is as. high as 100 : 1 with single stage. The ratio is 100 : 1, means when worm completes one rotation, the worm wheel rotates by only one tooth or when worm completes 100 rotations, the worm wheel rotates through one rotation only.

This is generally used for cranes (lifting purposes), machine tools and material handling equipments.

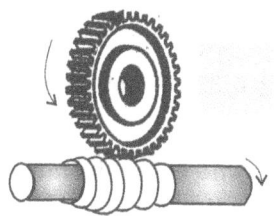

Fig. 5.31 : Worm and Worm wheel

Advantages and Disadvantages of Gear Drives over Other Drives :

Advantages :

1. It provides constant velocity ratio as it is positive drive.

2. It transmits more power than other systems.

3. Its transmission efficiency is high.

4. It transmits power with very low velocity.

5. It requires minimum space as it is compact in size.

Disadvantages :

1. This system requires lubrication for smooth working.

2. Its manufacturing cost is considerably high and manufacturing is also complicated.

Types of Gear Trains : Different types of gear trains in use are discussed below :

(i) Simple gear train.

(ii) Compound gear train.

(1) Simple Gear Train :

An arrangement of such gear train (with 3 gears) is shown in Fig. 5.32. In this type of gear trains these is only one gear on each shaft. Take N_1, N_2, N_3 are the speeds of gears 1, 2 and 3 respectively and number of teeth on respective gear is T_1, T_2 and T_3.

As gears 1 and 2 are engaged with each other, then their speed ratio is given by,

$$\frac{N_2}{N_1} = \frac{T_1}{T_2}$$

Similarly, for gears 2 and 3 we can also write

$$\frac{N_3}{N_2} = \frac{T_2}{T_3}$$

From the above two equations, we can write

$$\frac{N_2}{N_1} \times \frac{N_3}{N_2} = \frac{T_1}{T_2} \times \frac{T_2}{T_3}$$

$$\therefore \quad \frac{N_3}{N_1} = \frac{T_1}{T_3} = \frac{\text{Number of teeth on driver}}{\text{Number of teeth on follower}}$$

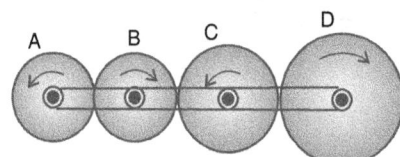

Fig. 5.32 : Simple Gear Train

(2) Compound Gear Train :

When there are more gears on one shaft as shown in Fig. 5.33 then such gear train is known as compound gear train.

Consider N_1 and T_1 are the speed (rpm) and number of teeth on the driven gear.

N_2, N_3, N_4 and T_2, T_3, T_4 are the speeds (rpm) and number of teeth on the respective gears.

Then speed ratio for gears 1 & 2 is given,

$$\frac{N_2}{N_1} = \frac{T_2}{T_1}$$

Similarly, for gears 3 and 4 we can write,

$$\frac{N_4}{N_3} = \frac{T_3}{T_2}$$

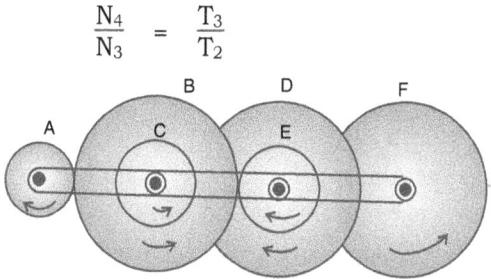

Fig. 5.33 : Compound Gear Train

The speed ratio of the gear train can be obtained by multiplying above two equations as :

$$\frac{N_2}{N_1} \times \frac{N_4}{N_3} = \frac{T_1}{T_2} \times \frac{T_3}{T_4}$$

∴ $\quad\dfrac{N_4}{N_1} = \dfrac{T_1}{T_2} \times \dfrac{T_3}{T_4}$ As $N_2 = N_3$

∴ $\quad$ Speed Ratio $= \dfrac{\text{Speed of the last follower}}{\text{Speed of the first driver}}$

(3) Epicyclic Gear Train :

When these is relative motion of axis in the given gear train, the gear train is known as Epicyclic gear train. In this system, the axis of at least one of the gears also move relative to the frame.

The arrangement of this type of train is shown in Fig. 5.34. Consider two gears wheels B and C, whose axes are connected by an arm A. Assume the wheel B is fixed and arm A rotates about axis of gear B, then gear C will also move around B along with arm. This is known as epicyclic as wheel C moves outside another wheel B and follow epicyclic path. This is generally used where large reduction in speed is essential.

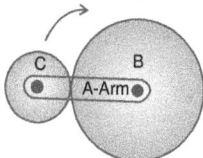

Fig. 5.34 : Epicyclic Gear Train

Part B

5.8 INTRODUCTION TO AIR COMPRESSORS

Compressed air is widely used in industry and in commercial equipments. It is very commonly used for the operation of pneumatic drills, riveters, hammers, hoists, paint spraying and many other operations. It is also used for starting I.C. engines and for supercharging. Some other applications of compressed air are in pneumatic tyres, lift gates, air lift pumps and glass blowing. The compressors are mainly divided as reciprocating and rotary compressors. The reciprocating compressors are mainly used where small quantity of air at high pressure is needed (even 100 bar) and rotary (mainly centrifugal). Compressors are mainly used where large air quantities are needed at considerably lower pressure (2 bar)

Reciprocating compressors are used in chemical industries, fertilizer plants, refrigeration industry and metallurgical industry. They are used to compress air, gas or vapour. Rotary compressors are mainly used in Gas-Turbine power plants.

The object of an air compressor is to raise the pressure of air with the minimum amount of energy. An air compressor sucks air from the atmosphere, compresses it and delivers the same to the storage tank. From the storage tank, it is conveyed by the pipelines where the supply of compressed air is needed. A compressor has to be driven by some prime mover (diesel engine, electric motor) as compression of air requires some work to be done on it.

5.8.1 Working of Single-Stage Reciprocating Air Compressor

A reciprocating compressor consists of a cylinder, piston, crank shaft, connecting rod, inlet and outlet valves as shown in Fig. 5.36. During the downward motion of the piston, the pressure inside the cylinder falls below the atmospheric pressure and the spring loaded inlet valve is opened due to the pressure difference. The air is drawn into the cylinder until the piston reaches the bottom dead centre position.

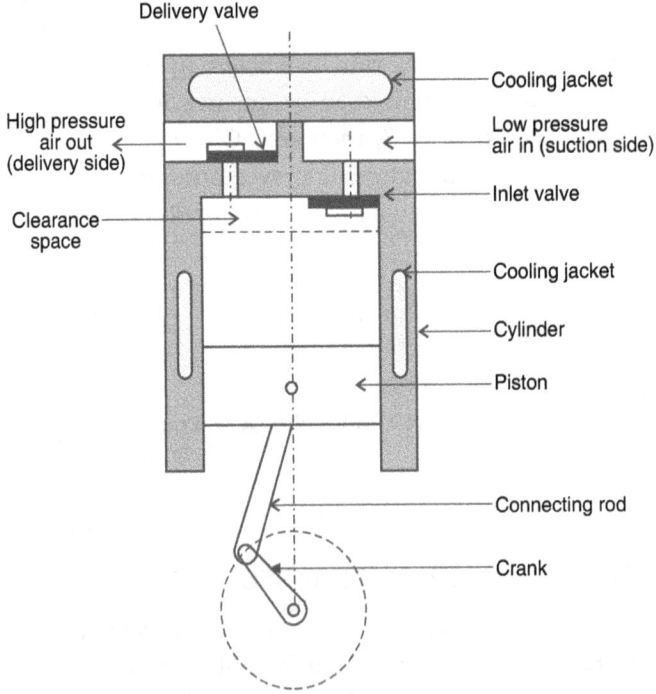

Fig. 5.36 : Single Stage Compressor

As the piston starts moving upwards, the inlet valve is closed and the pressure starts increasing continuously until the pressure inside the cylinder is above the pressure of the delivery side which is connected to the receiver. Then the delivery valve opens and air is delivered to the receiver during the remaining upward motion of the piston. At the end of the delivery stroke, a small volume of high pressure air is left in the clearance space. The high pressure air left in the clearance expands as the piston starts moving downwards and the pressure of the air falls until It is just below the atmospheric pressure. The inlet valve then opens as the pressure inside the cylinder falls below atmospheric pressure and the air from atmosphere is taken in and the cycle is repeated. The suction, compression and delivery of air takes place within two strokes of the piston or one revolution of the crank. The suction takes place during one stroke and compression and delivery take place during the second stroke.

5.8.2 Classification of Reciprocating Air Compressor

1. **Single Acting – Single Cylinder Compressor :** The arrangement is shown in Fig. 5.37 (a). In this compressor, the air is taken in at pressure P_1 and compressed to the required pressure and delivered to the receiver at a higher pressure (P_2). The delivery is once in one revolution of the compressor.

2. **Single Cylinder – Double Acting Air Compressor :** The arrangement is shown in Fig. 5.37 (b). In this case, the top and bottom of the piston are used for suction, compression and delivery of the air. Therefore, delivery is twice in one revolution of the compressor and the mass of air delivered is twice the mass of air delivered by single acting-single cylinder compressor.

3. **Single Acting, Multicylinder Compressor :** The arrangement is shown in Fig. 5.37 (c). It consist of 'n' number of cylinders mounted on the same shaft and each cylinder works similar to single cylinder compressor. The mass delivered by the compressor is 'n' times the mass delivered by single cylinder compressor.

The arrangement can be made as double acting for each cylinder. The purpose of this arrangement is to deliver more quantity of air at the same pressure.

4. **Multistage Compressor :** The arrangement is shown in Fig. 5.37 (d). This is generally used when the required delivery pressure (P_3) is considerably high.

The delivery of the first cylinder becomes the suction of the second cylinder as shown in Fig. 5.37 (d). The diameter of the second cylinder (d) is less than the first cylinder (D) as the mass of air in the second cylinder occupies less volume than the volume occupied in the first cylinder by the same mass as $P_2 > P_1$.

The following terminology is commonly used with air compressor.

1. **Pressure Ratio :** It is the ratio of delivery pressure to the suction pressure. For single stage compressor. It is (P_2/P_1) and two stage compressor, it is (P_3/P_1).

2. **Displacement of the Compressor :** The swept volume of the single cylinder is known as displacement volume and it is $\frac{\pi}{4} D^2 L$, where, D is diameter and L is stroke.

The swept volume of the first cylinder in two stage compressor is $\frac{\pi}{4} D^2 L$ and the swept volume of the second stage is $\frac{\pi}{4} d^2 L$.

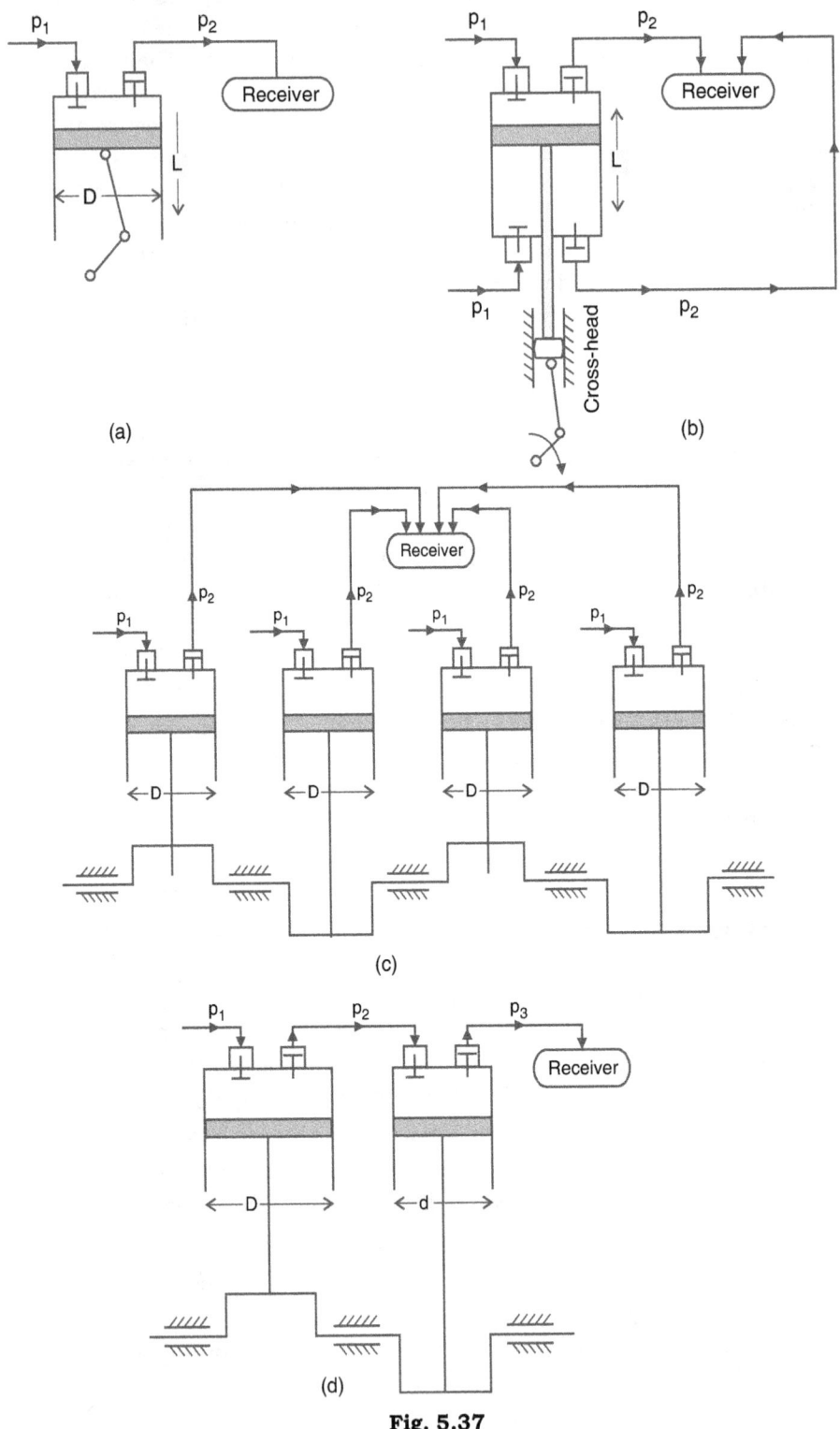

Fig. 5.37

3. Free Air Delivered : The inlet and outlet conditions for different compressors (single stage or multi-stage) are always different. For example, the inlet condition of air (P_1, T_1) at Simla is different from the inlet condition at Delhi. Similarly, the delivery pressure depends upon the requirement and pressure ratio for which the compressor is designed. Therefore, it is common practice to specify the compressor by volume at atmospheric conditions or it is also known as Free-Air-Delivery (FAD).

4. Size and strength of cylinders can be adjusted to suit the pressure of air in L.P. and H.P. cylinders. This reduces the overall cost of the compressor.

5. Effective lubrication is possible due to lower temperature range.

6. The loss of air leakage is less as the pressure range is reduced in each cylinder.

5.8.3 Rotary Compressors

Air compressors are classified as reciprocating and rotary type. The reciprocating types are mainly used for high pressure ratio and comparatively small volume of air supplied as compared with rotary compressors.

In reciprocating compressors, the pressure is increased by means of variation in the volume of cylinder with the help of of moving piston.

Rotary compressors are further classified as positive displacement type and dynamic type. In positive displacement type, the air is entrapped between two sets of engaging surfaces and the pressure rise is either by back flow of air (root blower) or by squeezing action and back flow of air (vane type). In dynamic type air compressor, the air is not trapped in specified boundaries but it flows continuously through the compressor. The energy from the impeller is transferred to the air as the air flows through the machine and the rise in pressure is primarily due to dynamic effects. The rotary compressors are generally preferred where large quantity of air at moderate pressure is required.

1. Centrifugal Compressors : Centrifugal compressors are used to supply large quantities of air but at a lower pressure ratios. It consists of a rotating impeller, diffuser and casing is as shown in Fig. 5.38.

The impeller consists of a disc on which radial blades are attached. Centrifugal compressors can run at as high speed as 20,000 to 30,000 r.p.m. The diffuser is the other important part of the compressor which surrounds the impeller and provides diverging passages for air flow thus increasing the air pressure. The air coming out from the diffuser is collected in the casing and taken out from the outlet of the compressor.

Air enters the eye of the compressor at low velocity and atmospheric pressure. The air moves radially outward passing through the impeller and is guided by the impeller vanes. The impeller increases the momentum of the air flowing through it, causing a rise in pressure and temperature of the air. The air leaving the impeller enters the diffuser where its velocity is reduced by providing more cross-sectional area for the air flow. Part of the kinetic energy of the air is converted into pressure energy and pressure of the air is further increased.

Nearly half of the total pressure rise is achieved in the impeller and remaining half in the diffuser. A pressure ratio of 4 can be achieved with single stage centrifugal compressor. For higher pressure ratios, multistage compressors are used. In multistage compressors, the outlet of the first stage is passed to the second stage and so on. A pressure ratio of 12 is possible with multistage centrifugal compressors.

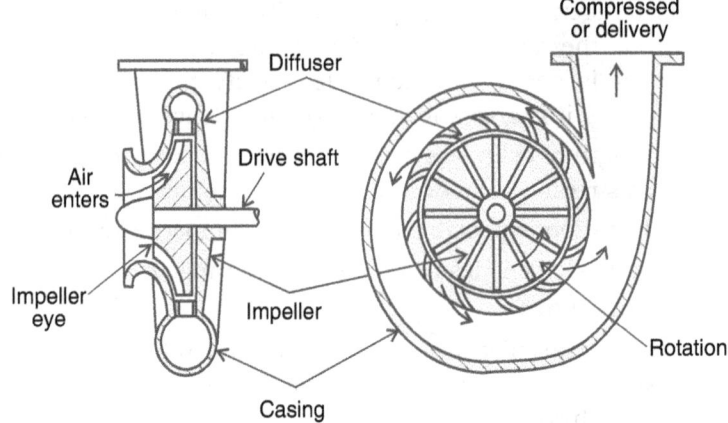

Fig. 5.38 : Centrifugal Compressor

2. **Axial Flow Compressor :** In axial flow compressors, the air essentially flows parallel to the axis of the shaft. It consists of a number of rotating blade rows fixed on a rotating drum and stator blade rows fixed on casing as shown in Fig. 5.39.

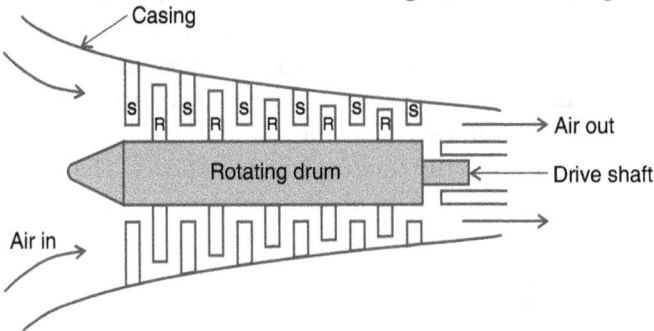

Note: S means stationary & R means rotating

Fig. 5.39 : Axial Flow Compressor

Each stage consists of one moving row of blades and one fixed row of blades. The enthalpy and pressure of air rise as it passes through the rotating blades. This happens at the expense of a reduction in relative velocity of the air. The absolute velocity of the air increases along the axis of the rotor due to the work input. This increase in kinetic energy is partly converted into the pressure energy as the air passes through the diverging stator blades. Fixed blades also help to guide the air into the next stage of rotating blades to reduce the losses caused by shock.

The blades are made of aerofoil section to reduce the losses caused by turbulence and boundary separation.

This type of compressor can give a pressure ratio of 1.2 and 1.3 per stage. A pressure ratio upto 10 can be obtained by using multistage. The number of stages used vary from 4 to 16. These compressors are commonly used in gas turbine plants and aeroplane systems.

3. Root Blower : The arrangement of this blower is shown in Fig. 5.40. It consists of two rotors, rotating in opposite directions. The lobes of the rotors are of epicycloid, hypocycloid or involute profiles because this ensures correct mating. The high pressure side of the compressor is sealed from low pressure side. forall angular positions of the rotors. A small clearance is provided between the rotors and the cylinder surface to reduce wear. The leakage through this clearance increases with increasing pressure ratio and reduces the efficiency of the compressor.

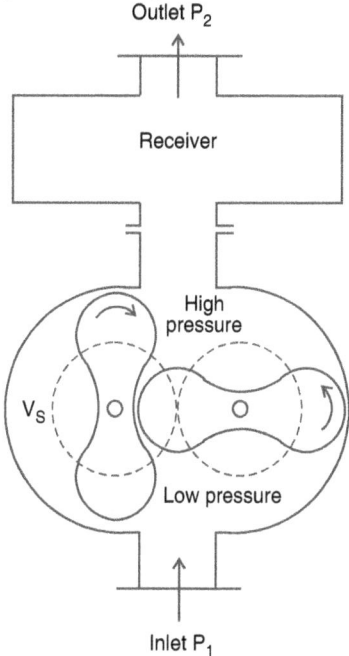

Fig. 5.40 : Root Blower

The volume of air V_s at atmospheric pressure P_1, is entrapped between the left hand rotor and casing. The volume of the air once entrapped does not decrease from entry to exit and therefore pressure is not developed till the exit port is uncovered. As the exit port opens, some high pressure air from receiver will rush back and mix with the air volume V_1 irreversibly until the pressure is equalized. The resulting pressure after mixing will be receiver pressure P_2 if the volume of receiver is assumed large. The air is then transferred to receiver. This happens four times in one revolution in case of two lobed rotor and six times in case of three lobed rotor.

Root blowers are designed to supply air from 0.15 m³/min to about 1500 m³/min and pressure ratios in the order of 1 to 5.6 for single stage machines. The maximum rotational speed used is 12500 r.p.m.

4. Vane Type Blower : It consists of a rotor located eccentrically in a cylindrical outer casing. The rotor carries a set of spring-loaded vanes in the slots of the rotor as shown in Fig. 5.41. The volume of air V_1 at atmospheric pressure P_1 is entrapped between two vanes as in root blower. As the rotation proceeds, the entrapped air is first compressed reversibly from condition V_a to V_d as the compression takes place due to the decrease in volume provided for the entrapped air. Then the air is compressed from the pressure P_1 to P_2 irreversibly. This irreversible compression is just similar to the compression as explained in root blower.

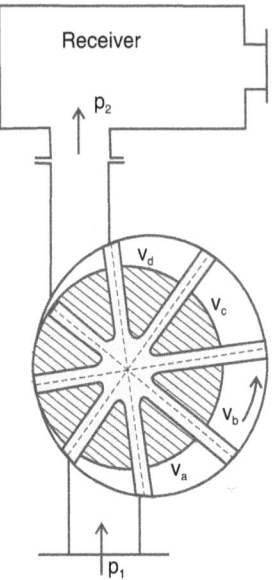

Fig. 5.41 : Vane Blower

5.8.4 Comparison between Reciprocating and Centrifugal Compressor

Ths differences between two types of compressors are tabulated in the following lable.

Reciprocating Compressor	Rotary Compressor
1. Provides low discharge at high pressure (100 to 500 Bar).	1. Provides large discharge at low pressure (5 to 6 bar).
2. The speed of compressor is low (200 to 500 rpm) because of balancing problem.	2. The speed is high enough (1000 to 5000 rpm) as there is no balancing problem.
3. The lubrication is complicated and costly.	3. Lubrication system is very simple.
4. There is no continuous air supply.	4. Air supply is continuous.
5. The size and weight are considerably higher than centrifugal compressor.	5. The size and weight are considerably small for the given discharge.
6. Air is contaminated as it comes in contact with lubricating oil.	6. The air is considerably clean as it does not come in contact with lubricating oil.

5.8.5 Uses of Compressed Air

The compressed air is used for many industrial and commercial purposes as listed.
1. Compressed air is used to charge the automobile tyres.
2. It is also used for air-washing the vehicles in the service stations.
3. It is used in operating lifts and hoists.

4. It is used for operating air brakes in automobiles and locomotives.
5. It is used in spray-painting.
6. It is used for supercharging the I.C. engines as supercharging increases the power generating capacity.
7. It is very commonly used in sand blasting industries.
8. It is used in pneumatic hammers and drills which are commonly used in coal mines as using the electric power or thermal power to operate these machines in mines is dangerous because any spark may blast the gas pockets in the mines.
9. It is used in air-lifted pumps to pump the water from deep-bores.

(B) WATER PUMPS

5.9 INTRODUCTION TO PUMPS

These are hydraulic machines which convert mechanical energy into hydraulic energy. It is immaterial, whether that energy is utilized for lifting purposes or for increasing the pressure. Pumps are driven by prime mover which can be I.C. engine, steam engine or an electric motor.

In most of the cases, pump is used for raising liquids from a lower to a higher level. This is achieved by creating a low pressure at the inlet or suction end and high pressure at the delivery end or outlet of the pump.

The pumps are mainly classified as :
1. Positive displacement or reciprocating pumps.
2. Centrifugal pumps.

5.9.1 Reciprocating Pumps

It consists of a piston or a plunger reciprocating inside a cylinder. The piston performs the suction and delivery strokes. These types of pumps deliver the required quantity of liquid against any head. A reciprocating pump works at low speed.

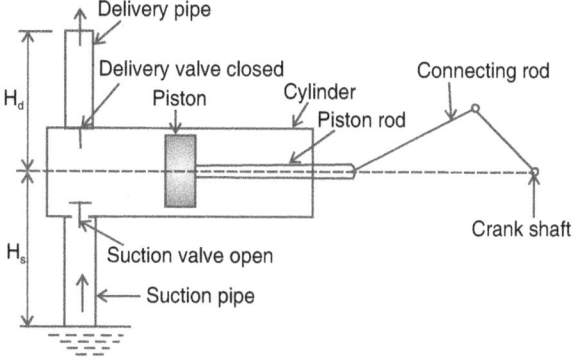

Fig. 5.42 : Single acting piston pump

Piston pump : A piston pump maybe single acting or double acting. A single acting piston pump is shown in Fig. 5.42.

As the piston moves outwards (towards right in the figure) partial vacuum will be created inside the cylinder. The atmospheric pressure acting on the surface of the liquid, forces the liquid through the suction pipe into the cylinder. Liquid will enter the cylinder through the suction valve which will open into it.

When the piston moves backwards (inward stroke) the piston will compress the liquid in the cylinder and the pressure of the liquid will rise. This increased pressure of the liquid will automatically close the suction valve and open the delivery valve and the liquid will be pushed through the delivery pipe.

Double Acting Piston Pump : In double acting piston pump, in every stroke, there is suction on one side and delivery on the other side. When it moves from left to right, on the left side of the piston, there is suction and on the right side there is delivery. When it moves from right to left, on the right side of the piston, there is suction and on the left side there is delivery. A double acting piston pump is shown in Fig. 5.43. It has two suction and two delivery pipes.

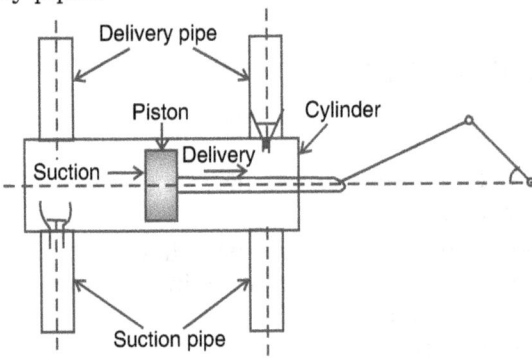

Fig. 5.43 : Double acting piston pump

Air-vessel : A air-vessel is a closed chamber made of cast iron. It contains compressed air at the top and liquid (to be handled by the reciprocating pump) at the bottom. Air vessel has an opening at the base through which liquid can enter into it or flow out of it.

One air vessel is fitted to the suction pipe near the suction valve (S) and another air vessel is fitted to the delivery pipe near the delivery valve (D). The air in the air vessel is either compressed due to entrance of liquid into it or is expanded due to flowing out of liquid from it. The air vessel thus absorbs pressure fluctuation. Hence, it acts like the flywheel of a reciprocating heat engine.

Working principle of an air vessel : At the beginning of delivery stroke, the liquid flowing through the delivery port (controlled by the delivery valve D), finds two passages open to it, one leading into the delivery pipe, and the other leading into the air vessel containing air. The total pressure in the delivery pipe being greater than that of air in the air vessel. The liquid, taking the path of least resistance, enters into the air vessel and compresses the air in it. In this way, during first few delivery strokes, the pressure of air in the air vessel gradually rises. This gradually increasing air pressure sets the liquid column in the delivery pipe in motion gradually without shock.

After that, during the first half of the delivery stroke, when the piston moves with acceleration, it forces the liquid into the delivery pipe with a velocity greater than the average velocity of flow, and excess liquid flows into the air vessel. During the next half of the delivery stroke when the piston moves with retardation, the velocity of the piston falls below the average velocity and rate of flow in the delivery pipe from the pump cylinder is reduced. The compressed air in the air vessel then forces some of the liquid from it to flow through the delivery pipe. In this way, constant rate of flow in the delivery pipe beyond the air vessel is maintained. This minimises shocks which would have been created in the delivery pipe due to sudden change of pressure.

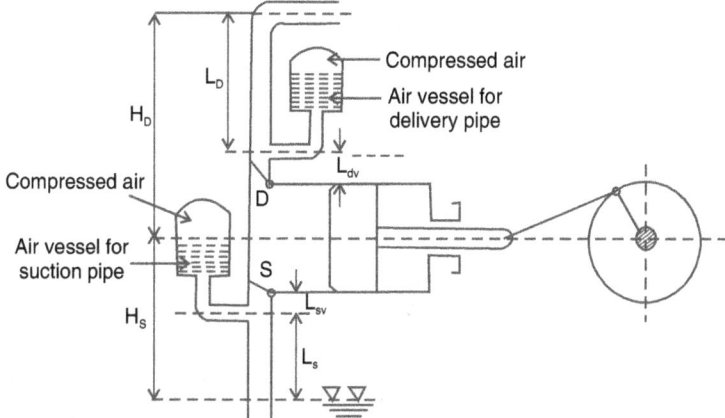

Fig. 5.44

During the first half of the suction stroke, the piston moves with acceleration, thus forcing the liquid in the suction pipe to move with a velocity greater than the mean velocity of flow, and the discharge of the liquid required into the cylinder will be more than the average rate of flow. This excess quantity of liquid will be supplied from the air vessel to the pump cylinder so that velocity in the suction pipe below the air vessel is equal to the average velocity of flow. During the second half of the suction stroke, the piston moves with retardation and the velocity of flow in the suction pipe is less than the mean velocity of flow. Hence, the discharge entering into the cylinder will be less than the mean discharge. The velocity of liquid in the suction pipe due to air vessel is equal to mean velocity of flow and the discharge required in the cylinder is less than the mean discharge. The excess liquid flowing in the suction pipe will be stored into the air vessel which will be supplied during the first half of the next suction stroke.

Functions of Air Vessel :
1. Uniform rate of discharge from the pump is ensured.
2. Less power is required to run the pump as considerable amount of work is saved which would otherwise be required in overcoming increased frictional resistance in the suction and delivery pipes.

5.9.2 Centrifugal Pumps

In a centrifugal pump, we create pressure with the help of a centrifugal action. The pump is driven by power from an external source by means of which the vanes are rotated. This creates a centrifugal head of water in the pump. The water leaves the vanes with a high velocity and pressure.

A partial vacuum is created at the centre, due to which the water will be drawn through the suction pipe. The high pressure created by the pump is utilized in overcoming the delivery head of the pump.

The rotating element of a centrifugal pump is called the impeller. Centrifugal pumps are usually of the radial-flow type but pump having a mixed flow and axial flow are also made. Axial flow pumps are known as propeller pumps and are used for low heads.

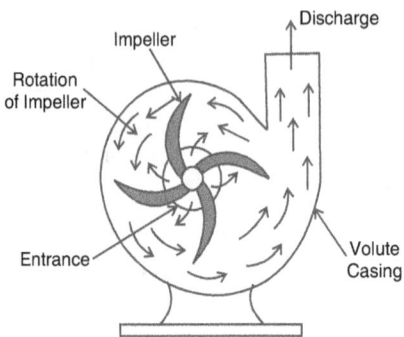

Fig. 5.45 : Centrifugal pump

Types of Centrifugal Pumps :

1. Pumps are classified according to the types of casing :

The casing of radial-flow pumps may be either (i) volute type, or (ii) turbine type.

(i) Volute Pump : It has got a volute casing which surrounds the impeller or the vane wheel. Volute is of a spiral form. A volute casing is designed to produce an equal velocity of flow around the circumference of the impeller and to reduce the velocity of the water as it enters the discharge pipe, consequently the pressure will be increased. It has been found that this type of chamber slightly increases the efficiency of the pump.

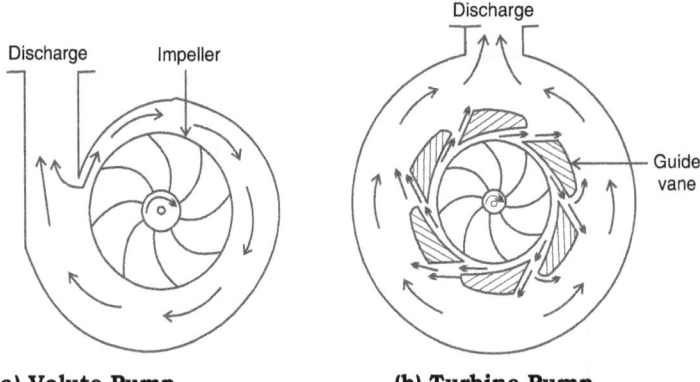

(a) Volute Pump   (b) Turbine Pump

Fig. 5.46 : Type of Centrifugal Pumps

Priming : Necessity of Priming

Centrifugal force produced by the rotation of the impeller is directly proportional to the density of the liquid to be handled by the impeller. So, if a impeller is to run in air, the density of which is low, centrifugal force imparted on the liquid will be small. Hence, rise of pressure developed will be small and liquid will not be delivered and will remain in the impeller. This will hamper suction of fresh liquid into the impeller. So, before starting the pump, the suction pipe, the impeller and the casing is completely filled with the liquid to remove air from the suction side of the pump. This operation is called priming. So priming is necessary in order that sufficient quantity of liquid is continuously sucked into the impeller through the suction pipe and delivered.

Different methods of priming. Various methods of priming are :

1. Manual priming : In this method, before starting the pump, the delivery valve (or regulating valve) is closed, priming cock is opened and the liquid is poured into the pump through the priming funnel until the liquid overflows through the funnel. This ensures removal of air from the suction pipe, impeller and the casing.

2. Vacuum priming : In this method, air is extracted from the suction side of the pump by an "ejector" to create vacuum in the suction side. Due to fall of pressure within the pump, the liquid in the sump which is under atmospheric pressure, is sucked into the pump.

3. Self priming : In this method, air removing device is incorporated in the pump itself. When the pump is started to cause rotation of the impeller, this device starts removing air from within the pump.

5.9.3 Comparison Between Centrifugal and Reciprocating Pumps

Reciprocating pump	Centrifugal Pump
1. Flow is intermittent.	1. Flow is smooth and even.
2. Weight of the pump is more for the same delivery rate.	2. Weight of the pump is less for a given delivery rate.
3. Floor space occupied is about 6 to 8 times the floor space occupied by a centrifugal pump for the same delivery rate.	3. It is compact and occupies less floor space for a given delivery rate.
4. Initial cost is about 4 times that of a centrifugal pump of the same capacity.	4. Initial cost is less.
5. Installation is difficult.	5. Installation is easy.
6. Number of valves is more. This makes construction difficult.	6. Number of valves is less. This simplifies construction.
7. Efficiency of low head pump is low, because of higher losses.	7. Efficiency of low head pump is high.
8. Maintenance cost is high, because parts like valves require constant attention.	8. Maintenance cost is less. Periodical check up is sufficient.
9. The pump cannot be run at high speed, because greater the speed of the pump, greater is the risk of cavitation.	9. The pump can be run at high speed, because cavitation does not depend upon speed of the pump.
10. Torque on the pump shaft is non-uniform.	10. Uniform torque acts on the impeller shaft.
11. It cannot handle viscous liquid, because valves and glands cause trouble when required to handle viscous liquid.	11. It can handle viscous liquid like paper pulp, muddy water.
12. Air vessel is required.	12. No air vessel is required.
13. It does not require priming.	13. It requires priming.
14. It is suitable for low discharge and high head.	14. It is suitable for large discharge and small head.

(C) TURBINES

5.10 HYDRAULIC TURBINES (WATER TURBINES)

The two types of hydraulic machinery of interest to hydraulic engineers are pumps and turbines. A pump converts mechanical energy into hydraulic energy, while a turbine serves the opposite purpose. There are many types of pumps and turbines. Each type has its own characteristics and for a given set of operating conditions, there is a type and size of hydraulic machine best suited to the job. In this article, the emphasis is laid on water turbines, used for power generation.

Water turbines are divided into two main classes as :
1. Impulse turbines.
2. Reaction turbines.

5.10.1 Impulse Turbines

In the impulse turbine, all the energy of the water is converted into velocity before entering the wheel by expanding through a nozzle or guide vanes. The pressure of water is atmospheric, hence the wheel must not run full, in which case, it must be placed at the foot of the fall and above the tail race. The water may be admitted over part of the circumference only or over the whole circumference. The impulse turbine may be radial flow or axial flow turbine. The pelton wheel is a type of impulse turbine.

The pelton wheel : The pelton wheel, also called pelton turbine. It is the special type of axialflow impulse turbine generally mounted on a horizontal axis. It can also be mounted with its axis vertical. It operates under a high head of water and therefore, requires a comparatively less quantity of water. Water is conveyed in penstocks from the head race in the mountains to the turbine in the power house. The penstock is joined to a branch pipe or lower bend fitted with a nozzle at the end. Water comes out of nozzle in the form of a free and compact jet at a very high velocity.

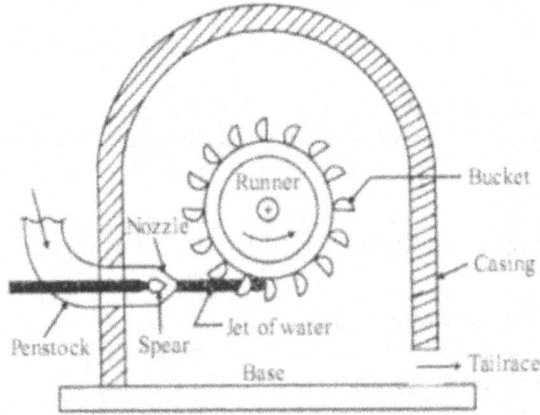

Fig. 5.47 : Pelton wheel

The number of nozzles required for a turbine depends on its specific speed. The water having a high velocity is made to impinge, on buckets fixed round the circumference of a wheel, the latter being mounted on a shaft. The impact of water on the surface of the bucket produces a force which causes the wheel to rotate, thus supplying a torque or mechanical power on the shaft. The jet of water strikes the double hemispherical cup-shaped buckets at the centre and is deviated on both sides, thus eliminating an end thrust. After performing work on the buckets, water is discharged into the tail race. The wheel must be so located that the buckets do not splash into the tail race water when it revolves. Overall efficiencies are obtained upto 88 per cent and single wheels have been constructed to produce 50 MW power.

5.10.2 Reaction Turbines

In the reaction turbine, water enters the wheel under pressure and flows over the vanes. In passing over the vanes, the pressure head is converted to velocity head and is finally reduced to atmospheric pressure before leaving the wheel. The water leaves the wheel with a large velocity but a small absolute velocity, practically the whole of its original energy have been given to the wheel.

In reaction turbine, total head consists partly of pressure head and partly of velocity head. As the water is under pressure, the wheel must run full and may, therefore, be entirely submerged below the tail race, it may also discharge into the atmosphere or discharge into a section or draft tube. The water must be admitted into a reaction turbine over the whole circumference of the wheel.

Francis Turbine : The Francis turbine is an inward flow radial reaction type. The water under pressure, enters the runner from the guide vanes towards the centre in radial direction and discharges out of runner axially. It operates under medium heads and also requires medium quantity of water.

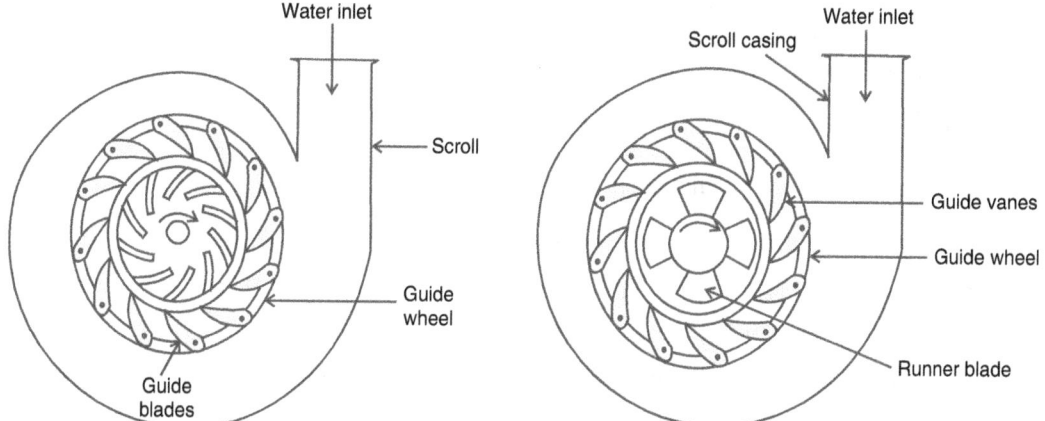

Fig. 5.48 : Outline of Francis turbine   **Fig. 5.49 : Outline of a Kaplan turbine**

A part of the head acting on the turbine is transformed into kinetic energy and the rest remains as pressure head. There is a difference of pressure between the guide vanes and the runner which is called the reaction pressure and is responsible for the motion of the runner. That is why a Francis turbine is also known as reaction turbine. In this turbine, the pressure at the inlet is more than that at the outlet. In the Francis turbine, the runner is always full of water. After doing work, the water is discharged to the tail race through a draft tube. The free end of the draft tube is submerged deep in the tail race.

Kaplan Turbine : The Kaplan turbine is a reaction turbine. It operates in an entirely close conduit from inlet to tail race. The turbine is used where comparatively low head and large quantity of water is available.

All parts such as spiral casing, guide mechanism and draft tube of the Kaplan turbine except the runner are similar to those of Francis Turbine.

IMPORTANT FORMULAE

The following formulae are used for solving the problems :

(A) Power Transmission by Belts :

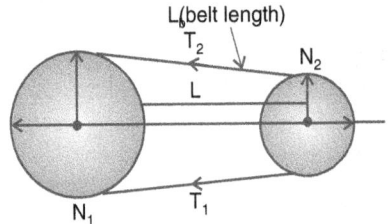

Fig.

1. $\dfrac{N_1}{N_2} = \left(\dfrac{D_1 + t}{D_2 + t}\right)\left(1 - \dfrac{S_t}{100}\right)$ where, $S_t = S_1 + S_2$

2. **Length of belt :**

   (a) **Open belt :** $L_o = \left[\pi(R_1 + R_2) + 2C + \dfrac{(R_1 - R_2)^2}{C}\right]$

   where C is centre distance.

   (b) **Cross belt :** $L_o = \left[\pi(R_1 + R_2) + 2C + \dfrac{(R_1 - R_2)^2}{C-}\right]$

3. $\dfrac{T_1 \text{(Tight side tension)}}{T_2 \text{(Slag side tension)}} - (e)^{\mu\theta}$

   where θ is belt contact angle or known as lap angel and μ is coefficient of friction.

4. **Angle of contact of belt drive :**

   (a) **Open belt :** $\theta = (180 - 2\phi)$

   where $\phi = \sin^{-1}\left(\dfrac{R_1 - R_2}{C}\right)$

   (b) **Cross belt :** $\theta = (180 - 2\phi)$

   where $\phi = \sin^{-1}\left(\dfrac{R_1 + R_2}{C}\right)$

5. **Centrifugal tension :**

   $T_c = mv^2$

Where, m is mass in kg/meter length of belt

$$T_{max} = T_1 + T_c$$

6. Condition for transmitting maximum power:

$$T_c = \frac{T_{max}}{3} \text{ and } V = \sqrt{\frac{T_{max}}{3m}}$$

When, power is maximum.

7. Velocity ratio of compound belt:

$$\frac{N_4}{N_1} = \frac{D_1 + t_1}{D_2 + t_1} \times \frac{D_3 + t_2}{D_4 + t_2} \left(1 - \frac{S}{100}\right)$$

Where, $S = S_{t1} + S_{t2}$

8. Power transmitted, $P = \dfrac{(T_1 - T_2) V}{1000}$ kW

9. Initial tension, $T_0 = \dfrac{T_1 + T_2}{2}$ neglecting centrifugal tension

$$= \left(\frac{T_1 + T_2}{2} + T_c\right) \text{ if centrifugal tension is considered}$$

(B) Power Transmission by Gears:

1. Circular pitch, $P_c = \dfrac{\pi D_p}{T}$

where D_p is pitch circle diameter and T is number of teeth.

2. Diametral pitch, $P_d = \dfrac{T}{D_p}$

3. $\quad P_d \cdot P_c = \pi$

4. Module, $m = \dfrac{1}{P_d} = \dfrac{D_p}{T} = \dfrac{P_c}{\pi}$

$\therefore \quad P_c = \pi \cdot m$ and $D_p = mT$

when two gases are in mesh,

$$P_{c_1} = P_{c_2}, \quad P_{d_1} = P_{d_2} \text{ and } m_1 = m_2$$

5. Velocity ratio $= \dfrac{N_1}{N_2} = \dfrac{D_2}{D_1} = \dfrac{T_2}{T_1} =$ Gear ratio

6. Centre distance, $C = \dfrac{D_1 + D_2}{2} = \dfrac{m}{2}(T_1 + T_2)$

7. Power transmitted, $P = \dfrac{F \cdot \pi DN}{1000 \times 60}$ kW $= \dfrac{2\pi TN}{1000 \times 60}$ kW

where torque, $T = F \times R$ (Nm)

(**Note**: In solved examples, D or D_p is used for pitch diameter of the gear.)

SOLVED PROBLEMS

Problem 5.1 : Determine the rotational speed, and direction of rotation of the follower in the open and crossed belt drive as shown in Fig. 5.50.

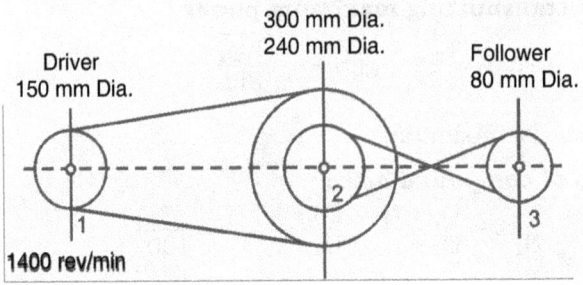

Fig. 5.50

Solution : Since, the 300 mm and 240 mm pulleys rotate together on the intermediate shaft, all the same rotational speed assume that the drive is rotating clockwise direction.

$$\frac{1400}{N_2} = \frac{300}{150}$$

N_2 is the rotational speed of the intermediate shaft

$$\therefore \quad N_2 = \frac{1400 \times 150}{300} = \mathbf{700 \text{ rev/min.}}$$

The rotational speed of the follower is N_3

$$\frac{N_2}{N_3} = \frac{d_1}{d_2} \text{ and } \frac{700}{N_1} = \frac{80}{240}$$

$$N_3 = \frac{700 \times 240}{80} = \mathbf{2100 \text{ rev/min.}} \text{ (Anticlockwise)}$$

The speed of the follower (cross belt)

$$= \frac{\pi d_3 N_3}{60}$$

$$= \frac{\pi \times 80 \times 2100}{60} = 8800 \text{ mm/sec.}$$

$$= \mathbf{8.8 \text{ m/sec.}}$$

Problem 5.2 : A flat belt 8 mm thick and 100 mm wide transmits power between two pulleys, running at 1600 m/min. The mass of the belt is 0.9 kg/m length. The angle of lap in the smaller pulley is 165° and the coefficient of friction between the belt and the pulley is 0.3. If the maximum permissible stress in the belt is 2 MN/m². Find (i) Maximum power transmitted and (ii) Initial tension in the belt.

Solution :

Centrifugal Tension, $T_c = mV^2$

Velocity, $V = 1600 \text{ m/min} = 26.67 \text{ m/sec.}$

$$T_c = 0.9 \times 26.67^2$$
$$= 640 \text{ N}$$

Maximum tension, $T_{max} = T_1 + T_c$

and $T_{max} = \sigma \times t \times b$
$$= 2 \times 10^6 \times \frac{8}{1000} \times \frac{100}{1000} = 1600 \text{ N}$$
$$T_1 = T_{max} - T_c$$
$$= 1600 - 640 = 960 \text{ N}$$

Also $\dfrac{T_1}{T_2} = e^{\mu\theta}$
$$= e^{0.3 \times 165 \times \pi/180} = 2.373$$
$$T_2 = \frac{T_1}{2.373} = \frac{960}{2.373} = 404.7 \text{ N}$$

Power, $P = (T_1 - T_2) V$
$$= (960 - 404.7)\, 26.67 = 14807.6 \text{ W} = \mathbf{14.807 \text{ kW}}$$

Initial tension, $T_i = T_1 + T_2 + 2T_c$
$$= 960 + 404.7 + 2 \times 640 = \mathbf{1.32 \text{ kN}}$$

Problem 5.3 : Two pulleys, one 450 mm diameter and the other 200 mm diameter are on parallel shafts 1.95 m apart and are connected by a crossed belt. Find the length of the belt required. What power can be transmitted by the belt when the larger pulley rotates at 200 r.p.m., if the maximum permissible tension in the belt is 1 kN and the coefficient of friction between the belt and the pulley is 0.25.

Solution :

Length of the cross belt, $L = \left[2C + \pi (R_1 + R_2) + \left(\dfrac{R_1 + R_2}{C}\right)^2\right]$
$$= 2 \times 1.95 + \pi (0.225 + 0.1) + \left(\frac{0.225 + 0.1}{1.95}\right)^2$$
$$= 4.975 \text{ m}$$

Since, $R_1 = \dfrac{450}{2}$ mm = 225 m

And $R_2 = \dfrac{200}{2}$ mm = 0.1 m

The angle of lap for smaller pulley
$$\theta = 2\left[\pi - \cos^{-1}\left(\frac{R_1 + R_2}{C}\right)\right]$$
$$= 2\left[\pi - \cos^{-1}\left(\frac{0.225 + 0.1}{1.95}\right)\right]$$
$$= 2\,(180° - 80°\,52') = 199°\,10'$$

We know that $\dfrac{T_1}{T_2} = e^{\mu\theta}$

$= e^{0.25 \times \frac{199° \; 10' \times \pi}{180}} = 2.385$

$T_1 = 1000$ N (given)

$T_2 = \dfrac{T_1}{2.385} = 419.31$ N

Power, $P = (T_1 - T_2) V$

Velocity, $V = \dfrac{\pi d_1 n_1}{60}$

$= \dfrac{\pi \times 0.45 \times 200}{60} = $ **4.17 m/sec.**

$P = (1000 - 419.31) \, 4.17 = 2736.2 \text{ W} = $ **2.736 kW.**

Problem 5.4 : A leather belt transmits 30 kW power from a pulley 750 mm dia. which rotates at 500 r.p.m. The belt is in contact with the pulley over an arc of 160° and the coefficient of friction is 0.3. If the permissible stress in the belt is not to exceed 2 MN/m², find the maximum cross sectional area of the belt.

Solution :

Velocity, $V = \dfrac{\pi dn}{60} = \dfrac{\pi \times 0.75 \times 500}{60} = 19.63$ metre/sec.

$P = (T_1 - T_2) V$

∴ $T_1 - T_2 = \dfrac{P}{V} = \dfrac{30 \times 100}{19.63} = 1528.27$ N ....(1)

$\dfrac{T_1}{T_2} = e^{\mu\theta} = e^{0.3 \times 160 \times \pi/180} = e^{0.8377} = 2.311$ ....(2)

$T_2 = \dfrac{T_1}{2.311} = 0.4327 \, T_1$

$T_1 - 0.4327 \, T_1 = 1528.27$ N   from equation ....(1)

$0.5673 \, T_1 = 1528.27$ N

$T_1 = \dfrac{1528.27}{0.5673} = 2693.9$ N $= 2.6939$ kN

Cross sectional area of the belt can be calculate from

$T_1 = \sigma \cdot t \cdot b = 2.6939 = t \times b \times 2 \times 10^6 \text{ Nm}^2$

Cross sectional are of belt, $(A_c) = t \times b = \dfrac{2693.9}{2 \times 10^6} \text{ m}^2 = \dfrac{2693.4 \times 10^4}{2 \times 10^6} = $ **13.46 cm²**

Problem 5.5 : A 'V' belt having a lap of $\pi/2$ radians has cross sectional area of 6.5 cm² and runs in a groove which has an included angle of 45°. The density of the belt is 2.5×10^6 kg/m³ and the maximum stress is not exceed 50×10^6 N/m². The coefficient of friction is 0.16. Find the maximum power that can be transmitted if the wheel has a mean diameter of 30 cm and runs at 1000 r.p.m.

Solution :

$$\frac{\mu\theta}{\sin\frac{\alpha}{2}} = \frac{0.16 \times \frac{\pi}{2}}{\sin 22.5°} = \frac{0.16\,\pi}{2 \times 0.3827} = 0.6567$$

$$\frac{\mu\theta}{\sin\frac{\alpha}{2}} = e^{0.5667} = 1.928$$

$$\text{Velocity} = \frac{\pi\,dN}{60} = \frac{\pi \times 0.3 \times 1000}{60} = 15.7 \text{ m/sec.}$$

$$T_1 = \text{Area} \times \text{Stress}$$
$$= \frac{6.5}{10^4}\,(m^2) \times 50 \times 10^6\,\frac{N}{m^2} = 32250\,N = \mathbf{32.25\ kN.}$$

$$\text{Maximum power} = (T_1 - T_2)\left(1 - \frac{1}{e^{\mu\theta}}\right) V$$

For maximum power, $T_c = \dfrac{T_1}{3}$

∴ $\quad$ Maximum power $= \dfrac{2}{3} T_1 \left(1 - \dfrac{1}{1.928}\right) \times 15.7$ m/sec.

$$= \frac{2}{3} \times \frac{32.25 \times 0.4813 \times 15.7}{1.9^3} = \mathbf{167.7\ kW}$$

Problem 5.6 : In an a assembly of spur-gear having a velocity ratio 0.2, the centre distance between the gears is 500 mm and module is 5 mm. Find the following :

(a) Number of teeth on pinion and gear.

(b) Pitch circle diameter of pinion and gear.

Solution : The given data is L = 500 mm and m = 5 mm

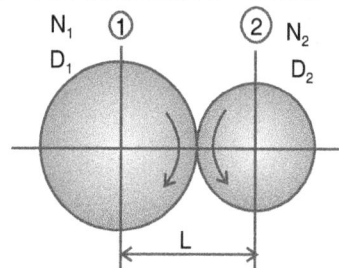

Fig. 5.51

V. R. (Velocity Ratio) $= \dfrac{N_1}{N_2} = 0.2$

$$L = \frac{m}{2}(T_1 + T_2)$$

$$500 = \frac{5}{2}(T_1 + T_2)$$

∴ $\quad T_1 + T_2 = 200 \qquad\qquad\qquad\qquad\qquad\qquad\qquad\qquad ......(a)$

$$\frac{N_1}{N_2} = \frac{T_2}{T_1} = 0.2$$

∴ $T_2 = 0.2\, T_1$ ....(b)

From equations (a) and (b),

$$T_1 + 0.2\, T_1 = 200$$

∴ $T_1 = \dfrac{200}{1.2} = 166.7 \approx 167$

∴ $T_2 = 200 - 167 = 33$

The pitch circle diameter is given by

$$P_d = \frac{T_1}{D_{P_1}} = \frac{T_2}{D_{P_2}} \quad \text{Where } P_d \text{ is diameteral pitch}$$

∴ $\dfrac{D_{P_1}}{T_1} = \dfrac{D_{P_2}}{T_2} = m \text{ as } p_d = \dfrac{1}{m}$

∴ $D_{P_1} = m \times T_1 = 5 \times 167 = 835 \text{ mm} = \mathbf{83.5\ cm}$

∴ $D_{P_2} = m \times T_2 = 5 \times 33 = 165 \text{ mm} = \mathbf{16.5\ cm}$

Problem 5.7 : If the gear ratio of a spur-gear pair is 5 and a gear with 100 teeth is rotating at 500 r.p.m., find the following :

(a) Circular and diameteral pitch.

(b) Pitch circle diameter of gear and pinion.

(c) Centre distance.

(d) Velocity ratio. Take module = 1 cm.

Solution : The given data is G.R. (Gear Ratio) = 5, T_2 = 100, N_2 = 500 r.p.m., and m (module) 1 cm.

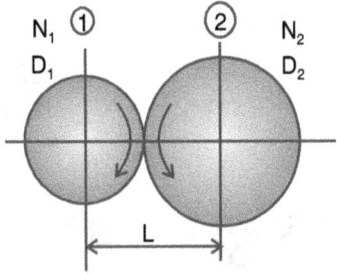

Fig. 5.52

(a) Circular pitch, $P_c = \pi \cdot m = \pi \times 1 = 3.14 \text{ cm}$

$P_d = \dfrac{\pi}{P_c} = \dfrac{\pi}{31.4} = \mathbf{1\ teeth/cm}$

(b) $D_2 \text{ (gear)} = mT_2 = 1 \times 100 = 100 \text{ cm}$

But gear ratio, $\text{G.R.} = \dfrac{T_2}{T_1} = 5$

$D_1 \text{(pinion)} = mT_1$

∴ $T_1 = \dfrac{100}{5} = 20$

∴ $D_1 = 1 \times 20 = \textbf{20 cm}$

(c) Centre distance, $L = \dfrac{D_1 + D_2}{2} = \dfrac{100 + 20}{2} = \textbf{60 cm}$

(d) Velocity ratio, $\text{V.R.} = \dfrac{D_2}{D_1} = \dfrac{T_2}{T_1} = \dfrac{N_1}{N_2}$

∴ Velocity ratio $= \dfrac{T_2}{T_1} = \dfrac{100}{20} = \textbf{5}$

Problem 5.8 : A spur gear shaft is rotating at a speed of 400 r.p.m. and transmits power to pinion shaft rotating at 2000 r.p.m. If the number of teeth on pinion is 50 and module is 10 mm, find the following terms :

(a) Diameteral pitch,

(b) Pitch circle diameter of gear and pinion,

(c) Gear ratio,

(d) Velocity ratio.

Solution : The given data is $N_1 = 400$ r.p.m., $N_2 = 2000$ r.p.m., $T_2 = 50$, and $m = 1$ cm

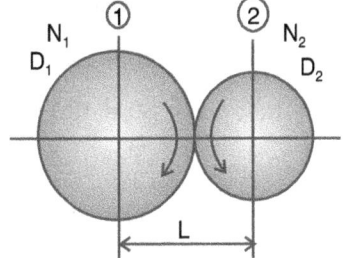

Fig. 5.53

(a) $P_d = \dfrac{1}{m} = \dfrac{1}{1} = \textbf{1 cm}$

(b) $P_c = \dfrac{\pi D_{P_1}}{T_1} = \dfrac{\pi D_{P_2}}{T_2}$ or $\dfrac{D_1}{T_1} = \dfrac{D_2}{T_2}$

Velocity ratio $= \dfrac{N_1}{N_2} = \dfrac{D_2}{D_1} = \dfrac{T_2}{T_1}$

∴ $\dfrac{D_2}{D_1} = \dfrac{N_1}{N_2} = \dfrac{400}{2000} = \dfrac{50}{T_1} = \dfrac{1}{5}$

∴ $T_1 = \dfrac{2000 \times 50}{400} = 250$

$m = \dfrac{D_{P_1}}{T_1} = \dfrac{D_{P_2}}{T_2}$

∴ $1 = \dfrac{D_{P_1}}{250} = \dfrac{D_{P_2}}{50}$ where D_{P_1} & D_{P_2} are pitch circle diameters

∴ $D_{P_1} = 250$ cm and $D_{P_2} = \textbf{50 cm.}$

Gear ratio $= \dfrac{T_1}{T_2} = \dfrac{250}{50} = \textbf{5}$

Problem 5.9 : A pair of spur gear consists of 20 teeth pinion meshing with 80 teeth gear. The module is 6 mm. Calculate :

(a) Circular pitch and diameteral pitch,

(b) Pitch circle diameter of pinion and gear,

(c) Velocity ratio,

(d) Centre distance.

Solution : The given data is $T_1 = 20$, $T_2 = 80$, $m = \dfrac{D_1}{T_1} = \dfrac{D_2}{T_2} = 6$ mm, $P_{c_1} = P_{c_2} = \dfrac{\pi D_1}{T_1} = \dfrac{\pi D_2}{T_2}$.

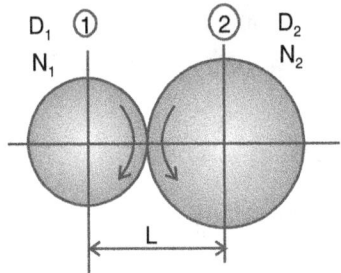

Fig. 5.54

(a) and (b) $D_1 = mT_1 = 6 \times 20 = 120$ mm $= 12$ cm

$D_2 = mT_2 = 6 \times 80 = 480$ mm $= 48$ cm

∴ $P_c = P_{c_1} = P_{c_2} = \dfrac{\pi D_1}{T_1} = \dfrac{\pi \times 120}{20} =$ **18.85 mm**

$P_d = P_{d_1} = P_{d_2} = \dfrac{T_1}{D_1} = \dfrac{20}{120}$

$= 0.17$ teeth/mm $=$ **1.7 teeth/cm**

(c) Velocity ratio $= \dfrac{N_1}{N_2} = \dfrac{D_2}{D_1} = \dfrac{48}{12} = 4$

(d) Centre distance, $L = \dfrac{D_1 + D_2}{2} = \dfrac{12 + 48}{2} =$ **30 cm.**

EXERCISES

1. Differentiate with the help of diagrams, the simple gear train and compound gear train and give the examples for their use.

2. When gear drive is essentially used ? List out the advantages and disadvantages of gear drive over belt drive.

3. When the chain drive is preferred over belt drive. List out five examples of chain drive.

4. What do you understand by coupling ? List out the different couplings. Mention the use of each.

5. Draw the neat diagrams of the following couplings and mention the specific application of each (a) Oldham, (b) Flexible, and (c) Universal.

6. A diesel engine shaft running at 1500 r.p.m. is required to drive another shaft with the help of belt. The pulleys on engine shaft and machine shaft are of 1m and 0.5 m diameters respectively. If the belt thickness is 6 mm, find out the speed of the machine shaft when (a) there is no slip, and (b) when there is 2.5% slip.

7. A leather belt 12 cm wide and 5 mm thick transmit power from a pulley of 60 cm diameter running at 600 r.p.m. The lap angle is 15° and coefficient of friction is 0.325. Find out the maximum power that can be transmitted by the belt. Take $\rho = 920$ kg/m^3 (for belt material).

8. A flat belt of 10 cm wide and 5 mm thick transmits power between two pulleys when running at 25 m/sec. The lap angle on the smaller pulley is 15° and μ (coefficient of friction between belt and pulley) = 0.3. If the maximum permissible stress in the belt is 20 kN/cm^2, find (a) Initial tension in the belt and (b) Maximum power transmitted. Take mass of the belt = 0.85 kg/m length.

9. A simple gear train consists of three wheels having number of teeth 40, 50 and 60 respectively. Find its velocity ratio. If the driving wheel having 40 teeth is rotating at 3.5 r.p.s., find the speed of the driven wheel.

10. Two parallel shafts whose centre to centre distance is nearly 34 cm and velocity ratio required is exactly 11 : 3. The module is 6 mm. Find (a) The number of teeth on each wheel and (b) Exact centre distance between the two shafts.

11. Draw the neat diagrams of different bearings and menions the specific use of each.

12. Draw a neat diagram of a single cylinder, single stage air compressor and explain its working.

13. Explain the different types of reciprocating compressors with the help of diagrams.

14. Draw a neat line diagram of a single stage centrifugal air compressor and explain its working.

15. List out the different uses of compressed air.

16. How the pumps are classified ?

17. Explain the working of reciprocating water pump with the help of neat sketch. What do you understand by priming. ? Why it is necessary for reciprocating pump ?

18. Compare the reciprocating pump with centrifugal pump.

19. How the water turbines are classified ?

20. Explain the working of Impulse and Reaction water turbines with the help of diagrams.

21. Name the different types of water turbines and list out the field of application of each giving proper justification.

6

MANUFACTURING PROCESSES

6.1 Introduction To Manufacturing Processes

(A) Casting

6.2 Casting Methods
6.3 Casting Defects
6.4 Advantages and Limitations of Casting Method

(B) Machine Tools

6.5 Introduction to Machine Tools
6.6 Lathe Machine and its Principal Parts
6.7 Different Operations Performed on Lathe
6.8 Drilling Machine
6.9 Operations carried out on Drilling Machine

(C) Joining Processes

6.10 Introduction to Metal Joining Process
6.11 Classification of Welding Methods
6.12 Electric Resistance Welding
6.13 Arc Welding
6.14 Gas Welding
6.15 Brazing
6.16 Soldering
Exercises

6.1 INTRODUCTION TO MANUFACTURING PROCESSES

A engineering process used to manufacture the required product is known as manufacturing processes.

There are different types of processes used for manufacturing different products. The processes used are mainly classified in three different classes a casting, cutting and Joining.

In casting processes, the metal which is used for the purpose is melted and then poured in the cavity (formed by pattern known as mould) and the required product is formed. This is generally used to form complicated shape products and the product need not bear high forces This is also used to form smaller product like cobbler stand or biggher product like lathe base structure.

The second common manufacturing process is cutting the material to give the required shape try different machine tools like Lathe, Drilling machines, Shaping machines and Milling machines. The Lathe is used for cutting the raw piece into required diameter and many other purposes. The drilling machine is used to generate the hole of the required diameter and depth in the given piece. The shaping machine is used to form the surface and key slots in the shaft. The milling machine has wide range of operations to be carried out as required.

The third method which as welding is commonly used for joining two metal pieces of the same materials or different materials. According to the temperature generated for joining, the methods are classified as arc welding, Gas welding, Brazing and Soldering.

All these manufacturing processes are discussed in this chapter.

(A) Casting

A casting can be simply defined as a molten material that has been poured into a prepared cavity and allowed to solidify. Many casting processes have been developed over the years to fulfill specific needs. These processes include sand casting, shell-mould casting, plaster-mould casting, investment casting, permanent mould casting, centrifugal casting and die-casting. Sand casting is the most common of these processes.

6.2 Casting Methods

The various casting processes are as given below :

1. Sand Mould Casting.
2. Plaster Mould Casting.
3. Metallic Mould Casting.
4. Centrifugal Casting.

1. Sand Mould Casting

In sand mould casting, the moulds are prepared in of required shape and size the sand as described earlier and molten metal is poured into it. The metal is allowed to solidify and casting is taken out and dressed. Metals and their alloys must be poured at the correct temperature, otherwise defective castings are likely to result from such causes as porosity, distortion or low mechanical properties. The production of sand castings is carried out by :

(a) Green Sand Moulding.

(b) Dry Sand Moulding.

(c) Loam Moulding.

(d) Shell Moulding.

The Sand Casting (Green Sand) molding process utilizes a cope (top half) and drag (bottom half) flask set-up. The mold consists of sand (usually silica), clay and water. When the water is added, it develops the bonding characteristics of the clay, which binds the sand grains together. When applying pressure to the mold material, it can be compacted around a pattern which is either made of metal or wood, to produce a mold having sufficient rigidity to enable metal to be poured into it to produce a casting. The process also uses coring to create cavities inside the casting. After the casting is poured and has cooled, the core is removed.

The details of the casting are given below.

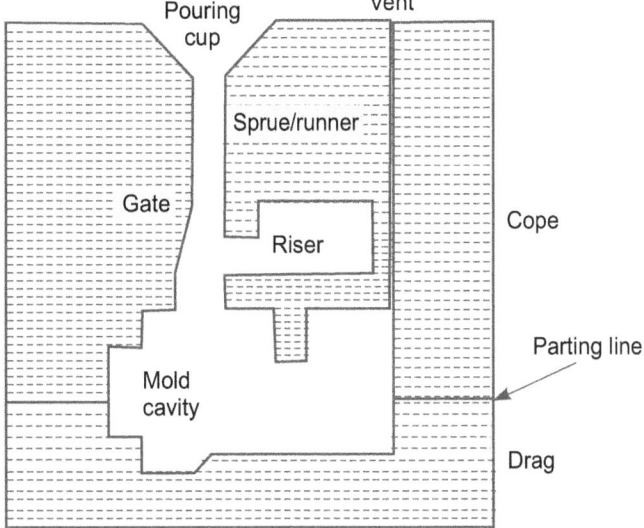

Fig. 6.1 : Sand casting mold

1. **Pouring Cup :** This is where the metal is poured into the mold.

2. **Sprue :** The vertical channel from the top of the mold to the gating and riser system. Also, a generic term used to cover all gates, runners and risers.

3. **Runner :** The portion of the gate assembly that connects the sprue to the casting in gate or riser.

4. **Gate :** The end of the runner in a mold where molten metal enters the mold cavity.

5. **Riser** : A reservoir of molten metal provided to compensate for the contraction of the metal as it solidifies.
6. **Mold Cavity** : The impression in a mold produced by the removal of the pattern. When filled with molten metal it forms a casting.
7. **Cope** : Upper or top most section of a flask, mold or pattern.
8. **Parting Line** : A line on a pattern or casting corresponding to the separation between the parts of a mold.
9. **Drag** : Lower or bottom section of a flask, mold or pattern.

The sand must exhibit the following characteristics :

(i) **Flow Ability** : The ability to pack tightly around the pattern.

(ii) **Plastic Deformation** : Have the ability to deform slightly without cracking so that the pattern can be withdrawn.

(iii) **Green Strength** : Have the ability to support its own weight when stripped from the pattern. and also withstand pressure of molten metal when the mold is cast.

(iv) **Permeability** : This allows the gases and steam to escape from the mold during casting.

The material costs for the process are low and the sand casting process is exceptionally flexible. A number of metals can be used for castings in sizes from ounces to many thousand kilograms. The mold material is reclaimable, with between 90 and 95% of the sand being recycled, although new sand and additions are required to make up for the discarded loss. These features, combined with the relative ease of mold production, have ensured that the green sand molding process has remained as the principal method by which castings are produced.

The sand used for green sand molding is critical and determines the favorable or unfavorable outcome of the casting. It controls the tolerances, surface finish and the repeatability while in production.

Advantages of Sand Casting

➢ Use is widespread; technology well developed.

➢ Capable of holding detail and resist deformation when heated.

➢ Can achieve very close tolerances if uniform compaction is achieved.

➢ Mould preparation time is relatively short in comparison to many other processes.

➢ Handles a more diverse range of products than any other casting method.

➢ Less expensive than machining shapes from bar stock.

- Can cast intricate shapes.
- Can be used with most pourable metals and alloys
- High levels of sand reuse are achievable.

Limitations
- Typically limited to one or a small number of moulds per box..
- Sand : metal ratio is relatively high.
- High level of waste is typically generated, particularly sand, baghouse dust and spent shot.

Shell Mould Casting : In its simplest form, a shell mould is made by fixing together (as described earlier in shell moulding) two such sand shells, the flat faces, reproduced from the pattern, allowing intimate contact so that the mould impression is completely enclosed apart from the pouring channel. The metal is poured in rapidly until the mould is full. The casting heat begins to burn the resin binder out of the mould, and the gases evolved escape through the permeable shell wall. Normally by the time the metal has set, the binder has completely burned out, leaving only a deposit of loose sand on the face of the casting. On tapping the shell mould with an iron bar disintegrates, and loose sand is removed from the casting.

2. Plaster Mould Casting

This process should be used only for casting non-ferrous materials. The cope and drag method used in sand casting may be used in this process. Once dried, the mould (described earlier) is assembled and pouring may take place.

3. Metallic Mould Casting

It consists of :

(a) Gravity or permanent mould casting.

(b) Slush casting.

(c) Pressed casting.

(d) Die casting.

(a) Permanent Mould Casting : Permanent mould casting refers to the process of die casting in which the molten metal is fed into the cavity by gravity. The head pressure of the molten metal forces the metal into the mould. This process is also known as **gravity die casting.**

The moulds are coated with a refractory material and lamp black. The dies are closed, and the metal is poured into the dies and allowed to solidify. The dies are opened and the casting is ejected. The dies are then cleaned and the process is repeated.

Cores may be positioned in the dies before they are closed and removed as soon as solidification starts.

This process is used for making steel and cast iron castings. It is also used to make alloy castings having a copper, aluminium or magnesium base.

(b) Slush Casting : In this process, the melt is poured into the die cavity. At a predetermined period of time, the mould is inverted to permit the part of the metal still in the molten state to flow out of the cavity. The hollow shell casting which has solidified is then removed. Ornaments, toys, etc., may be cast by this process. The inside wall of the casting is usually rough and irregular.

(c) Pressed Casting : This process is also known as Carthias process. It is still another variation of the permanent mould process. In this process, the cavity is filled with a precalculated quantity of metal. A core or plunger is inserted under low pressure to force the melt into the cavity. As the metal sets, the core or plunger is withdrawn. A hollow casting is the result.

(d) Die Casting : The die casting processes are permanent mould casting methods which force the metal into the mould under high pressure. The pressures vary from 20 to 2000 bar and it is maintained till solidification stage. A smooth and accurate casting is obtained. Die casting is used for mass production and is most suitable for non-ferrous metals and alloys of low fusion temperature. The principal base metals most commonly employed in die casting are zinc, aluminium, copper, magnesium, lead and tin.

As metal flows under high pressure, it fills the entire cavity quickly and intricate castings can be produced successfully. Also as the die is metallic, the cooling rate is high. It has high initial cost and is advantageous only in mass production. There are various die casting machines which make use of either (i) hot chamber method or (ii) cold chamber method.

(i) Hot Chamber Die-casting Machine : This machine, as shown in Fig. 6.2 consists of a hot chamber and a gooseneck type metal container.

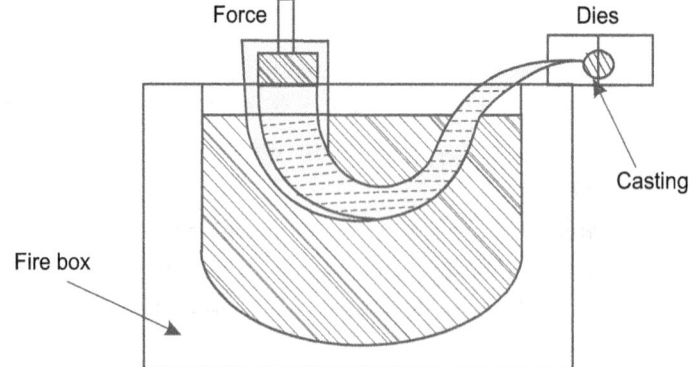

Fig. 6.2 : Hot chamber method

The gooseneck either remains totally immersed in the melt or is lowered into the melt to fill it. The metal is then forced out of the small end of the gooseneck by a pressure cylinder or by air pressure applied at the large end. The molten metal leaves the small end of the gooseneck, enters the die and is maintained under pressure in the die until it solidifies. Once solidified, the die is forced open and the casting is forced out of the die.

Since the gooseneck and the crucible pot are made of iron and since most metals react with iron at elevated temperatures, only the low melting point metals may be cast with this process. Alloys of lead, tin and zinc may be cast by this method.

Advantages and Limitations of Die Casting

Advantages

- True shapes of die cavity can be obtained.
- Thin sections of complex shape can be cast.
- Most of the non-ferrous alloys can be cast.
- It provides greatly improved surface finish when compared to other casting methods.
- The rate of production is very high.
- Well defined and distinct surface details can be obtained.
- Castings produced by die-casting are usually less defective.
- The true shape of die can be retained for a longer period.
- Die-casting requires less floor area than is required by other casting process.

Limitations

- The initial cost of the die and equipment used is high.
- The size of castings produced by this method is limited.
- There is limited scope of non-ferrous alloys that can be used for die casting.
- Special skill is required for maintenance and supervision of dies.
- It is not economical for small quantity production.

4. Centrifugal Casting

In this process, the mould is filled to a revolving disc and rotated at about 1500 r.p.m. The centrifugal force causes the molten metal to be distributed to all parts of the mould. The casting that results has a high degree of detail and superior density. Impurities in the melt collect at the inner wall of the casting because the mass of impurities is lower than the mass of the molten metal. This tends to localize the impurities and, to some extent, purify the metal melt.

Cylindrical parts and pipes are most adaptable to this process. Centrifugal casting finds its best use in mass production operation. There are three recognised centrifugal casting processes.

(a) True centrifugal casting.

(b) Semi-centrifugal casting.

(c) Centrifuged or pressure casting.

(a) True Centrifugal Casting : This process is used to cast symmetrical objects such as

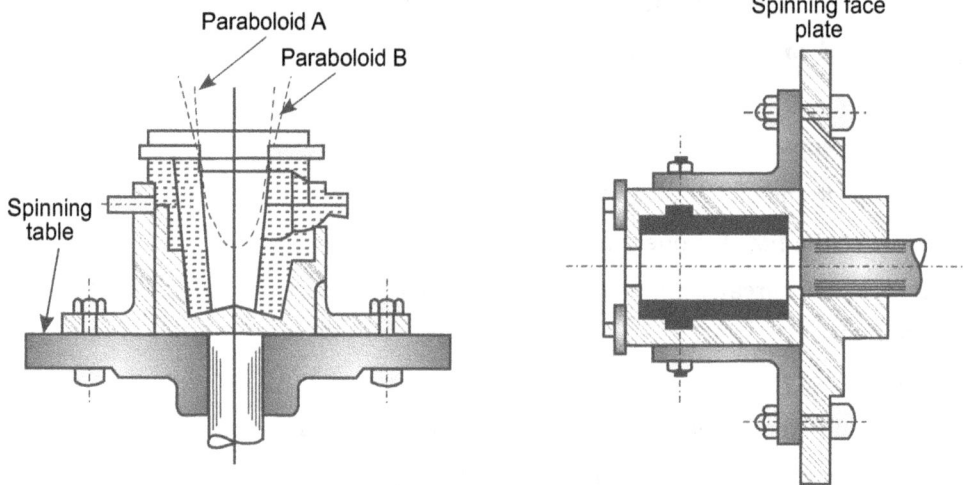

Fig. 6.3 : True centrifugal method of casting radial engine cylinder barrels

pipe. The metal is forced against the mould wall by the centrifugal force until it solidifies. No core is needed to form the hole in the casting. Molten metal distributed by this process may be forced into moulds where rapid solidification takes place before the freezing process starts.

Centrifugal castings may be rotated about a vertical or horizontal axis. At low speeds, the vertical-axis rotation leaves the inner hole parabolic. At high speeds this effect disappears.

(b) Semi-Centrifugal Casting : This process is used to ensure purity and density at the extremities of a casting such as a cast wheel. The sand mould (cope, drag and centre core) is rotated at a lower speed (350 rpm) than in the centrifugal casting process. Several moulds may be stacked one on top of the other and rotated. The molten metal is fed through a centre pouring basin. Rotation takes place about a central axis. The number of moulds which may be rotated at one time depends upon the conditions prevailing at the time and the size of the mould. The centrifugal force is used to feed the metal outwards to fill the mould cavities completely. Due to lower speed of rotation, pressure developed is too low and the impurities are not directed towards the centre as effectively as in true centrifugal casting.

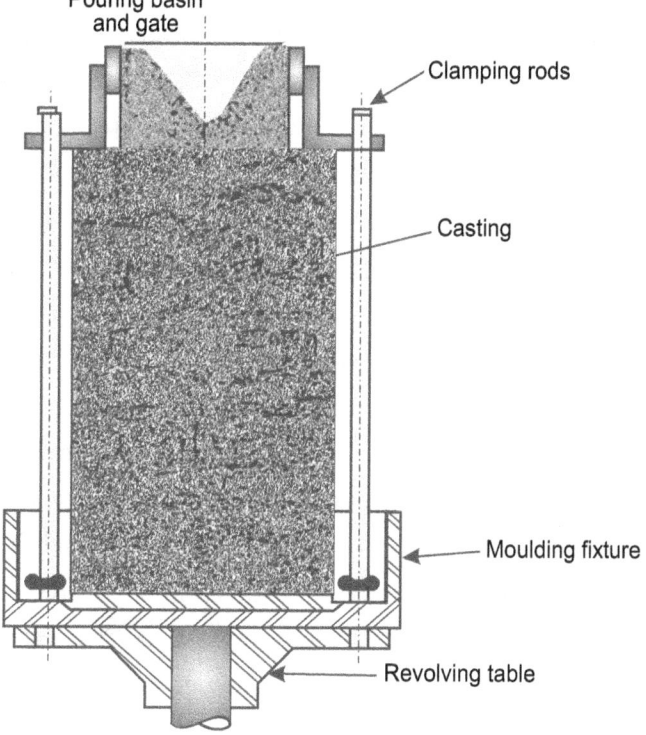

Fig. 6.4 : Semi-Centrifugal Casting

Advantages and Limitations of Centrifugal Casting

Advantages

- The castings produced are very sound and clean.
- Simplified inspection techniques can be employed and rejection is less.
- Castings with improved mechanical properties are obtained.
- Parts are produced closer to finished dimensions with consequent saving in machining.
- Use of runners and risers and cores is eliminated.
- Production rate is sufficiently high.
- Thin sections, intricate shapes can be easily cast.

Limitations :

- The process is limited to only cylindrical and annular parts with a limited range of sizes.
- It requires high initial cost.
- Its maintenance also is quite expensive and requires skilled labour.

6.3 CASTING DEFECTS

Some of the important casting defects, their causes and remedies are described below :

1. Blow Holes : These are in the form of internal voids, dispersed internal porosity or surface depression as a result of excessive gases which cannot escape. They are caused by hard ramming, excessive moisture, improper venting, low temperature of mould and excess other organic materials. These can be controlled by taking care of the above mentioned points.

2. Surface Roughness : Too coarse a moulding sand or when pouring temperature is high lead to rough surface castings. Proper quality of moulding sand and correct pouring temperatures should be used.

3. Scabs or Buckles : These defects occur due to some sand shearing from the cope surface and as a result, a layer of metal is separated from the casting by a layer of sand. Scabs are relatively small particles and buckles are big defects. These can be avoided by pouring metal rapidly and by using sand with high hot plasticity.

4. Shrinkage : Shrinkage refers to the condition of voids in the casting resulting from concentration of the metal during solidification. This defect occurs on account of improper location of gates and runners and inadequate filleting of corners.

5. Hot-tear : It is due to the discontinuity in the metal casting resulting from hindered contraction, occurring just after the metal has solidified. It is due to the poor collapsibility of mould, poor design and very hard ramming of sand. Hot-tear can be eliminated by an improvement in the above shortcomings.

6. Sand Spots : These are irregularly shaped depressions spaced randomly or clustered on casting and are due to impurities collected at one or more vortices developed by the metal. By adopting proper moulding, gating and melting techniques, these can be minimised.

7. Cold Shots : These are external defects and are caused by two streams of metals that are too cold to fuse properly. These occur due to slow pouring, poor design and small gate. These can be eliminated by improving the design and adjusting the pouring temperature to ensure proper fluidity.

8. Sponginess or Honey-Combing : It is also an external defect, consisting of a number of cavities in close proximity. It is caused by dirt held in the molten metal, imperfect skimming and poor quality of molten metal.

9. Porosity : These are rounded voids with smooth walls and occur due to gases dissolved in metal during melting and pouring. Imperfect feeding causes angular voids.

10. Metal Penetration : This defect occurs when the molten metal penetrates into the interstices of sand grains and holds some of the sand tightly with it. This causes a rough and uneven external surface on the casting. It is caused because of soft ramming, use of coarse sand, having high permeability and low strength. By using fine sand, hard ramming and proper metal temperature, this defect can be minimised.

11. Swells : The bulges found on the casting surfaces are known as swells. It is due to the enlargement of mould cavity when the molten metal is poured into the mould. It is caused by either insufficient ramming or by pouring the metal too rapidly.

12. Run-outs : Run-outs occur when the molten metal leaks out of the mould during pouring, resulting in an incomplete casting. These are caused by too large pattern, uneven match plate surfaces, defective moulding boxes, which do not fit properly and excessive pouring pressure. Corrective measures in respect of these causes will prevent this defect.

13. Misruns : When molten metal fails to reach all sections of mould, certain cavities and corners are improperly filled resulting in an incomplete casting, the defect is known as misrun. It occurs because of low pouring temperature and lack of fluidity of the metal. This defect is eliminated by adjusting pouring temperature to ensure proper fluidity.

14. Sand Inclusions or Dross : These inclusions may be in the form of oxides, dirt, slag, sand etc. Oxides are generally formed on the exposed surface of molten metal. These should be prevented from entering the mould cavity. Proper fluxing and effective skimming prevent their entry.

15. Pour-short : It refers to the condition of incomplete filling of mould due to insufficient metal in the laddle and interruptions during pouring operation.

16. Fins : A thin projection of metal, which is not a part of casting, is called fin. These usually occur at the parting of mould and core section. These are caused by run out of metal, poor fittings on moulds and cores, high metal pressure etc.

17. Warpage : It is an undesirable deformation in the casting which occurs during or after solidification. The deformation takes place due to internal stresses developed in the casting due to differential solidification in different sections. It is due to the faulty design of the casting.

18. Lifts and Shifts : These are caused due to misalignment of pattern parts, flask equipment, and improper handling of mould. These are external defects in castings.

6.4 ADVANTAGES AND LIMITATIONS OF CASTING METHODS

Advantages

- Large or small, simple or complicated shapes can be made with this casting.
- The objects can be casted from ferrous or non-ferrous materials.
- It is the cheapest method to produce the objects.
- Good finished objects can be produced.
- It can be used for mass production.

Limitations

- Dimensional accuracy and high quality finish cannot be achieved.
- The castings are always associated with some forms of defects.

The casting methods for producing objects are universally used for the following parts :

- Machine tool frames and beds.
- Rail wheel and housing.
- Automobile engine beds.
- Turbine vanes.
- Agricultural equipments.

(B) Machine Tools

6.5 INTRODUCTION TO MACHINE TOOLS

In the present advanced techological society, we use hundreds of equipments in our house, shops, industries, institutes and many others. Each equipment is of unique nature and requires engineering talent for its manufacturing. The idea of equipment configuration is cooked in the minds of engineers and they are manufactured in the work-shop using different types of machines or known as machine tools.

Each equipment is made of raw materials cutting excess material and given a shape as per the requirements. The machines used for giving the required shape to the raw material cutting excess material are known as machine tools. It is a power driven machine which holds the work-piece and gives the motion to the work-piece and tool to perform necessary operation of cutting.

The different manufacturing processes which are commonly used in paractice are shown in Fig. 6.5 and according to the nature of the process required a typical type of machine tool is used.

The following are the basic machine tools which are commonly used in every workshop.

1. Lathe machine (for turning and reducing the diameter).

2. Drilling machine (for generating hole).
3. Shaping machine (for producing flat surface).
4. Milling machine (metal is removed as work is fed against a rotating multi-point cutter as per requirements).
5. Grinding machine (for producing smooth surfaces).

The purpose of this chapter is to introduce the students the configuration of first two simple machines, their different parts and different processes which are carried out on each machine.

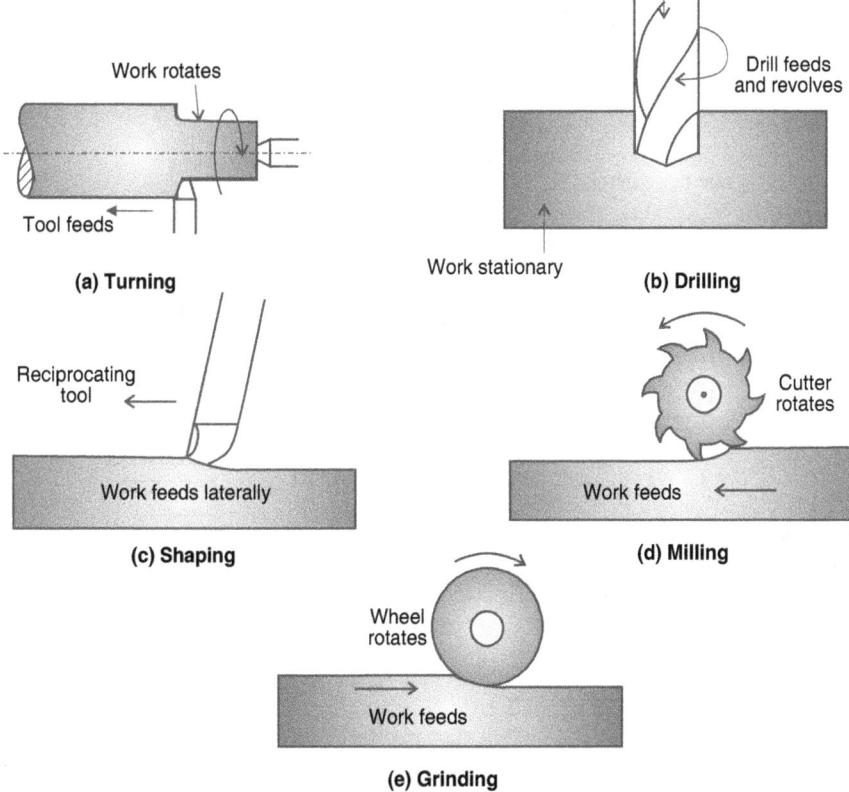

Fig. 6.5 : Different cutting operations

6.6 LATHE MACHINE AND ITS PRINCIPAL PARTS

The configuration of a lathe commonly used in work-shop is shown in Fig. 6.6. The different parts and their functions are described below :

1. Bed : The bed is the basic component of the lathe and all the parts are mounted on it. The head stock, tail stock and carriage are mounted on bed. It provides guide ways for sliding the tail stock and carriage. It is generally casted as one piece and made of gray cast iron.

2. Headstock : It is mounted at the left hand end of the machine and houses the driving mechanism ether pulley or gears — for providing different speeds to the work-piece as per requierment. The head stock provides a support to the work-piece either with the centre fitted into the spindle or by a chuck.

3. Tailstock : It is mounted on the bed opposite to head stock. It can slide along the bed to hold the work-piece accroding to the length of work-piece. The very purpose of tail stock is to support long jobs to avoid vibrations. It can also hold drill, reamber or tab when required for drilling, reaming and taping.

4. Carriage : It is located between tailstock and headstock and can be moved in longitudinal direction. It can be fixed at any desired position. It also carries cross-slide and tool post as shown in figure. The tool post is used to hold the tool and position the tool as per requirements. The tool post-slide helps to rotate the tool post in the horizontal plane.

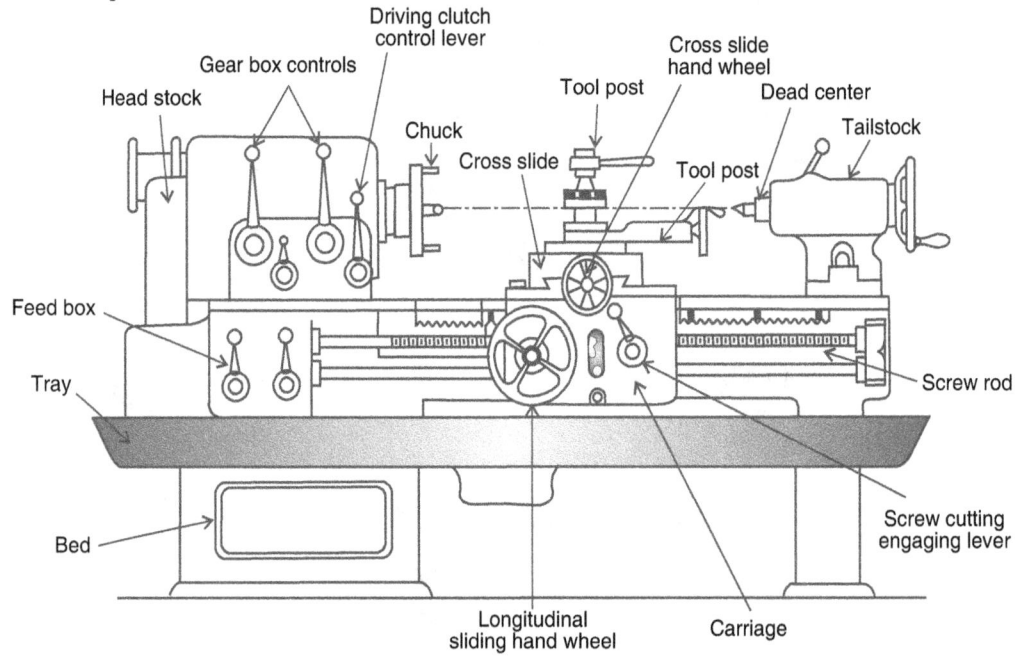

Fig. 6.6 : Important parts of lathe

5. Lead Screw : It is a threaded long part as shown in figure driven by driving mechanism and used for thread cutting purposes.

6. Tray : It is fitted to cover the whole lathe parts and fitted as shown in Fig. 6.6 This is used to collect the coolent which falls on the job during cutting operation. The collected coolent is taken out from the holes provided at the bottom of the tray and recirculated again after filteration.

Job Holding Device

A part which is to be turned on the lathe is to be hold in some device fitted on the lathe is known as a chuck. The common chucks which are used are described below.

(a) 3-Jaw or Universal Chuck : The configuration of 3-jaw chuck is shown in Fig. 6.7 (a). It is known as self-centering check as all the three jaws move towards the centre simultaneously. This helps the operator to load and unload the job quickly and easily.

(b) 4-Jaw Independent Chuck : It has four independent jaws as shown in Fig. 6.7 (b). The loading operation is slower as jaws must be adjusted separately. The advantage of this chuck is, its holding power is more and it is used for holding both on and off centre work. It can also be used to hold odd-shaped pieces also.

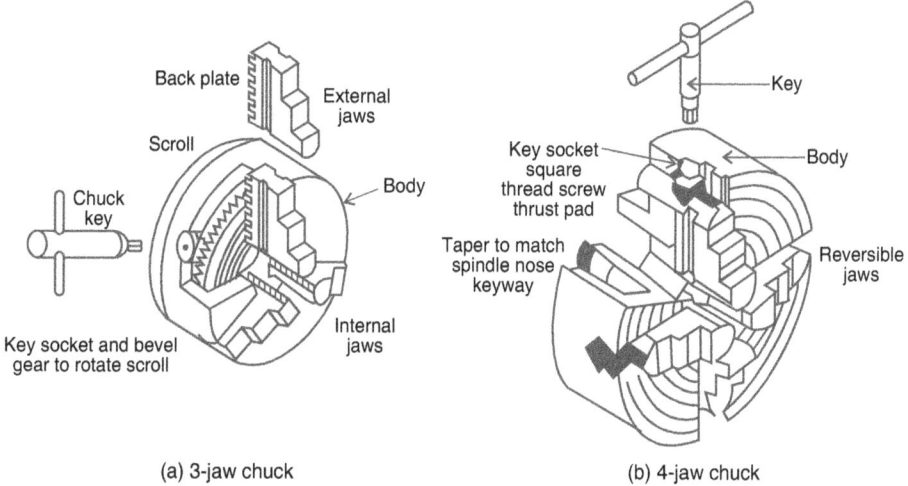

(a) 3-jaw chuck (b) 4-jaw chuck

Fig. 6.7 : Chuck

6.7 DIFFERENT OPERATIONS PERFORMED ON LATHE

The different cutting operations performed on the lathe are described below.

(a) Turning Operation : The positions of the work-piece and the cutting tool are shown in Fig. 6.8 (a). In this operation, the diameter of the work-piece is reduced to a desired diameter. During this operation, the workpiece is fixed in the chuck and the tool is clamped in the tool post. The work-piece is rotated and cutting tool is fed parallel to the axis of rotation.

The surface of the piece can be rough or smooth according to the depth of cut and feed of the tool. Higher depth of cut and high feed are used for rough cutting and lower depth of cut and lower feed are used for finished surface.

If the diameter is reduced uniformly throughout the length of workpiece, it is known as straight turning and where the work-piece is made of different diameters, then it is known as step-turning.

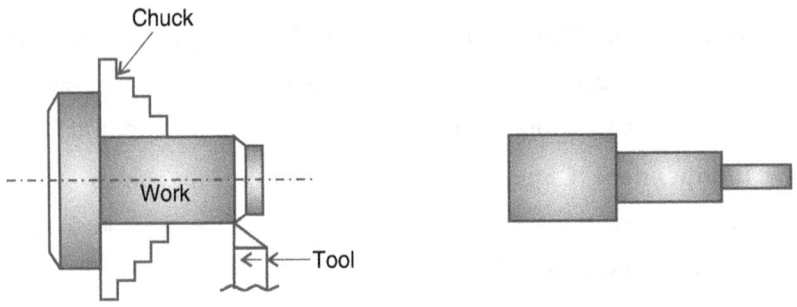

Fig. 6.8 (a) : Turning operation   Fig. 6.8 (b) : Step-turning

(b) Facing Operation : This machining operation is used to produce flat surface at the end of work-piece. The tool is fed perpendicular to the axis of rotation. The tool is held slightly inclined as shown in Fig. 6.8 (c). The movement to the tool is given with the help of cross-slide.

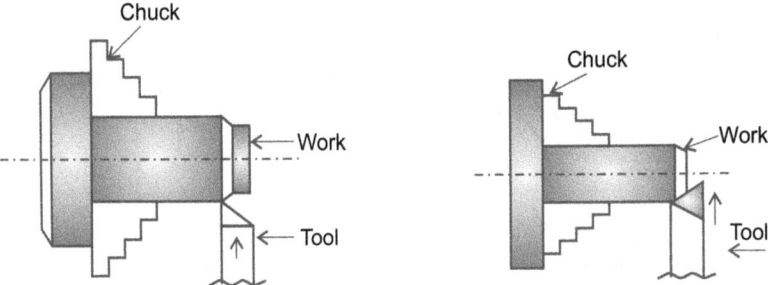

Fig. 6.8 (c) Facing operation   Fig. 6.8 (d) : Chamfering operation

(c) Chamfering : This operation is used to provide small tapered shape at the end of the work-piece as shown in Fig. 6.8 (d). The work is fitted in the chuck and rotated and tool is fed perpendicular to the axis of rotation.

(d) Forming : This operation is used to give required profile to the work-piece. The required profile is obtained by pressing the form tool against the surface of work-piece as shown in Fig. 6.8 (e). This operation is used to produce convex, concave or any other shape as required.

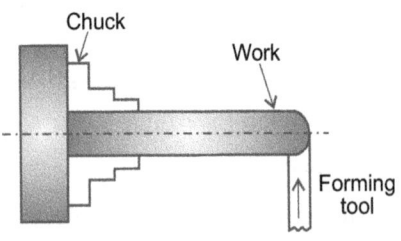
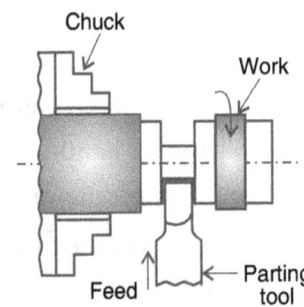

Fig. 6.8 (e) : Forming operation   Fig. 6.8 (f) : Grooving or Parting operation

(e) Grooving or Part-off : With the help of this operation, groove is formed in the work-piece, if required. Grooving tool of the desired groove width is fed in the work-piece as shown in Fig. 6.8 (f), perpendicular to the axis of rotation.

The parting-off operation from the work-piece of required length can also be carried out. A parting tool is used for this purpose.

(f) Knurling : This process is used for embossing a required shape-pattern on the surface of the work-piece. This is done to provide firm gripping to the work-piece. A kurling tool as shown in Fig. 6.8 (g) of required pattern is used for the purpose.

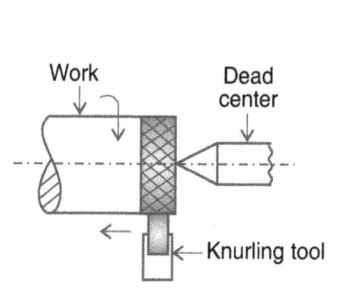

Fig. 6.8 (g) : Knurling operation

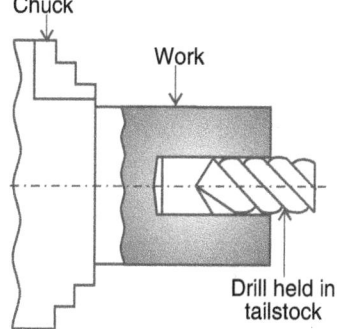

Fig. 6.8 (h) : Drilling operation

(g) Drilling or Reaming : Using drilling operation, a hole is produced in the work-piece by using a tool known as drill. The work-piece is fitted in the chuck and drill is fitted into the tail strock spindle as shown in Fig. 6.8 (h). The drill is fed in the work along the axis of the work-piece and removes the material from the work-piece and produces a hole of drill diameter size.

If drilled hole is to be corrected to a desired size after drilling, a reaming operation is carried out as shown in Fig. 6.8 (i). For this purpose a reaming tool is used. This operation also provides the smoothness to the drilled hole.

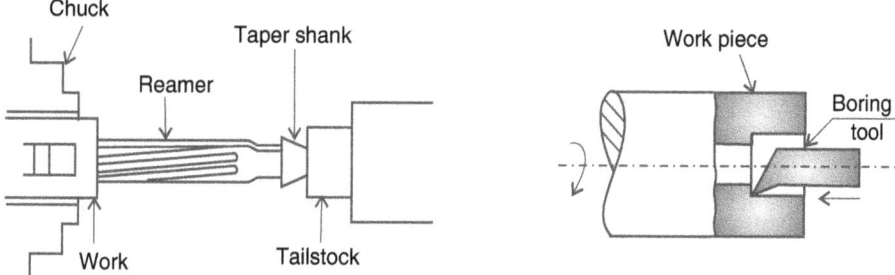

Fig. 6.8 (i) : Reaming operation

Fig. 6.8 (j) : Boring operation

(h) Boring Operation : This operation is used for enlarging the drilled hole by using boring tool as shown in Fig. 6.8 (j). The work-piece is held in the chuck and is rotated. The boring tool fitted on tool post is fed in the work-piece along the axis for enlarging the drilled hole. If this boring operation is carried out upto certain length of the work-piece, then it is called counter boring.

(i) Filing : After turning operation on the work-piece, a finishing operation on the surface is done by using filing. A fine file is pressed on the surface of work-piece and pressed with the hand on the rotating work-piece.

(j) Taper Turning : A taper is defined as a uniform increase or decrease in diameter along the length of the work-piece. The taper turning operation on the lathe produces a conical shape work-piece.

The taper turning operation is carried out by using different methods as described below.

(a) Taper Turning by Form Tool : In this method, a tool with straight cutting edge making half the taper angle with respect to lathe axis is fixed on tool post. The work-piece is held in the chuck and rotated. Then the tool is fed against the rotating work-piece where taper is to be produced. This method is used to provide taper on short-lenght work-piece as shown in Fig. 6.9 (a).

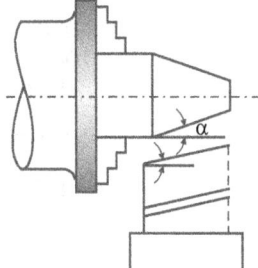
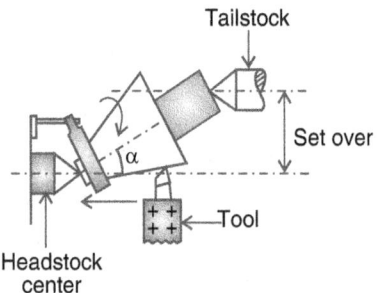

(a) Taper turning by a form tool   (b) Taper turning by tailstock set-over

Fig. 6.9

(b) Using Tailstock Set-over : In this method, the tailstock body is made to slide on the base as when in Fig. 6.9 (b) towards or away from the operator by a set-over screw. The work-piece is held between two centres which itself provides an angle to the work-piece. The tool is fed straight along the axis as shown in figure. During the motion of the tool, the material is removed from the surface of the work-piece and generates taper surface.

This method is suitable only for small taper on long jobs as tailstock set-over is limited.

(k) Threading Operation : This is a special operation carried out on the lathe as special mechanism is provided. The threads are formed either on internal surface or external surface of a cylinder. The principle of thread cutting operation is to generate a helical groove on a cylinderical surface by feeding the tool longitudinally when the work-piece is rotating between two centres. The longitudinal feed must be equal to the pitch of the thread.

The lead screw of the lathe, through which saddle receives its traversing motion, has a definite pitch. Definite ratio between longitudinal feed and speed of spindle is to be calculated so that the relative speed of work-piece and lead-screw will result in cutting of threads of desired pitch. This is effected by gear mechanism provided with the lathe. Once the change-gears are set, then half-nut is engaged with lead-screw. This engagement moves the cutting tool through a distance equal to pitch of the thread in one revolution of the spindle. The shape of the tool is according to the type of thread desired. For obtaining threads of different pitches, the speed of lead-screw is changed by engaging proper change-gears.

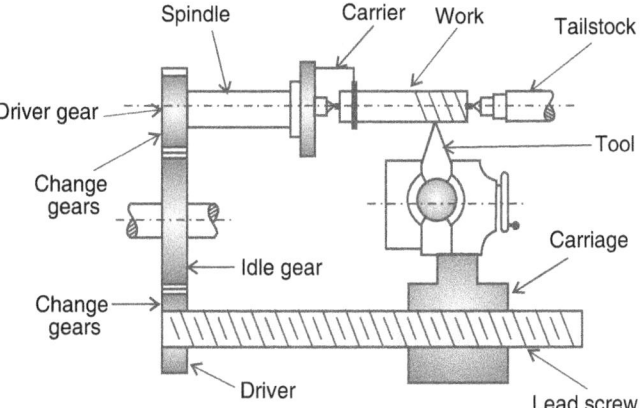

Fig. 6.10 : Threading operation

6.8 DRILLING MACHINE

This machine is commonly used for making hole of required diameter in the blank work-piece. This process of making hole is known as drilling.

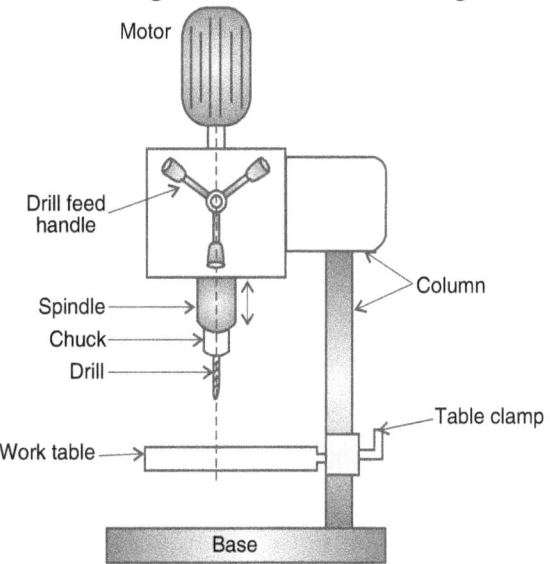

Fig. 6.11 : Drilling machine

The holes in the workpiece are essential for many purposes like fasting the object with bolts and nuts for fixing.

A conventional drilling machine is shown in Fig. 6.11.

It consists of a spindle, drilling tool, and a work-piece fixing table and all these components are supported by a frame as shown in Fig. 6.11.

The spindle is rotated by a motor and transmitting mechanism. The drill is press-fitted into the spindle and work-piece is fixed on the table. As the drill is fed into work-piece, the hole is created by removing the material in the form of chips.

The column is a vertical part fixed to the base which supports the driving and feed mechanism. The work table has two types of motion as it can move up and down and it can swing about the column.

The drilling machines are classified as listed below as per their use and configuration.

1. Portable Drilling Machine : This is small and compact machine which can be

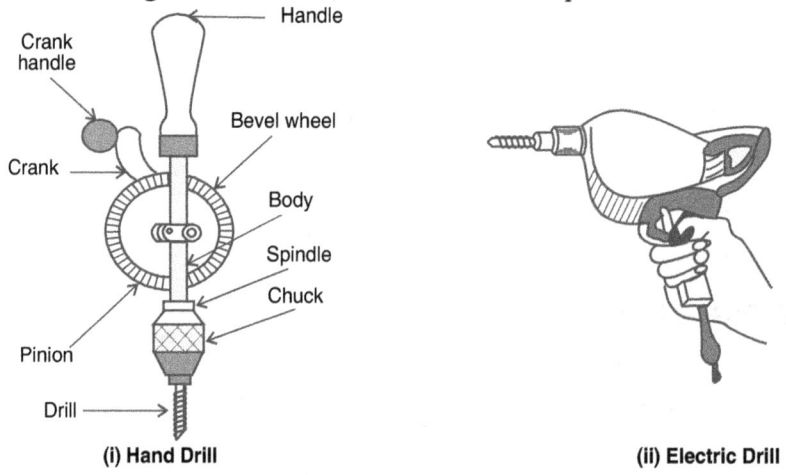

(i) Hand Drill   (ii) Electric Drill

Fig. 6.12 (a)

carried easily at the work place and used for the purpose. A hand operated drill is shown in Fig. 6.12 (a), which is used for drilling small diameter holes in sheet metal or wooden sheet. It is fitted with a chuck to take small straight shank drills and operated by turning the large bevel wheel which is geared with pinion.

Another portable machine is shown in Fig. 6.12 (b), which is known as electrical drill as it is operated by using small electric motor. It is operated by means of a switch fitted into the hand grip and a small high speed motor geared to drive the spindle.

2. Sensitive Drilling Machine : This machine is small in size and it is provided with high speed mechanism of simple construction with belt drive as shown in Fig. 6.12 (b). It consists of standard horizontal table and vertical spindle for holding and rotating the drill. This type of machine is hand-feed, usually by means of rack and pinion arrangement. This arrangement helps the operator to sense the force applied and therefore it is known as sensitive drilling machine. This is generally suitable for light work and drills upto 15 mm diameter.

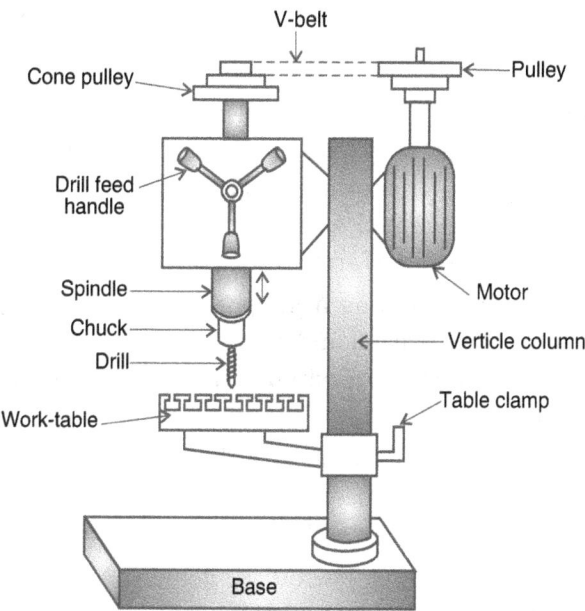

Fig. 6.12 (b) : Sensitive drilling machie

3. Piller or Column Upright Drilling Machine : This is similar to sensitive drilling machine except the column is more rigid and therefore, can be used for heavy duty

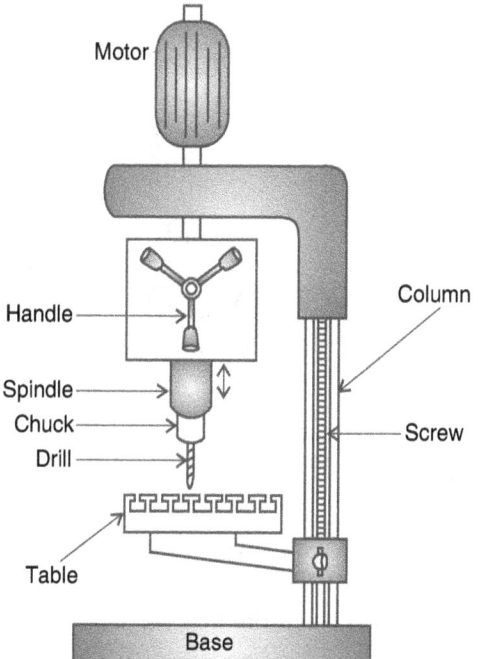

Fig. 6.12 (c) : Piller drilling machine

work. It is provided with power feed and a speed change gear box. A universal table is used instead of standard T-slot table, providing accurate lateral and longitudinal movement as its movement is controlled by lead screw. The machine is of heavier construction and better suited for a wide range of jobs. It is used to drill upto 40 mm diameter. The configuration of the machine is shown in Fig. 6.12 (c).

4. Radial Drilling Machine : When work-piece is large and requires several holes, then it is difficult to position the work-piece for each operation. To avoid this difficulty, it is equipped with radial arm as shown in Fig. 6.13, that can swing through an arc 180° and therefore, can be positioned at any desired place easily and accurately. The drilling head is mounted on the radial arm.

The column of the machine acts as a support for radial arm which can be easily raised or lowered (as it is power driven) and swing to any position as required. It is used to drill number of holes on a work-piece without changing the position of the work-piece which is fixed on the table.

The major advantages of this machine are, the cutting tool can be located at any desired point easily and the arm can be raised or lowered along the column which helps to accommodate a wide range of works with wide range of heights.

In addition to the above drilling machines, gang drilling machine (two or more drilling heads are mounted), multi-spindle drilling machine (number of holes can be drilled simultaneously) and deep hole drilling machines (as hole in connecting rod and rifle barrel) are also used. The details are not included in this text as it is out of the scope of this text.

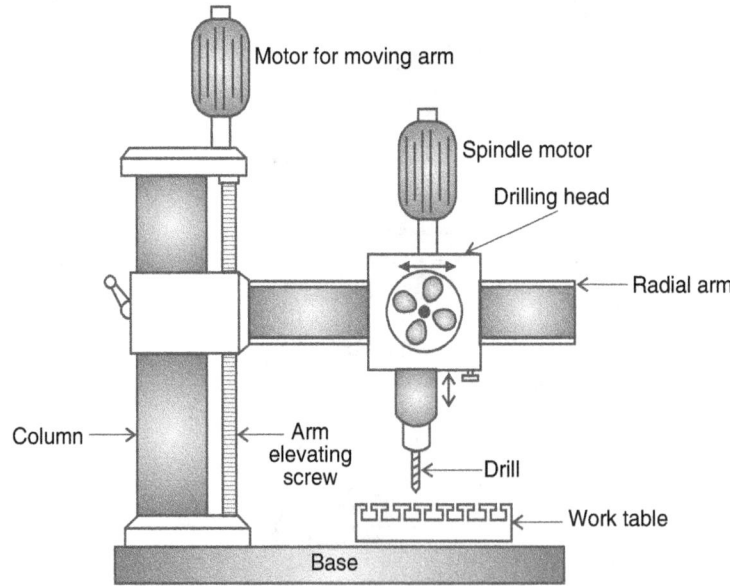

Fig. 6.13 : Radial drilling machine

6.9 OPERATIONS CARRIED OUT ON DRILLING MACHINE

The different opeations carried out with the help of drilling machine are described below.

1. Drilling : Drilling operation is carried out to produce a cylindrical hole in the work-piece with the help of drill-tool as shown in Fig. 6.14 (a). The job is fixed on the table and revolving drill removes the metal in the form of chips and generates the hole in work-piece.

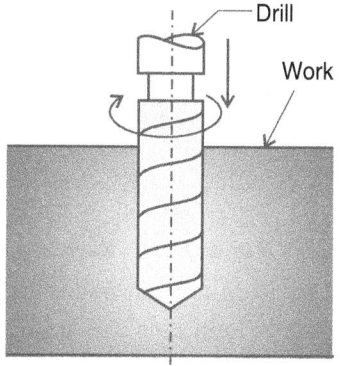

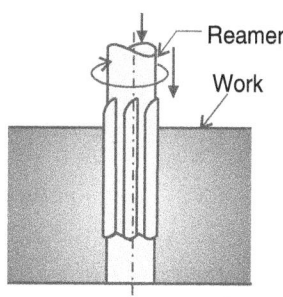

Fig. 6.14 (a) : Drilling   Fig. 6.14 (b) : Reaming

2. Reaming : The drilling cannot produce the hole of exact diameter, therefore a reaming is used which finishes the drilled hole to accurate size and gives fine surface finish. The tool used for the purpose is known as reamer, which is shown in Fig. 6.14 (b).

3. Boring : This is generally used to enlarge the already drilled hole to bring it to the required size and gives better finish. A boring tool is used for this operation as shown in Fig. 6.14 (c).

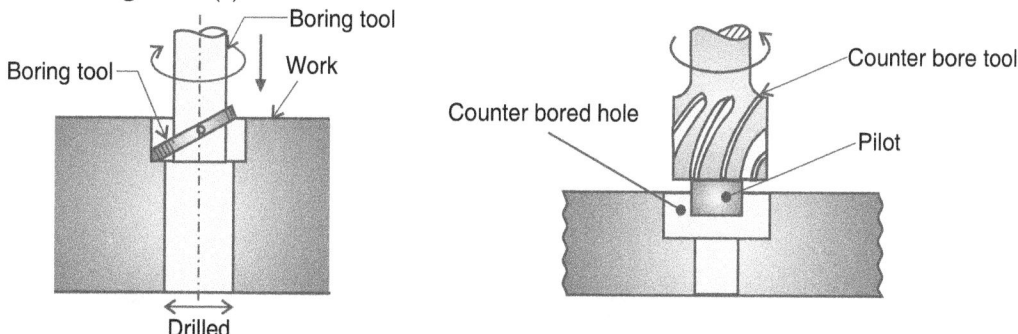

Fig. 6.14 (c) : Boring   Fig. 6.14 (d) : Counter boring

4. Counter Boring : This operation is used to enlarge the already drilled hole upto certain depth only as shown in Fig. 6.14 (d). It is performed by using counter boring tool. This counter bored hole can be used as a seat for bolt or nut etc.

5. Counter Sinking : By using this operation, a cone shaped enlargement of the drilled hole is done by using a tool known as counter sink tool as shown in Fig. 6.14(e). This is used for providing seat for counter sink screws.

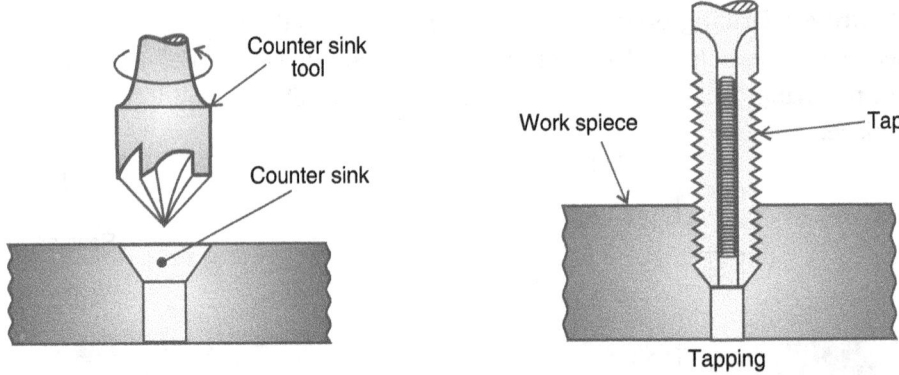

Fig. 6.14 (e) : Counter sinking   Fig. 6.14 (f) : Tapping

6. Tapping : With the help of tapping, internal threads are cut in the drilled hole. Thi tool used for the purpose is known as tap. Tie tap is held into the spindle and fed into the drilled hole with the help of hands and the threads are cut as shown in Fig. 6.14 (f).

7. Spot Facing : With the help of this operation, finishing of the surface around and at the end of the hole is carried out. A special spot facing tool is used for the purpose as shown in Fig. 6.14 (g).

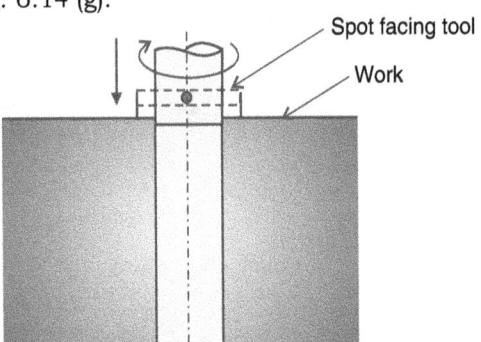

Fig. 6.14 (g) : Spot facing

(C) Joining Processes

6.10 INTRODUCTION TO METAL JOINING PROCESSES

Welding is a process of joining two similar metal pieces by applying pressure on the surfaces in the plastic state or without pressure in the fusion state. This is also done with or without the use of filter metal as per requirement.

In welding, two similar metal pieces are permanently joined together through localized function by providing the heat and pressure.

Welding process is very commonly used in our daily life as well as in industries for fabricating boiler sheets, oil tanks, bridge structures, house grills, automobile parts and many others. Therefore, the basic purpose of this chapter is to introduce the basic principles of different welding methods which are commonly used in practice.

The required heat for welding is applied by different methods and using different equipments. This heat is applied by using a gas, so the welding method is known as gas welding and when heat is applied by electric arc, then it is known as arc welding.

Different types of welding which are commonly used are described in this chapter.

6.11 CLASSIFICATION OF WELDING METHODS

The welding process is mainly classified as plastic and fusion welding.

In plastic welding method, the metals to be joined are heated to the plastic state and then forced together by external pressure without the addition of filler material. Forged welding, resistance welding and thermic welding with pressure fall under this category.

In fusion welding method, a high temperature is produced near the joint which is above the melting point of the joining metal without any pressure. The metal at the joint is heated to the molten state and then allowed to solidify. The required heat is generated either by producing an electric arc or by burning the gases. These methods are known as arc welding and gas welding respectively.

The general classification of welding method is shown below

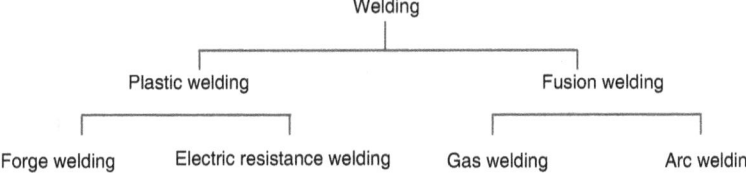

The above mentioned methods are also further classified which will be discussed in detail.

The forge welding is the oldest method of welding. In this process of welding, the parts to be welded are heated in a furnace till the metal comes in plastic state and then they are removed from the furnace and placed end to end and then hammered either manually or by power hammer until they form a solid structure. This method is used for welding low carbon steels and wrought iron. This method is rarely used now a days for mass production processes.

6.12 ELECTRIC RESISTANCE WELDING

In this method of welding, heat required for welding is generated by the resistance of workpiece keeping it in the electric circuit. During welding, a pressure is applied. No filler material is required for this type of welding.

The heat generated for welding is given by $Q = C\ I^2 R_e$ watts

where R_e is the electric resistance offered by the joint in Ohms and I is the current through the contact surfaces in ampers. The C is a factor which takes into account the heat losses.

The advantages and disadvantages of this system are listed below.

Advantages

1. The production rate is fast.
2. The filler material is not required.

3. Skilled worker is not required.
4. Practically, all metals can be joined.

Disadvantages
1. The capital cost of equipment is high.
2. It is suitable only to weld thin sheets.

This method is commonly used for joining sheets, making tubes, air-craft and automobile parts, making tanks of cars and tractors and many others.

The electric resistance welding is further classified as spot welding and seam welding.

(a) Spot Welding : This is the most widely used method of resistance welding. In this process of welding, two sheets of metal are held between metal electrodes and a low voltage current is passed between the electrodes. A pressure is applied over the electrode which squeezes the metal together and forms the weld.

The configuration of the system is shown in Fig. 6.15 and its principle of operation is described below.

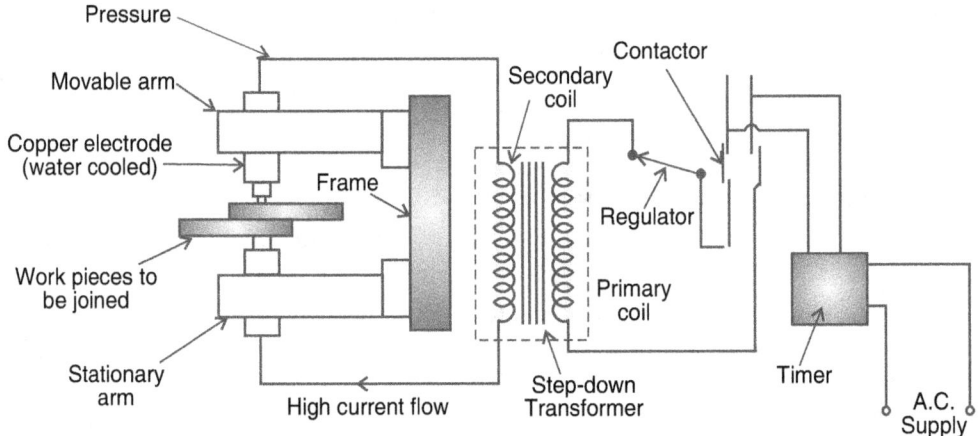

Fig. 6.15 : Circuit for spot welding machine

First the electrodes are brought together against the overlapping work-pieces and high pressure is applied to make perfect contact between the sheets. Then very high current of the order of 5×10^3 to 100×10^3 amperes is passed through the electrode for a predetermined time (a few seconds) depending upon the type of metal and its thickness. The temperature at the point of weld ranges from 800°C to 1000°C. Then the current is switched off and pressure is released allowing to cool down and form the firm joints. This process of welding along the length of the sheet is continued. The number of welded points per unit length is earlier decided and for the same, the procedure described above is continued.

It is the simplest form of resistance welding and widely used for manufacturing automobile and refrigeration and air-conditioning parts.

(b) Projection Welding : Projection welding is just similar to spot welding method, except one of the metal piece among the two to be welded has projections on its surface as shown in Fig. 6.16. Two plates which are to be welded are held in position between fixed and movable electrodes and current and pressure are localised at welding points by making projections for the upper sheet of the metal.

In this case, the electrodes are flat instead to tips in spot welding and therefore, the surface area in contact with electrode is relatively large. The electrical power and mechanical pressure required are more compared with spot welding as number of welds are more.

The projection provided in upper piece is held in contact with lower piece under pressure given by the electrode. When the current is switched ON, the heat produced brings the metal projection in plastic state and weld is formed because of the pressure applied by the electrode.

This is more preferred for forming refrigerator condensers.

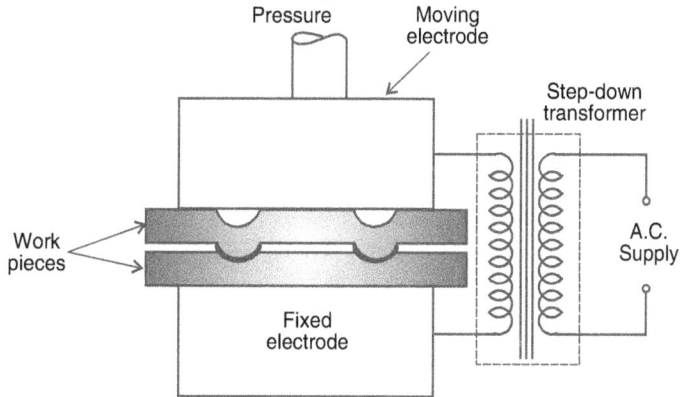

Fig. 6.16 : Projection welding principle

(c) Seam Welding : This process of welding is just similar to spot welding method, except the electrodes used in spot welding are replaced by roller type rotating electrodes which are operated by power drive as shown in Fig. 6.17. The work-sheets which are to be welded are passed through the rotating electrodes.

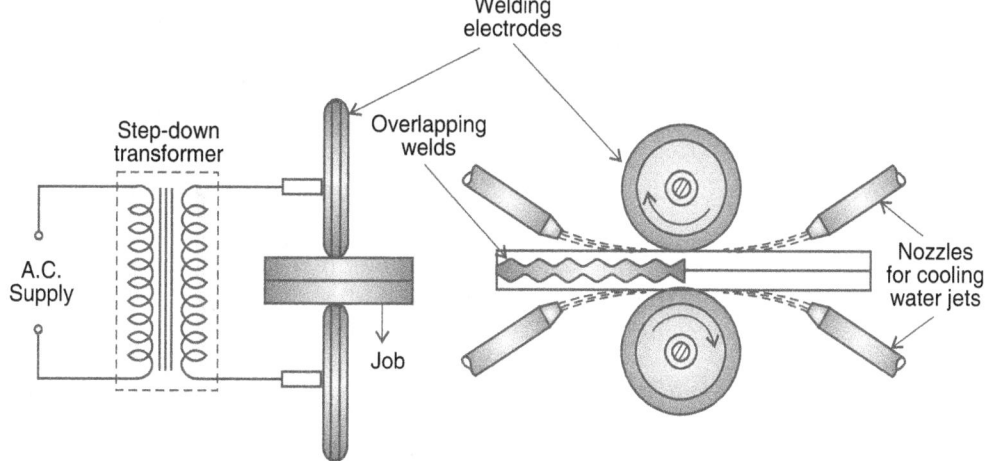

Fig. 6.17 : Seam welding principle

When the metal sheets are passed through the rotating electrodes, a current impulse is applied to the electrodes to generate heat to bring the metal in plastic region. The pressure applied by the electrode roller completes the weld.

The current applied is 'ON' for a definite length of time and is OFF for another definite length of time. Due to this intermittent current, overlapping spot welds are obtained and therefore, it is known as seam welding.

This method of welding is very commonly used for manufacturing tanks of ferrous and non-ferrous metals where liquid or air-tight joints are essential.

To prevent the overheating of the surfaces of sheets, a water cooling is provided through the water nozzles as shown in Fig. 6.17.

6.13 ARC WELDING

In arc welding process, fusion of metal is produced by heating the work-piece and the electric arc sets up between the electrode and work-piece. The electrode used during the process melts and supplies the filler metal for joining the two pieces together.

Different equipments which are commonly used with arc welding process, are listed below.

1. D.C. Generator or Transformer : For welding, using the A.C. supply, a step-down transformer is used which reduces the supply voltage from main supply to 80-100 volts. A current regulator is provided (operated by hand) which ranges from 30 to 500 amperes. If the D.C. voltage is used, then D.C. generator is used which develops direct current of 80-100 volts.

2. Electrodes and Electrode Holders : A heavy coated electrodes of length 25 cm to 45 cm and a diameter of 1.5 mm to 10 mm diameter are used as per requirements. A well insulated electric holder is used to grip the electrode by lever held in operator's hands.

3. Cables, Cable connector and Earthing Clamp : The cables and cable connectors are used to carry the current from the transformer to the point of welding. The earthing clamp is used to complete the electric circuit.

4. Face Shield and Hard Gloves : The arc produced emits ultra-violet and infra-red rays because of very high temperature produced during arcing. It is necessary to protect the face of the operator from these rays, therefore, face shield or safety goggle is used for this purpose.

Hand gloves are used to protect the hands of the operator from the sparks during arcing.

5. Clipping Hammer and Wire Brush : A light hammer is used to remove the slag from the weld and brush is used for cleaning the weld after chipping.

(A) Arc Welding :

In arc welding, an electric arc is produced by passing large electric current between the electrodes separated by a small gap. The welding rod behaves as one welding electrode and the metal-piece which is to be welded becomes the second electrode.

A general arc welding set-up is shown in Fig. 6.20. The electrodes (welding rod and job to be welded) are connected to the supply. When one electrode (welding rod) just touches the work-piece, arc is started and then it is separated by 3 to 4 mm by hand and moved along the line of the work-piece which is to be welded. The arc produces the temperature of about 5000°C which melts the metals and forms the weld when solidified. The arc voltage lies between 20 to 40 V and current lies between 50 to 1000 amperes.

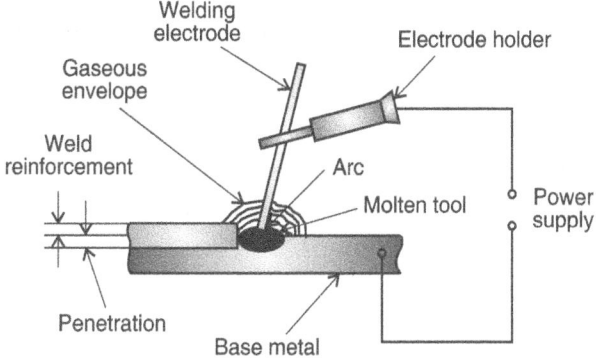

Fig. 6.18 : Arc welding set-up

Different types of arc welding commonly used, are described below.

Metal Arc Welding :

It is a simple arc welding method as described earlier, where coated metal electrode is used instead of base electrode. The electrode melts and provides necessary filler metal for forming the joint. The welded joint during this process is shown in Fig. 6.19 where the arc created forms the molten metal and further forms the weld. The coating over the core rod also melts and forms a protective layer over the molten surface. During welding, a gaseous film is also formed and surrounds the arc which also works as protective shield for oxidation of the molten metal.

The joint to be welded, the edges of the joint and adjoining area is cleaned from scale, rust, dust or any other foreign materials. Before starting the welding, suitable welding voltage and current are set and then welding is started.

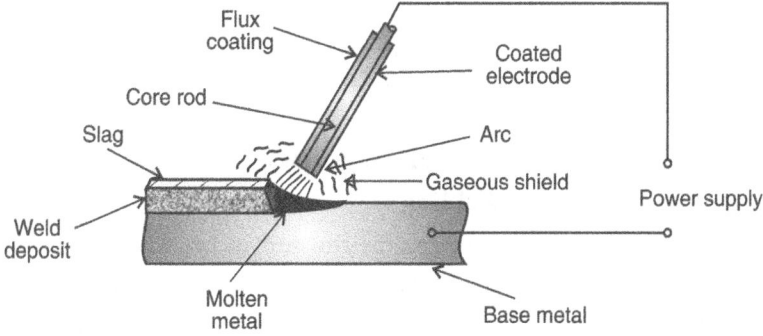

Fig. 6.19 : Metal arc welding

(B) Inert Gas Welding

In this method of welding, fusion is produced by an arc like conventional arc welding, except the welding electrode and work-piece are shielded by some inert gas like argon, helium or carbon dioxide. This protects the weld totally from the oxidation as the chance of oxidation of the weld is very high because of very high temperature produced by the arc (5000°C) during welding.

There are two types of inert gas welding known as MIG and TIG-welding.

1. Metal Inert Gas (MIG) Welding :

The configuration of the system is shown in Fig. 6.20. In this process of welding, the arc is maintained between consumable electrode and work-piece which are surrounded by inert gas atmosphere. The coil electrode wire is fed by drive rolls as shown in Fig. 6.20 as it melts at the tip for welding purposes. The D.C. supply is commonly used except for aluminium with the consumable electrode as positive terminal. This method of welding is used for thick plates and fillet welds.

The advantages and disadvantages of this method are listed below.

Advantages :

1. There is no slag formation.
2. Deeper penetration is possible.
3. It produces better quality weld.
4. It is more suitable for welding thin sheets.
5. It forms faster welding.

The major disadvantage is, its capital and running costs are considerably high.

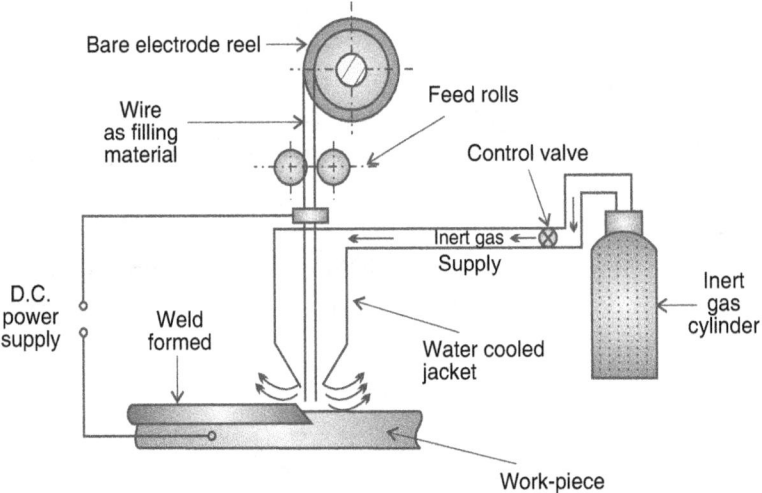

Fig. 6.20 : Metal inert gas (MIG) welding

2. Tungsten Inert Gas (TIG) Welding :

It is exactly same as arc welding, except the arc is produced between a tungsten electrode and work-piece. No filling material is fed and the arc produced melts the work-piece and forms the weld. In this case also, the inert gas is supplied to shield the molten metal to avoid other chemical reactions on the weld surface. Welding current, inert gas and cooling water supply are started simultaneously. The configuration of the system is shown in Fig. 6.21.

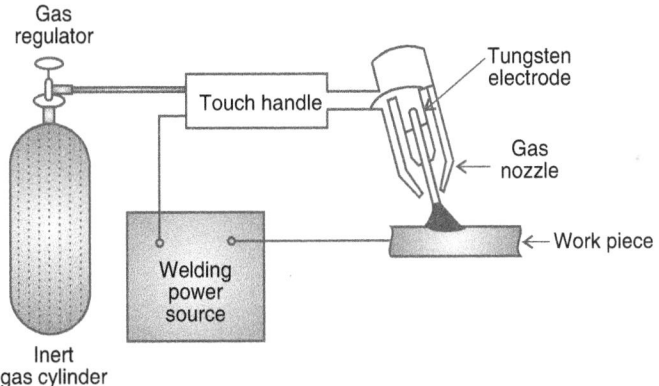

Fig. 6.21 : TIG welding equipment

The advantages and disadvantages of this process of welding are listed below.

Advantages :
1. The possibility of flux entrainment is totally eliminated as flux is not used.
2. The operator has better control over the process as the visibility of arc and job is clear.
3. High quality welding is produced (clean and uniform welding).
4. It is used for non-ferrous metals such as aluminium and stainless steel.
5. Very thin welding, as thin as 0.125 mm, can be produced. It also produces quality welding joints of magnesium and copper alloys.

Disadvantages
1. TIG welding is slow compared to MIG welding, as filler rod is not used.
2. The TIG weld surface becomes hard and brittle if tungsten is mixed with molten metal of the weld.
3. It is very costly.

This is very commonly used for welding very thin section like transistor cases; diaphragms of electronic equipments, air-craft industries and atomic reactors.

The comparison between MIG and TIG welding is given in the following table.

Sr. No.	MIG welding	TIG welding
1.	Uncoated metal electrode is used.	Tungsten electrode is used.
2.	Electrode is consumed during operation.	Electrode is not consumable.
3.	Electrode feeding mechanism is required.	Electrode feeding mechanism is not required.
4.	D.C. power source is used with work-piece as negative polarity.	D.C. power source is used with work-piece as positive polarity.
5.	A.C. power source can be used.	A.C. power source can be used.
6.	Used for joining similar metals.	Used for joining dissimilar metals.

Advantages of Arc Welding :
1. It gives excellent and strong weld quality.
2. Wide range of metals and their alloys can be welded.
3. It provides higher speed of welding.
4. It provides uniformity of weld of higher strength.
5. Higher metal deposition rates can be achieved as well as joints with deep penetration can be produced.

6.14 GAS WELDING

This is a fusion welding method which joins the metal together with the help of heat generated by the combustion of gaseous fuel (acetylene or hydrogen) and oxygen. The heat is produced in the form of flame and melts and fuses together the edges of the parts to be welded. The filler material is added to complete the weld.

Gas Welding Equipments :

The following equipments are commonly used for gas welding purposes:
1. One oxygen cylinder and one fuel gas cylinder with pressure regulators on each cylinder.
2. Blow torch with blow pipes.
3. Welding rods.
4. Goggles and hand-gloves.

Oxy-Acetylene Welding System :

This system is very commonly used in practice. The components of this system are shown in Fig. 6.22. The oxygen and acetylene are mixed in correct proportion with the help of gas control valves in the welding torch. The mixture is ignited and forms a flame at the tip of the torch. The temperature of the flame is sufficiently high (3200°C) to melt the parent metal. The filling metal (filler rod) is added to the molten metal to form the seam and helps for filling the gap between the metals to be joined. Thus the required weld is formed.

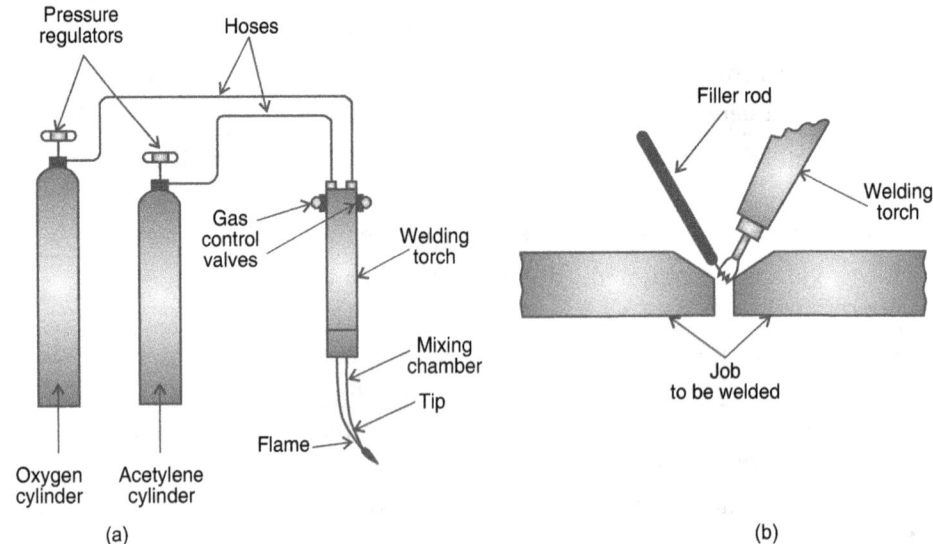

Fig. 6.22

The oxygen cylinder is charged with a required pressure (50-100 bar) but acetylene is supplied to the cylinder in the form of dissolved acetylene. The acetylene cylinder is filled with porous material in the form of charcoal and charged with acetone. This liquid has a property of absorbing 25 times its own volume of acetylene for each atmosphere of pressure applied. The pressure of acetylene is usually 15 bar and cylinder size varies from 2 to 10 m^3.

Types of Flames

The nature of welding flame plays very important role in gas welding. By changing the proportion of O_2 and acetylene in mixture. three types of flames are formed as shown in Fig. 6.23.

1. Neutral Flame : This flame is named as neutral flame as it has no effect on the chemical composition of the molten metal formed. Therefore, neither it will oxidize nor carburise the metal. Such type of flame is formed by mixing oxygen and acetylene in equal proportion. This type of flame is generally used for forming the welds of mild steel, copper and stainless steel. [Fig. 6.23 (a)]

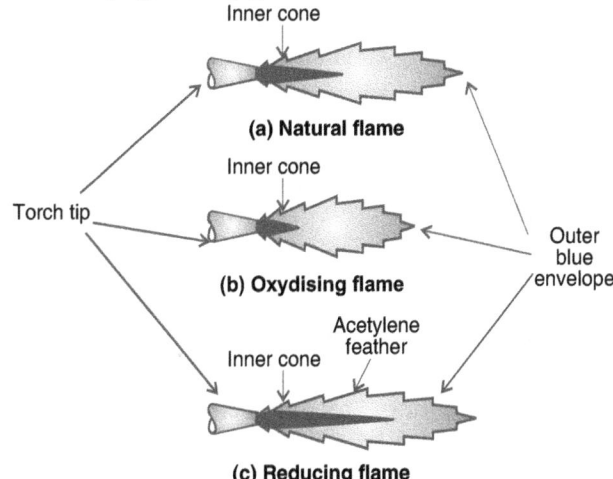

Fig. 6.23 : Types of welding flames

2. Oxidizing Flame : This flame contains more percentage of oxygen than acetylene in the mixture. The flame temperature is about 3500°C because of excess oxygen. It burns with roaring sound. This is commonly used for copper-base and zinc-base metals.

Excess oxygen available at high temperature combines with many metals and forms brittle and low strength oxides. It is never used for stainless steel. Fig. 6.23 (b).

3. Reducing Flame : This flame is rich in acetylene and forms a temperature of 3000°C. During welding, excess carbon is forced into the molten metal and makes the weld weak. Therefore, this is never used with the metals which tend to absorb carbon. Fig. 6.23 (c).

Welding Torch : This is most important part of the gas welding system. The configuration is shown in Fig. 6.24. One end of the hose is connected to the cylinder and other end to the torch. There are two such hoses for two cylinders. This type of torch delivers oxygen and acetylene to equal pressures. Both gases mix in the mixing chamber before coming to the tip of the burner. The amount of each gas is controlled with the help of needle valve as per requirement.

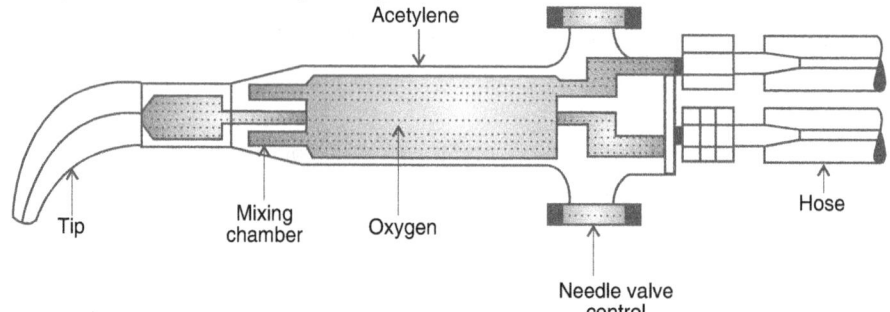

Fig. 6.24 : Construction of oxygen-acetylene torch

Advantages of Gas Welding :
1. The equipment is simple and less costly.
2. This method is used to join most of the metals.
3. It can also be used for cutting steel slabs using special torch.
4. It can be easily transported at the site of operation.

Comparison between Gas Welding and Arc Welding :

A comparison between these two welding methods is given in the following table

Sr. No.	Gas welding	Arc welding
1.	Heavy sections cannot be joined.	Best suited for heavy sections.
2.	Flame temperature (3500°C) is always less than the arc	The arc temperature formed is considerably high (5500°C)
3.	Refractory metals cannot be welded.	This can be used for refractory metals.
4.	It is slow welding process as the flame takes long time to heat the metal	It is taster5 method of welding as are temperature is higher.
5.	Flux shielding is not so effective compared with inert gas shielding used in MIG and TIG welding.	Inert gas shielding is very effective for obtaining good and strong joint.
6.	Prolonged heating period creates more distortion and less resistance to corrosion.	These problems are totally avoided in arc welding because of intense heating.

6.15 BRAZING

The brazing is a simple method of joining two similar and dissimilar metals by non ferrous fusible filler metal. The melting temperature of the filler metal (450°C) is always less than the melting temperature of the base metal. The common filler metals are

COPPE and silver alloys. The compositions and applications of these filling materials are listed below.

Filling material	Composition			Melting point	Use
Brazing brass	Cu 60	Zn 40	-	885-89°C	Ferrous metals
Silver brazing alloy	Cu 30	Zn 20	Silver 50	670-740°C	Ferrous and non-ferrous metals

The filler materials are available in the form of rod, strip or powders. The method cf joining gives quite good strength. The basic difference between welding and brazing is, the filling materials melt but base material is not melted in brazing: whereas, in welding both are melted and therefore the joint is more strong compared with brazing.

The procedure used tor brazing is shown in Fig. 6.25 and outlined as follows.

The joint which is to be brazed is first cleaned with the help of brushing and grinding. Then the base metal parts which are to be joined are aligned and then the joint is heated and filler metal is used for filling the joint. The joint is formed after cooling. It can be used for any types of metals as cast iron, wrought iron, and any ferrous and non-ferrous materials.

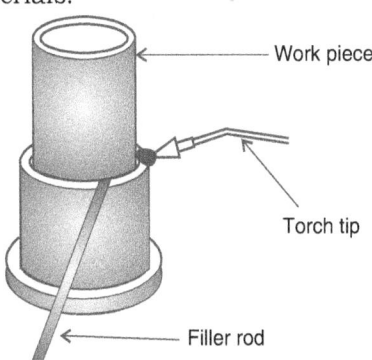

Fig. 6.25 : Brazing

The flux used for brazing is borax-powder. The main purpose of flux is to dissolve and absorb oxides which are formed during heating. It also controls the fluidity of filler metal.

The brazing torch which is normally used is oxy-acetylene gas flame. Torch used for brazing is known as brazing torch.

Advantages :

1. It is used for joining large variety of similar and dissimilar metals.
2. Pieces of different thickness can be joined satisfactorily as there is no danger of fusion.
3. It can easily join light gauge sheets and thin walled tubes which is not possible with welding.
4. It can be used to form complex and multi-component assemblies most

economically.

5. It preserves the basic metallurgical characteristics of base metals.

Limitations :
1. It cannot be used for thick and large sections as it can not be brought up to the required (brazing) temperature.
2. It requires light mating parts to ensure capillary flow of the filler metal. This requires expensive machining.
3. The possibility of corrosion exists if flux residues are not removed properly.
4. Brazing fluxes evolve toxic fumes during brazing.
5. A certain degree of skill is required to perform the brazing operation.

Applications :
1. It is very commonly used for joining thin sections like radiators of automobiles and condensers of refrigerators.
2. It can be easily used for brazing brass, bronze, copper steel and stainless steel.
3. If metallurgical characteristics of the joined material are to be preserved, then brazing is preferred over welding.
4. It can be easily used any-where, where the lightness is required but strength is not a major consideration.
5. It is very commonly used for repairing the heat exchangers used in refrigeration and air-conditioning plants.

6.16 SOLDERING

It is similar to brazing except the filler melting point temperature is considerably low. Instead of brazing torch, an electrical handy heater is used for soldering purposes as shown in Fig. 6.26. A common solder (filling material) used is composed of lead (Pb) and Tin (Sn) with low melting temperature (150-300°C).

Similar to brazing, the joint is first cleaned and heated to the required temperature and then flux is applied and solder material is filled in the joint by melting with the help of heater. The cooling makes the joint tight.

The filler material temperature is much below the temperature of the base material even compared with brazing material.

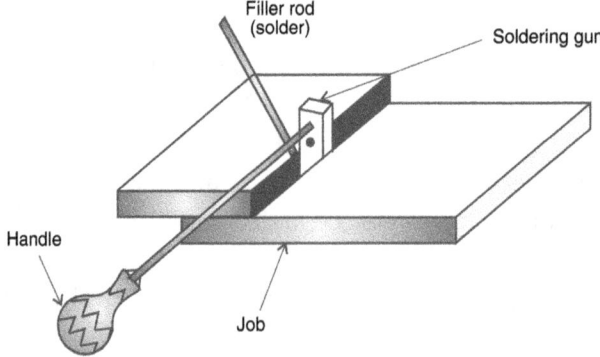

Fig. 6.26 : Soldering operation

Advantages :
1. It is cheaper and quick method of joining.
2. The equipments required are cheap and handy compared with brazing.
3. Less skill is required to carry out the job.
4. It produces pressure tight joint.
5. The base metal is not distorted at all.

The only disadvantage is, joint has less strength and less corrosion resistance compared with brazing.

It is very commonly used for electrical equipments and printed circuit boards in electronic equipments as strength of joint is not at all a consideration.

Comparison of Brazing and Soldering

Sr. No.	Brazing	Soldering
1.	The joint has more strength.	The joint has less strength.
2.	Melting point of filler is high.	Melting point of filler is low.
3.	It offers high resistance to corrosion.	It offers less resistance to corrosion.
4.	A special brazing torch is required.	A simple and handy electrical heater can be used.
5.	A skilled person is required to carry-out the job.	Any person can do the job.

EXERCISES

1. Draw a neat line diagram of lathe and describe the functions of each part.
2. Draw the neat diagrams of 3-jaw check and 4-Jaw cheak and mention the situation when one is preferred over the other.
3. Describe the different operations carried out on the leath with neat sketches.
4. How the taper turning is carried out on the lathe? Explain the operation with the help of sketch.
5. How the threading is done on the lathe. Explain with the neat sketch.
6. Draw a neat diagram of conventional drilling machine and explain the purpose of each part.
7. Describe the different operations carried out on the drilling machine with neat sketches.
8. Describe with neat sketch the spot welding process. Explain the principle of this welding.
9. Describe with neat sketch the seam welding method and explain how it differs from spot welding.

    Give five applications of spot welding and seam welding methods.
10. Describe and differentiate between TIG and MIG welding methods and list out

applications of each method.

11. Discuss the advantages and applications of TIG method of welding and compare with MIG method.
12. Describe the gas-welding method with neat sketch and discuss its advantages and disadvantages with arc welding method.
13. Give list of five industrial applications where only gas welding is preferred over arc welding and five applications where arc welding is preferred over gas welding.
14. Compare resistance welding with arc welding.
15. How brazing method is different from gas welding? Discuss its advantages and disadvantages over gas welding.
16. Explain the soldering method and give five specific applications of soldering.
17. Compare soldering with brazing as a method of joining the metal parts.
18. Describe briefly the defects generally occurring in arc welding. Explain how they can be avoided and corrected.
19. When riveting is used in practise? What is the difference between cold and hot riveting
20. List out the types of riveting joints and mention the two applications of each.
21. What are the different bolt joints? Give an example of each with the help of figure.

www.ingramcontent.com/pod-product-compliance
Lightning Source LLC
Chambersburg PA
CBHW080243170426
43192CB00014BA/2550